Understanding The Epigenetics Revolution:

A Plain English Guide to DNA Methylation, Biological Aging, and why Identical Twins can have Completely different Health Outcomes

C. Louis-Charles, PhD

Cybersoft Publishing LLC

Cybersoft Publishing LLC

First Edition, May 2026

This book is for general educational purposes and is not medical advice. The members of the Kessler Institute for Epigenetic Research who appear in its scenes are illustrative composites used to ground the science in a human story. They do not depict any real persons or organizations. Specific study findings, clinical trials, drug names, and diagnostic tests reflect the publicly documented state of the science as of 2026. Always consult a qualified healthcare professional before making decisions about your health.

Table of Contents

Introduction

James Okafor arrived at the Kessler Institute on a gray Tuesday in October, carrying a travel mug of coffee and a notebook he had not yet opened. The building sat on the edge of the Longwood Medical Area in Boston, a quiet brick facade tucked between two hospitals that never seemed to sleep. He had spent ten years covering medicine for a national outlet, interviewing researchers, sitting in on clinical trials, translating jargon into sentences his readers could follow. He was good at the surface of science. The machinery beneath it was another matter. And this morning, on his first day as Director of Science Communications at Kessler, he was about to confront that gap head-on.

Dr. Maya Chen was already at her desk when he found her office. She was the Executive Director, a former oncologist with a reputation for moving quickly and expecting clarity. She did not look up when he knocked. She slid a single printed page across the desk toward the empty chair. James sat down, set his coffee on the floor, and looked at the paper. It was a chart from a twin study, a Scandinavian registry that followed more than a thousand identical twin pairs from birth into their fifties. The chart showed health outcomes, including cancer diagnoses, cardiovascular disease, and metabolic conditions. James scanned the columns. The twins shared the same DNA. That much he knew. But the outcomes diverged sharply. One twin developed type 2 diabetes; the other did not. One developed breast cancer; her sister never did. One was lean and energetic at fifty-four; the other was not. James looked up from the page.

"Same DNA," Maya said, finally looking at him. "Different lives. Different diseases. Different biological ages, even." She let that sit for a moment. Outside her window, a pigeon landed on the ledge and immediately left again. "That is the question this institute exists to answer," she said. "And it is the question this book exists to explain." James picked up his notebook. He wrote three words at the top of the first page: If DNA is the same, why are the lives different? He would spend the next year at Kessler finding out.

Diagram I.1 - DNA Is Not Destiny

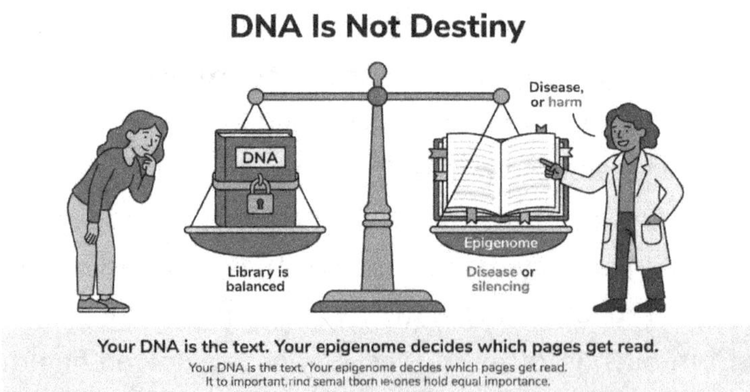

Why This Book Exists

Walk into the science section of any bookstore, and the epigenetics shelf will tell you two very different stories. On one end sit the books that promise you can reprogram your DNA with positive thinking and the right morning routine. These are well-intentioned, but they are not telling you what the science actually says. On the other end sit graduate-level textbooks written for people who already know what a methyl group is. This book takes the rigorous middle path. It respects both the science and the reader.

The central metaphor of this book is one that James will hear from Dr. Lena Fischer, Kessler's Lead Research Scientist, on his second day at the institute. Think of your DNA, Lena will tell him, as a library. A vast, encyclopedic library with roughly twenty thousand books on its shelves. Every cell in your body carries the same library, the same complete collection. But not every book is open. Not every page is being read. Some shelves are locked. Some volumes are dog-eared and read constantly. Others have never been touched. The epigenome is the system of bookmarks, highlights, sticky notes, and librarian decisions that determines, in any given cell at any given moment, which books get opened and which stay shut. Change the bookmarks, and you change what the cell does, without ever changing a single word of the text. That is epigenetics. That is the story this book tells.

The word "epigenetics" itself means "above the genome." The prefix epi comes from Greek and means "on top of" or "in addition to". Epigenetics is the study of changes in how genes are expressed, meaning turned on or off and how loudly, without any change to the underlying DNA sequence. These changes are real and measurable. They are driven by chemical tags, called methyl groups, that attach to DNA and signal a gene to quiet down. Modifications drive them to the proteins called histones that DNA wraps around in the cell nucleus; these can be loosened to allow a gene to be read more easily or tightened to keep it silent. These are not metaphors. These are biochemical events happening right now in every cell of your body. And they respond, in ways researchers are still working to fully understand, to how you live.

The gap between what headlines promise and what readers actually understand is not the reader's fault. The science is young, fast-moving, and genuinely complex. Its coverage, especially in popular media, has oscillated between overselling and under-explaining. This book exists to fill that gap honestly. Every mechanism in these pages is explained through analogy and story before any terminology is introduced. The terminology, when it does appear, is defined immediately, in plain English, in the same sentence. No science degree is required. High school biology is more than enough. All that is genuinely needed is curiosity, and you already have that.

Who This Book Is For

This book is for parents. If you have read something about childhood stress affecting your children's biology and felt a complicated mix of guilt and curiosity, this book will give you the real story. Not the alarming version. The accurate version, which turns out to be considerably more hopeful than the headlines suggest.

This book is for patients. If your doctor has mentioned an epigenetic therapy, an epigenetic clock, or an epigenetic drug, and you wanted a real explanation of what any of those words mean, you deserve one. This book gives it to you without condescension and without hand-waving.

This book is for nurses, dietitians, therapists, and teachers. If you work every day at the intersection of biology and human experience, and epigenetics keeps appearing in your professional world, this is the rigorous but readable account you have been looking for. It will not talk down to you. It will not oversimplify. It will give you a framework you can actually use.

And this book is for the curious reader who saw a headline, something like "Researchers Find That Childhood Poverty Leaves Marks on DNA" or "Twins Study Reveals Epigenetic Aging Differences," and thought: I want actually to understand that. Not the headline version. The real version. You are in exactly the right place.

You do not need to remember every enzyme name or modification type. The book introduces those tools as you need them, always through story and analogy first. What you will build over these ten chapters is a mental model you can actually use, and the ability to evaluate epigenetics claims around you with clear, confident eyes.

How To Read This Book

The book moves in a deliberate arc. It begins with the big question, the one James wrote in his notebook on that first morning, and it answers that question layer by layer, building your understanding the way a good teacher builds it: one solid concept at a time, always connected to the one before it.

Chapter 1, "DNA Is Not Destiny," sets the foundation. It introduces the library metaphor in full, explains what genes actually are and what it means for a gene to be expressed, and makes the case, through real twin studies and real data, that DNA is not the sole author of your biological story. Maya leads this chapter. James is there, asking the questions you are already forming.

Chapter 2, "A Brief, Remarkable History," traces how scientists discovered epigenetics without initially realizing it. You will meet the Dutch Hunger Winter of 1944 and 1945, a famine that left biological fingerprints on the children born during it. You will meet Conrad Waddington, whose landmark diagram gave the field its first conceptual map. Lena guides this chapter.

Chapter 3, "The Control Room," goes inside the cell. DNA methylation, histone modification, and chromatin remodeling are the three main mechanisms by which the epigenome controls gene expression. By the end of this chapter, you will understand all three through stories and analogies that actually hold up.

Chapter 4, "Reading the Epigenome," explains how scientists study these processes. How do you see a methyl group on a piece of DNA? What are epigenetic clocks, and how do they measure biological age? The tools of the field are explained through discovery rather than as a list of techniques.

Chapter 5, "You Are What You Eat," explores the connection between diet and the epigenome. Certain nutrients are literally the raw material from which methyl groups are made. What you eat affects which genes get methylated. Maya leads this chapter, bringing her clinical perspective to a topic where the science is real but the popular claims have often run far ahead of the evidence.

Chapter 6, "Stress, Trauma, and the Marks We Carry," is where Sofia's story begins to take shape. Chronic stress, adverse childhood experiences, and trauma all leave measurable epigenetic marks, particularly on genes involved in the stress response system. This chapter explains how that happens, what it means, and, crucially, what the evidence says about reversibility. The news here is more nuanced and more hopeful than most headlines suggest.

Chapter 7, "Inherited Echoes," is the book's most emotionally resonant chapter. It examines the evidence for transgenerational epigenetics, the possibility that the experiences of your parents and grandparents left biological marks that reached you. Sofia's thread comes fully into focus here, anchored by her grandmother's survival of the 1985 Mexico City earthquake and the question Sofia has carried her whole life: did those experiences travel forward, not as memory, but as biology?

Chapter 8, "The Aging Code," explores what epigenetic research has revealed about how and why we age. Biological age and chronological age are not the same thing, and epigenetic clocks can now measure the difference. Maya leads this chapter.

Chapter 9, "Rewriting Cancer and Your Epigenetic Blueprint," covers the role of epigenetic disruption in cancer and the FDA-approved drugs that now target those disruptions. It also introduces your personal epigenetic blueprint as a real and growing clinical tool.

Chapter 10, "The Road Ahead," looks at the horizon: CRISPR-based epigenetic editing, partial cellular reprogramming, and the ethical questions that come with the ability to rewrite biological instructions across generations. All four Kessler characters bring the story to a close.

Diagram I.2 - The Kessler Institute Cast

Meet the Kessler Institute Cast

Every chapter of this book opens with a scene from the Kessler Institute for Epigenetic Research, a fictional nonprofit in Boston where four people are working to translate the science of epigenetics into knowledge that can actually help people. They are not here to be heroes or cautionary tales. They are here to be guides, each one carrying a different piece of the story, each one asking a different kind of question.

Dr. Maya Chen is the institute's Executive Director. She is 48, a former oncologist who spent fifteen years at Mass General watching identical twin patients diverge in ways the genetics textbooks could not explain, and who eventually followed that question all the way to Kessler. She is the voice of clinical urgency in these pages, the one who keeps reminding you that this science has real consequences for real patients right now.

James Okafor is the Director of Science Communications. He is 35, a former health journalist who spent a decade covering medicine for a national outlet without ever feeling that he fully understood the biology underneath the stories. He is your primary companion in this book. He asks the questions you are thinking but might feel embarrassed to say out loud. He pushes back when explanations feel incomplete. He is the reader's closest friend in these pages, and he will grow alongside you chapter by chapter.

Dr. Lena Fischer is the Lead Research Scientist. She is 42, a molecular biologist who did her doctoral work on chromatin remodeling at the Max Planck Institute in Freiburg before her postdoc years in Boston revealed that she had an unusual gift: she could explain the most complex molecular mechanisms through stories that non-scientists found genuinely fascinating. At Kessler, she is the scientific backbone of everything, the voice that ensures every analogy is vivid and, more importantly, accurate.

Sofia Reyes is a Graduate Research Fellow studying intergenerational epigenetics. She is 29, the first person in her family to pursue a science career, and she arrived at this field through a question that was never purely academic. Her grandmother survived the 1985 Mexico City earthquake, and Sofia has spent much of her life wondering whether those experiences left marks that traveled forward, to her mother, and then to her. Not as a memory or a story. As biology. That question is her engine, and it is the book's most emotionally resonant thread.

Takeaway

Here is the promise of this book, stated plainly: by the time you turn the last page, you will understand epigenetics. Not in a vague, headline-reading way. In a real way. You will be able to explain what epigenetic marks are and how they work. You will understand why identical twins can diverge so dramatically in their health, and why that divergence is actually good news for you. You will know how the food you eat, the stress you carry, and the experiences of the people who came before you can leave measurable biological traces, and what, if anything, you can do about that. You will understand what epigenetic clocks measure, why biological age and chronological age are not the same thing, and how a new class of drugs is already using epigenetic mechanisms to treat cancer with striking results. And you will be equipped to evaluate every epigenetics claim you encounter, in a magazine, on a podcast, in a doctor's office, with the clear and confident eyes of someone who actually knows what the science says.

That understanding begins on the next page. Chapter 1 opens on a morning at the Kessler Institute when Maya walks into James's office with a folder of twin study data and a question she has been asking for twenty years. The question is simple. The answer, it turns out, is one of the most extraordinary stories in modern biology. Turn the page, and let's find out together.

1 DNA Is Not Destiny

The morning James Okafor walked into the Kessler Institute for Epigenetic Research, he was carrying a paper coffee cup, a brand-new notebook, and a quietly nagging worry that he had accepted a job he did not fully understand. The building sat on the edge of Boston's Longwood Medical Area, tucked between two larger hospital towers, its lobby modest and bright. A bulletin board near the elevator displayed a rotating set of research findings in large, reader-friendly font. James stopped and read one of them. He read it again. He was still reading it when Maya Chen appeared beside him, already dressed in the sharp blazer she wore like a second skin, a printed paper in one hand and her own coffee in the other.

"Here," she said, and handed him the printout without preamble. It was a summary of findings from a Scandinavian twin study. The graphs were clean, the data unambiguous. Identical twins, the kind who share every last letter of their genetic code, had been followed for decades. And somewhere in their forties and fifties, they had diverged. Not just in minor ways. One twin had developed a serious illness, and the other never saw it. One pair had different cholesterol levels, different brain scan patterns, and different responses to the same medications. They had the same DNA. They had not had the same life. Maya set her coffee on the lobby's side table, folded her arms, and let the paper do its work. "That," she said, "is what this institute exists to explain."

James looked at the data, looked at her, and asked the question he suspected he was not supposed to need answered on his first day. "So what is actually going on? If their DNA is identical, what is different?" Maya smiled. It was a smile he would come to know well, the one that meant she had been waiting for exactly that question. She picked up her coffee, turned toward the hallway, and said, "Walk with me."

Diagram 1.11 - James and Maya at the Kessler Conference Room

James and Maya stan eemarrtemecpuuous for curtrrs and epigenetic surviver, lang conference, the rmentising conuneratiom.

Why It Matters

For most of the last century, the dominant story about biology was simple. Your genes were your fate. Doctors spoke of genetic risk with a gravity that felt almost theological, as if the sequence of letters in your DNA were a sentence already written, and your job was to find out what it said. Heart disease in your father's family meant heart disease was coming for you. Genes were the blueprint, and the blueprint was fixed.

That story was never entirely wrong. Genes do matter enormously. But it was far from complete. And the incompleteness has cost people something real, not just in medical accuracy but in a sense of agency. If your biology is written before you are born, why bother? If the blueprint is the building, what is left to choose?

Epigenetics is the science that changes the question. It does not erase genetics. It deepens it. And in doing so, it hands something back to everyone who has ever felt trapped by what their family medical history says about them. This chapter is the doorway. Once you walk through it, you will never think about your body, your choices, or your biology in quite the same way again.

Diagram 1.1 - Identical Twins, Different Outcomes

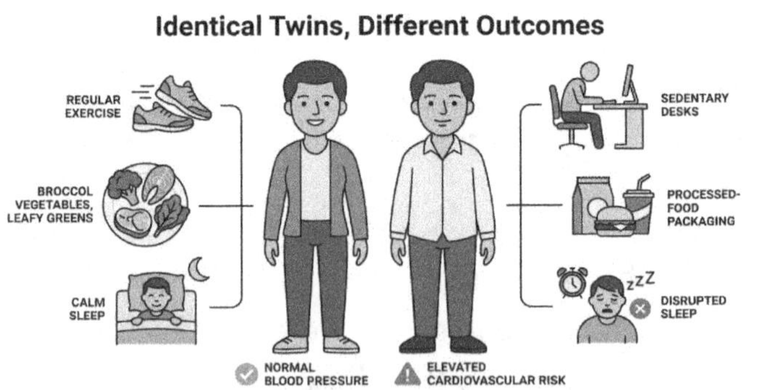

Identical twins, different outcomes that disease, harn, thenemeted on Pechnological silitograms.

The Twin Paradox

Twins have always fascinated scientists. They are, in a very real sense, nature's own experiment. When two babies develop from the same fertilized egg, they carry identical DNA sequences, all three billion base pairs. If genes were truly destiny, identical twins should have nearly identical health trajectories: same diseases, same ages, same responses to the same medications, same aging patterns.

For a long time, this idea held up reasonably well. Twin studies, in which researchers compared how often identical twins shared a trait versus how often non-identical twins shared it, became one of the main tools for estimating how "heritable" a condition was. The logic was elegant: if identical twins, who share all their DNA, are more likely to share a disease than non-identical twins, who share only half of it, then the difference must be genetic.

But a funny thing happened as researchers kept watching. The longer they followed identical twins, the more the twins diverged. Researchers working with the Nordic twin registries in Sweden, Denmark, Norway, and Finland have followed tens of thousands of twin pairs across decades. These registries track health outcomes, psychiatric diagnoses, physical measurements, and cause of death. The picture they paint is not one of genetic determinism. It is one of the genetic possibilities shaped by something else.

One landmark study looked at disease concordance across a range of conditions. Concordance means both twins developing the same condition. If genes were everything, concordance should approach 100 percent in identical twins. What researchers found was very different. For many conditions, including major depression, type 2 diabetes, schizophrenia, and several cancers, concordance in identical twins was often well below 50 percent. One twin developed the condition. The other, with the same DNA, did not. Something beyond the genetic sequence was at work.

There is another layer that researchers find even more striking. When scientists examined the full set of epigenetic marks on the DNA of identical twins, the young twins looked remarkably similar. But as the twins aged, especially if they had lived different lives with different habits and different stresses, their epigenomes drifted apart. By middle age, the molecular marks on their DNA had diverged substantially. Same genetic text. Different annotations. Different reading instructions.

Diagram 1.5 - Scandinavian Twin Study: Same DNA, Diverging Biology

Scandinavian Twin Study: Same DNA, Diverging Biology

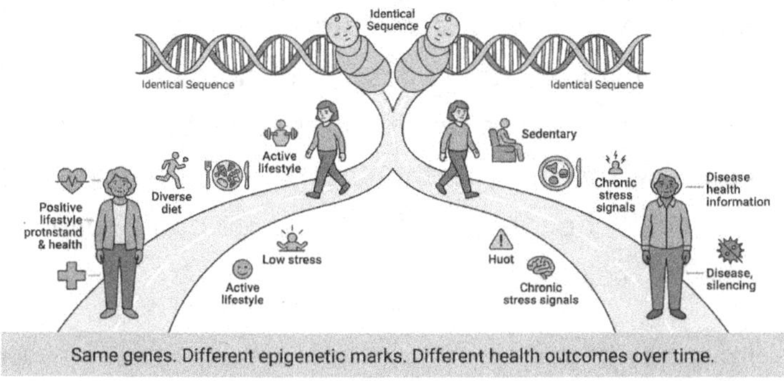

Same genes. Different epigenetic marks. Different health outcomes over time.

James read this with what he would later call productive confusion. Sitting with Maya in one of the institute's small meeting rooms, a whiteboard behind her half-covered in notes, he asked the obvious question. "So if their DNA doesn't change, what exactly is changing?" Maya pulled the cap off a marker. "That is precisely the right question," she said. "And answering it is going to take us the rest of the morning."

The answer is beautiful in its simplicity once you have the right metaphor. Maya Chen, who had spent fifteen years as an oncologist watching patients with the same genetic mutations take entirely different clinical journeys, had spent a long time finding that metaphor. She drew a book on the whiteboard. Thick, with a spine and pages. Then she started adding bookmarks.

What Epigenetics Actually Means

Imagine you are holding a very long novel. Not just any novel, but the most complex and detailed novel ever written, three billion letters long, encoded in a molecule so thin you could not see it without a microscope. This novel is your genome, your complete DNA sequence. Every cell in your body holds an almost identical copy. The text itself never changes. The letters in chapter three of your liver's copy are the same as the letters in chapter three of your brain cell's copy. The book is the same book, cover to cover, in every cell.

Now imagine that this book has been read by an extraordinarily attentive librarian who has spent years with it. Some pages are dog-eared. Some chapters have sticky notes. Entire sections are highlighted in yellow. Some passages are marked "skip this, not relevant right now." Others have a red ribbon bookmark saying, "Come back to this frequently." And critically, some chapters have been shut with a paper clip, sealed off, effectively locked: do not open, not needed here.

This is epigenetics. The text of the book, the actual DNA sequence, has not changed. But the system of marks, bookmarks, highlights, and closures sitting above the text determines which genes are read, which are skipped, and which are locked away. The word itself comes from the Greek prefix "epi," meaning "above" or "upon." Epigenetics is, quite literally, the science of what sits above the genetic text.

Diagram 1.2 - The Book-and-Bookmarks Metaphor: The Epigenome

The Book-and-Bookmarks Metaphor: The Epigenome

Same text in every cell. Different bookmarks tell each cell which pages to read.

Here is the part that should feel genuinely astonishing. Your liver cells and your brain cells contain the same DNA. Identical text. Yet they do completely different things. A liver cell makes enzymes that process the food you ate for lunch. A brain cell fires electrical signals that let you recall a conversation from years ago. The answer to how the same instruction manual produces such different machines is epigenetics. Each cell type has a unique set of epigenetic marks telling it which genes to express and which to ignore. The liver opens its relevant chapters and leaves the neuron chapters closed. The book is identical. The reading instructions are entirely different.

In practical molecular terms, these marks come in several forms. Some involve tiny chemical tags, called methyl groups, that attach directly to the DNA strand and act like a "do not read" signal. Others involve proteins called histones that wrap around the long DNA strand. Think of them as the spools that hold thread in a sewing kit. When the spool is wound tightly, the DNA is packed away and cannot be read. When it loosens, the DNA opens up and becomes accessible. The important thing for now is not the molecular detail but the logic: the text of your genes is not the whole story. The annotations on that text matter just as much.

Diagram 1.3 - DNA Double Helix with Methyl Tags

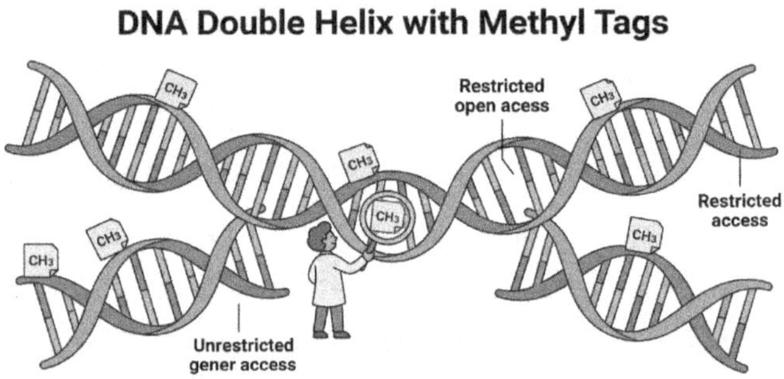

Methyl tags act like sticky notes on the DNA strand, signaling which genes to silence.

James sat back. "So the same person can have different gene-reading instructions at different points in their life? Can the marks change?" Maya nodded. "That is exactly what it is saying. And that, James, is the part that changes everything."

This is what makes epigenetics different from traditional genetics. The DNA sequence you inherited from your parents is essentially fixed, determined at conception. But your epigenome is dynamic. It has been changing since before you were born and will continue to change throughout your life. Experiences, environments, and choices leave molecular traces. Not as vague metaphors.

As literal, physical marks on the machinery of your genome.

Diagram 1.4 - Library Shelves: Open and Locked Gene Volumes

Every cell has the same library. Epigenetic marks decide which books get opened.

Why This Field Matters Now

Epigenetics is not a new idea. The term was coined in the 1940s by the British developmental biologist Conrad Waddington to describe how genes interact with the environment to produce an organism's characteristics. For most of the following decades, the molecular basis of those interactions remained murky. Researchers knew that something was happening above the level of the DNA sequence. But the tools to study it directly did not yet exist.

What happened in the last thirty years is something close to a scientific revolution. New sequencing technologies enabled researchers to map epigenetic marks across the entire genome, in every cell type and at every stage of development. The Human Genome Project gave science a reference text. Subsequent projects built the annotations on top of it, mapping the complete human epigenome across dozens of tissue types throughout the lifespan. The volume of data has been staggering, and so have the findings.

Diagram 1.7 - The Acceleration of Epigenetics Research: A Timeline

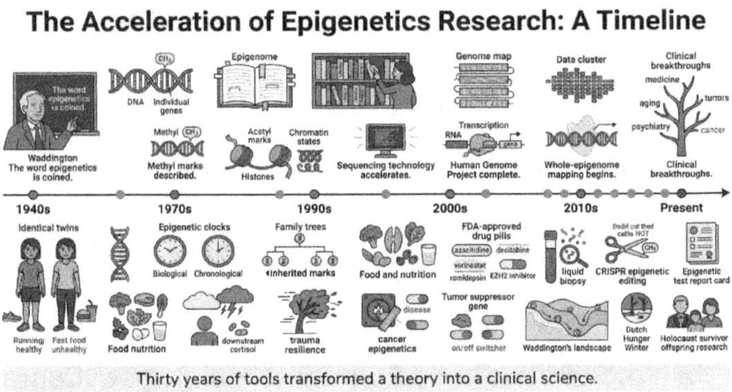

The pace of discovery has been remarkable. In the early 1990s, a search for the word "epigenetics" in the scientific literature would return a few hundred papers. Today, tens of thousands of new papers appear every year. Research groups in oncology, psychiatry, developmental biology, and nutrition have all converged on the same mechanisms. They are all reading the same book. They are all finding the same bookmarks.

For someone picking up a book on epigenetics today, the timing is good. The field has moved from theoretical curiosity to clinical application within a single scientific career. The FDA has approved drugs that modify epigenetic marks for cancer treatment. Researchers have built molecular clocks that estimate biological age with remarkable accuracy. Clinical trials are underway for epigenetic therapies targeting depression and autoimmune disease. The science is no longer waiting in the wings. It is on stage.

James found this part of the conversation almost dizzying. He had spent a decade writing about medicine and had developed a calibrated skepticism toward "revolutionary" claims. Most things described as revolutions turned out to be incremental improvements in dramatic language. But sitting with Maya in the Kessler meeting room, looking at the timeline of discoveries on her laptop screen, he felt something different. This did not feel incremental. It felt like a genuinely new layer of the story. Not a correction to genetics. An expansion of it.

Correcting the Myths

There is something understandable, even a little poignant, about how wellness culture has embraced epigenetics. Here was a science saying that environment and experience could leave marks on the genome, that what you did with your life was not biologically irrelevant, that your genes were not a prison. For people who had always suspected that attitude and meaning mattered to health in ways that reductive biology could not account for, epigenetics felt like a validation. A simplified, sometimes distorted version of the science found its way into books, podcasts, and social media feeds, passed along with genuine excitement.

Some of what circulates in wellness contexts about epigenetics is accurate in spirit. The idea that lifestyle, environment, and experience shape your biology at the molecular level is real. Science does support it, as we will see in detail throughout this book. But some of what gets said goes well beyond the evidence, and those overreaches are worth addressing clearly and warmly, not to embarrass anyone who believed them, but because the real science is genuinely more interesting and more empowering than the exaggerations.

Diagram 1.6 - Epigenetics Myth-Busting: What the Science Does Not Say

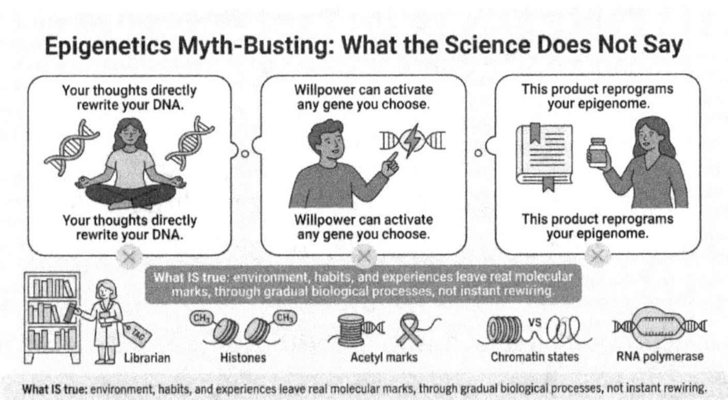

The most common myth is the idea that your thoughts can directly and immediately rewrite your epigenetic marks. It draws on a real truth: mental states do have physiological

consequences. Chronic stress genuinely affects your biology at the molecular level, and we will look closely at how in a later chapter. But the mechanism involves a long chain of events, hormones, inflammatory signals, cellular responses, and gradual epigenetic changes over time. It is not a direct, instant act. You cannot sit down, visualize a cancer gene switching off, and have it switch off. If that were true, oncology would look very different.

A related myth is that you can "activate" specific beneficial genes through willpower or supplements. Advertisements describe this as "epigenetic reprogramming" or "gene activation." Epigenetic marks are not light switches that flip on demand. They are the products of complex biological systems that respond to cumulative inputs over time. The good news is that those inputs do matter: diet, exercise, sleep, and stress management all genuinely shape the epigenome. The bad news is that there is no shortcut, no single supplement that instantly reprograms your genome.

Another area where the claims outrun the evidence is inheritance. A field called transgenerational epigenetic inheritance explores whether epigenetic marks can pass from parent to offspring without being encoded in the DNA sequence. Some findings are striking, particularly in plants and animal models. In humans, the picture is more complex. Some evidence suggests that a parent's stress or nutritional experiences may affect their children's biology through epigenetic channels. But the popular claim that your grandparents' traumas are fully imprinted on your genes is well beyond what current human evidence supports. Sofia, one of the researchers at Kessler, is studying exactly this question. We will hear her story in Chapter 7, and by then you will have the vocabulary to evaluate the evidence alongside her. For now: intriguing, partially supported, and actively being researched.

James asked Maya about this myth with some care. He had read a few of the popular accounts and found them compelling. "So, the trauma inheritance idea, is it real or not?" Maya chose her words carefully. "It is real in model organisms. It is real in some human studies. The wellness version of the story is usually forty steps ahead of the science. The actual science is still fascinating. It just requires more patience." That, James thought, was a useful sentence for his whole new job.

Environment, Lifestyle, and Experience Are Biological

There is a habit of thinking, deeply embedded in both everyday conversation and in some corners of medicine, that treats the biological and the environmental as two separate categories. "Is it genetic or is it lifestyle?" people ask. "Is it in their biology or is it stress?" The implicit assumption is that these are different kinds of causes: biological causes are real and hard, molecular, while environmental causes are softer, less fundamental, more amenable to simple fixes.

Epigenetics dissolves this distinction entirely, not as a philosophical claim but as a straightforward molecular description. When you eat a meal rich in folate, the nutrient found in leafy greens, it provides raw material for the methyl groups that regulate gene activity. When you exercise, you trigger molecular signals that include changes to the epigenetic state of genes involved in muscle repair and metabolism. When you experience prolonged stress, hormones circulate through your body and alter epigenetic marks on genes related to the immune system and mood regulation. These are not metaphors for biological events. They are biological events. The environment is not separate from biology. The environment is biology.

Diagram 1.8 - Environment as Biology: Choices Feeding Into the Body

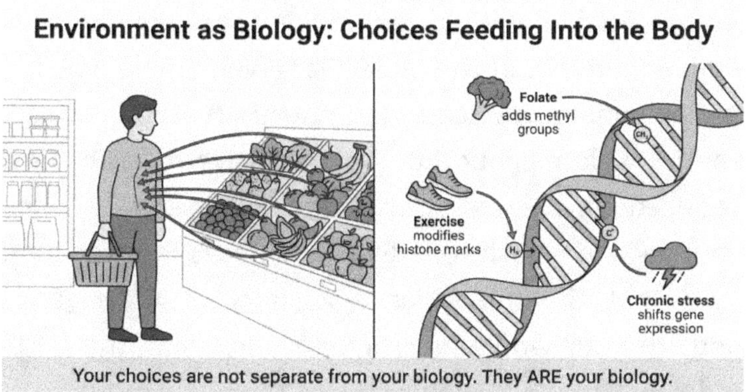

This is one of the most important moves science makes. For decades, one style of argument dismissed social and environmental factors in health as somehow less real than

genetic ones. If poverty correlates with worse health outcomes, perhaps poor people have worse genes. If stress correlates with heart disease, perhaps the relevant factor is a genetic predisposition to stress reactivity. The environment was noisy. Genetics was a signal.

Epigenetics does not dismiss genetic factors. Genetics remains enormously important. But it refuses the hierarchy. What you eat, how much you sleep, the neighborhood you grew up in, the stability or instability of your early childhood, the stress you have carried for years: all of these leave molecular traces. They are measurable. They are real. They are biological. The argument that "environment" somehow means "not really biology" has been dismantled not by philosophy but by data.

This reframing has practical and ethical consequences. If the experiences that shape epigenetics are themselves shaped by social conditions, improving those conditions is preventive medicine at the molecular level. Stable housing affects epigenetics. Access to nutritious food affects epigenetics. Safe neighborhoods, supportive relationships, and reduced chronic stress all affect epigenetics. Science does not reduce health to individual choices in a vacuum. It shows that the molecular machinery of your genes responds to your whole environment, including the parts that individuals cannot simply choose their way out of.

James found this quietly powerful. He had spent years as a health journalist frustrated by wellness advice that assumed unlimited personal control, as if every health outcome were purely a matter of the right breakfast. He had also spent years covering public health stories that, to some editors, felt insufficiently "actionable" because they pointed to structural causes. Epigenetics, he was starting to see, held both stories at once. Individual choices matter, genuinely and at the molecular level. And the conditions that shape those choices also matter, genuinely and molecularly. Neither truth cancels the other.

Diagram 1.9 - The Epigenetic Medicine Cabinet: FDA-Approved Drugs

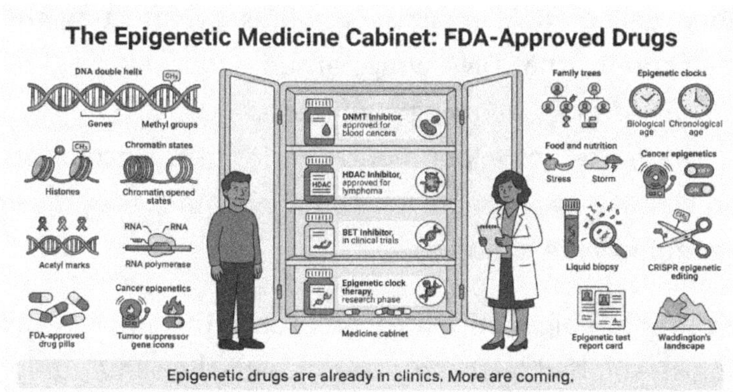

A Preview of Epigenetic Medicine

One of the most important things to understand about epigenetics at this stage of the book is that it is not a theoretical or speculative field. It is a clinically active one. Epigenetic discoveries have already produced approved medical treatments, diagnostic tools, and research programs that are transforming how doctors think about some of the most challenging diseases in medicine.

The clearest example is cancer. Researchers have known for decades that cancer cells have profoundly abnormal epigenomes. They silence genes that should be keeping the cell's growth in check. They open up genes that should be locked away. This is not a side effect of cancer. In many cases, it is one of the driving causes. And this insight led directly to a new category of cancer treatment. Drugs called DNMT inhibitors, which work by reducing the addition of methyl tags to DNA, allowing silenced genes to become active again, have been approved by the FDA and are in use today for certain blood cancers. A second category, called HDAC inhibitors, works by affecting the histone proteins that DNA wraps around, loosening tightly packed regions and allowing suppressed genes to be read again. These are not experimental curiosities. Oncologists are prescribing them, and for some patients, they have been genuinely life-changing.

Maya came to epigenetics through exactly this door. As an oncologist, she had watched patients with the same tumor type, the same genetic mutations, the same staging, respond to the same chemotherapy in completely different ways. One patient would go into remission. The next would not respond at all. For years, she attributed this to individual variation she did not fully understand. Then she began reading the epigenetics literature and found the missing layer. The epigenetic context of a tumor, not just its genetic mutations, influenced how cells behaved and responded to treatment. She left clinical practice to pursue that insight at the research level, and eventually, that pursuit led her to found the Kessler Institute. "I became a researcher," she told James, "because I had too many patients I could not explain. Epigenetics was the only framework large enough to hold what I was seeing."

Beyond cancer, epigenetic medicine is transforming aging research. Researchers have identified patterns of epigenetic change that correlate so reliably with age that they can be used to construct an epigenetic clock: a way of estimating biological age based on methyl-mark patterns across the genome. This biological age does not always match your chronological age. Some people's cells age faster than expected; others age more slowly. The gap has been linked to health outcomes, and crucially, the factors that influence it include the same lifestyle and environmental inputs we have been discussing. This is not a fixed track. It is a dial.

Diagram 1.10 - The Epigenetic Clock: Chronological vs Biological Age

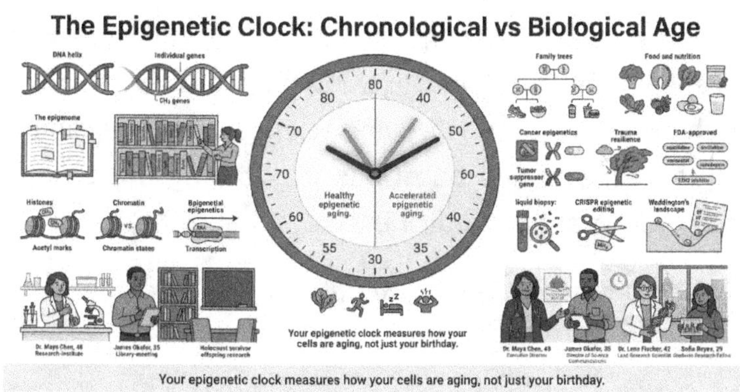

CRISPR-based tools, which many people have heard of in the context of gene editing, have been adapted to make epigenetic changes without altering the DNA sequence. Instead of cutting and replacing genetic letters, these tools add or remove epigenetic marks at specific locations. They are sometimes called epigenome editors, and clinical trials using them for genetic blood disorders, certain forms of blindness, and some cancers are underway. The pace of development is rapid.

Psychiatry is also beginning to engage seriously with epigenetic mechanisms. Research suggests that conditions including major depression and post-traumatic stress disorder involve epigenetic changes in brain cells that can outlast the original trigger. If a traumatic experience leaves a mark in the brain's stress-response circuitry, and that mark persists long after the immediate danger has passed, then the persistence of symptoms is not simply a failure of resilience. It is a molecular phenomenon. And molecular phenomena are, in principle, addressable by molecular medicine.

None of this means epigenetics has all the answers. The field is still young, and many exciting findings remain in the research phase. But this is a living science with real clinical consequences, and the questions it is asking are among the most important in medicine today.

Diagram 1.12 - The Reader as Active Participant

The Reader as Active Participant

You are not just reading about epigenetics. You are living it.

What This Means for You

It is worth pausing to make this personal. That is, after all, the reason you are reading this book.

The most important thing this chapter offers is not a set of facts. It is a shift in how you think about your biology. If the old story was that your DNA is your destiny, fixed before birth, the new story is more interesting. Your DNA is your starting library. Massive, detailed, and incredibly influential. But what gets read, when it gets read, and how actively different chapters are engaged is the product of an ongoing conversation between that library and everything that happens to you.

First, your medical history is not a verdict. A family history of heart disease, diabetes, or cancer is genuinely important information. It tells you which genes you carry and which epigenetic patterns are most relevant for you. But it does not tell you a particular outcome is inevitable. The twin data is not just a scientific curiosity. It is a message: same genes, different outcomes. The biology is real. The outcome is not predetermined.

Second, the lifestyle factors you have probably already heard about, sleep, nutrition, exercise, and stress management, are worth taking seriously, not because someone told you to, but because the mechanism is now visible. These are not vague wellness recommendations. They are molecular levers. When you sleep seven to eight hours, you are doing something measurable to your epigenome. When you eat a diet rich in vegetables and whole grains, you are providing your epigenetic machinery with the raw materials it needs. When you manage chronic stress effectively, you are reducing molecular signals that would otherwise push gene expression in unhealthy directions over time. Science does not turn these into guarantees. But it turns them from advice into biology.

Third, the parts of your life that felt like "just" psychology or "just" experience, your relationships, your neighborhood, the economic stability of your household, the accumulated stress or safety of your daily environment, are biological. They are leaving marks. The boundary between "real" medicine and "lifestyle" is much more porous than the old framework suggested. This should produce not anxiety but attention. And it should eventually produce a different conversation between patients and the healthcare system, one that takes the whole person seriously as a biological entity.

Try this, as a first exercise: think about one area of your life where you have felt the tension between "my genes make this hard" and "I should be able to change this." Maybe it is weight, or anxiety, or sleep, or a condition that runs in your family. Hold that tension as you read the following chapters. By the end of the book, you will have the molecular vocabulary to think about it more clearly, and perhaps to feel a little less stuck.

Takeaway

James spent the rest of his first day at the Kessler Institute reading. Not the grant reports or communications briefs he had been given. He read the twin study Maya had handed him, and then the papers it cited, and then three more from those references. By late afternoon, he was sitting in the window of the institute's small library, the Boston rooftops pale in the early spring light, the printout still in his hand. The question Maya had answered that morning had opened into a dozen more. All of them felt important. All of them felt like they were pointing toward something he genuinely wanted to understand.

That is the invitation this chapter extends to you. Epigenetics is not a threat to your sense of yourself or a new source of anxiety about your lifestyle. It is a window. It shows you that the story of your biology is longer and more interesting than you were told. That the fixed and the changeable in your health are arranged differently than the old genetics framework suggested. The distance between you and your genes is not zero, and the space in between is where your life takes place.

The next chapter takes a step back in time. To understand where the science is today, it helps to know how it got here, which requires a brief and genuinely remarkable journey through the history of ideas about genes, cells, and the layers of biology that were there all along, waiting to be found. The story begins, as so many good stories do, with something that seemed to make no sense until it did.

2 A Brief, Remarkable History

The photocopy was old enough to be yellow at the edges. Lena Fischer set it on the table between two coffee cups and smoothed it flat with both hands, as if it were something fragile. James Okafor leaned forward. The image showed a hilly landscape drawn in a style from a different era of science illustration: gentle slopes descending from a high ridge, branching into valleys below, and a collection of small circles, like marbles, perched at various points across the terrain. Some were at the top of the ridge. Others had already rolled partway down, settling into the grooves of particular valleys. At the bottom of each valley sat a label. Liver cell. Nerve cell. Skin cell. Heart cell.

"Conrad Waddington drew this in 1942," Lena said. She tapped the top of the ridge. "Every marble starts here. One fertilized egg. The same genome in every single cell." She moved her finger slowly down one of the valleys. "And by the time it reaches the bottom, it has become something specific. A liver cell. A neuron. It can never go back up the hill." James studied the diagram. "It looks like a marble run," he said. "The ones you build with your kids." Lena smiled. "Exactly. And Waddington drew this eighty years before anyone could explain the molecular machinery underneath it. He was just, somehow, right."

Outside the Kessler Institute's second-floor conference room, Cambridge was waking up in the gray light of a November morning. The Charles River was the color of pewter. Lena had pinned two more pages to the corkboard beside the window: a timeline of FDA approvals, and a journal article dated 2013, the year Steven Horvath published his epigenetic clock. The reason she always starts with history, she told James, is that this history is not background. It is the argument.

Diagram 2.12 - Lena and James in the Kessler Library

Why It Matters

History chapters in science books often feel like obligatory throat-clearing. Names, dates, a few Nobel prizes, and then, now that we have the context, let us get to the science. This chapter is not built that way. The history of epigenetics is not in context. It is the argument itself. Understanding how scientists came to recognize something that was hiding in plain sight tells you something important: this science is genuinely hard, it moves more slowly than headlines suggest, and when it does, it tends to move in surprising directions.

By the end of this chapter, you will understand why a British biologist's sketch from 1942 is still displayed in research institutes around the world. You will know about the Dutch Hunger Winter, a tragedy that became one of the most important natural experiments in the history of human biology. You will follow the discovery of the first chemical marks on DNA and the machinery that controls them. You will see how a global project mapped the human epigenome in staggering detail. And you will arrive at the present moment, where an epigenetic clock can estimate your biological age, and a new class of drugs treats cancer by targeting the epigenome directly. CRISPR is being adapted not to cut DNA but to change the marks sitting on top of it.

The reason all of this matters to you personally is simple. Every practical insight in the chapters ahead rests on the discoveries described here. The history is where the promises were made. The rest of this book is where they are being kept.

The Man with the Marble Sketch: Conrad Waddington, 1942

Conrad Hal Waddington was a developmental biologist at the University of Edinburgh, and he had a problem that other scientists of his era mostly chose to ignore. If every cell in your body contains an identical copy of your DNA, how do they end up being so remarkably different from one another?

Think about that for a moment. A liver cell and a neuron in your brain both carry the same thirty thousand or so genes. The same sequence. The same information. And yet a liver cell is flat and performs chemical processing tasks that a neuron would never dream of. A neuron extends long branches across millimeters of space and fires electrical signals thousands of times a second. These are radically different cells, doing radically different things, with the same instruction set. The dominant scientific view in the 1930s was focused entirely on the information in DNA itself. Waddington thought something else was doing important work, and he needed a way to describe it.

In 1942, he coined the word epigenetics. He built it from the Greek prefix epi, meaning "above" or "upon," and genetics. Epigenetics: the processes that sit above the genes and govern how they are used. At the time, the word had a slightly broader meaning than it carries today. Waddington used it to describe the entire set of developmental processes by which a fertilized egg becomes a complex organism. The modern usage has narrowed to refer specifically to heritable chemical marks on DNA and the proteins around it. But the core intuition was the same: there is more to biology than the sequence of bases in a gene.

Diagram 2.1 - Waddington's Epigenetic Landscape

Waddington's Epigenetic Landscape

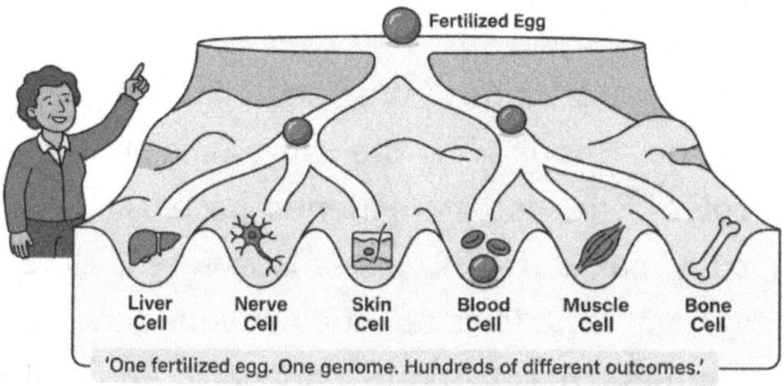

The epigenetic landscape diagram that Waddington drew, and refined over subsequent years, is a masterpiece of scientific intuition. A single ball sits at the top of a hillside. The slope below it is carved into branching channels, like a river delta seen from above, each channel leading toward a different valley at the bottom. The ball, as it rolls downhill, will follow whichever channel it is in. Once it has rolled into a valley, it stays there. The contours of the landscape represent the developmental possibilities available to any given cell. The ball is the cell. Each valley is a fate.

What made this diagram prophetic was not just the metaphor. It was the specificity of the claim underneath the metaphor. Waddington was saying something precise: cell fate is not random; it is directed. There are attractor states, biological destinations that cells are pulled toward. Once a cell becomes a liver cell, something is maintaining that identity across every division, every year of your life. He did not know what the mechanism was. That would take another forty years. But the map he drew pointed directly at the territory.

Lena sometimes describes Waddington's diagram by saying, "Imagine a book with the same text printed in a hundred copies." The words are identical across all copies. But each copy has different pages dog-eared, different passages highlighted. A liver-cell copy of your genome has certain chapters permanently opened and others permanently closed. A neuron copy has a completely different set of open pages. The text never changes. The reading of it changes everything.

The Winter That Changed Everything: The Dutch Hunger Winter, 1944 to 1945

In the autumn of 1944, the Nazi occupiers of the Netherlands imposed a blockade on the western part of the country in retaliation for a Dutch railway strike that had supported the Allied advance. Food deliveries stopped. The Dutch winter that followed was severe. By the time Allied forces liberated the country in May 1945, an estimated twenty thousand people had died of starvation, and the surviving population had subsisted on rations of as little as four hundred calories a day. It was a catastrophe of calculated cruelty, and it left a mark on the biological record that researchers are still studying.

The reason the Dutch Hunger Winter became one of the most important datasets in epigenetics has to do with timing and record-keeping. The Netherlands had meticulous public health records. It had a clearly defined famine period with a known start and end date. And it had something else: a large population of pregnant women, at different stages of pregnancy, exposed to severe nutritional deprivation at different moments in fetal development.

If you were a baby conceived in the summer of 1944, your first trimester took place during the worst of the famine. If you were conceived later, you were exposed in your second or third trimester. And if you were born just before the famine began, your mother was depleted during the last weeks she nursed you. These different exposure windows unintentionally created the kind of natural experiment that no ethics committee would ever deliberately approve.

Diagram 2.2 - Dutch Hunger Winter Timeline

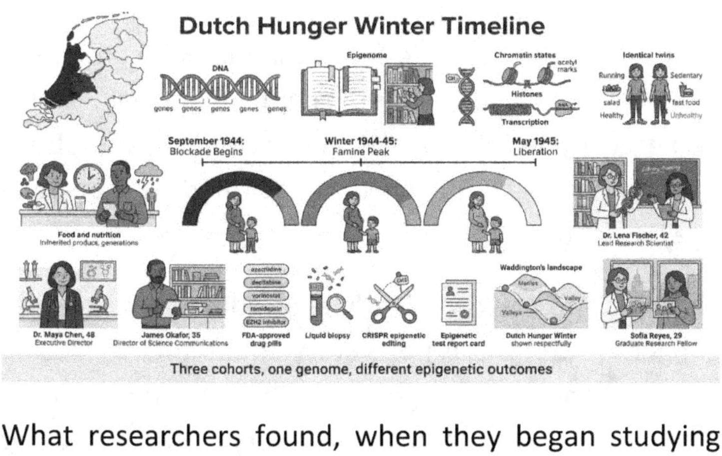

What researchers found, when they began studying the children of these cohorts decades later, was startling.

Babies who had been in their first trimester during the worst of the famine grew up to have significantly higher rates of obesity, diabetes, cardiovascular disease, and certain psychiatric conditions compared to siblings conceived after the famine ended. Crucially, many appeared normal at birth. The health consequences emerged over decades.

James asked Lena about this the first time she walked him through the data. "If the effects were not visible at birth, how did the biology hold on to them for decades?" It was, she said, exactly the right question. The answer is epigenetic. When a developing fetus experiences severe nutritional deprivation during critical windows of development, the epigenome responds. Methyl groups, the chemical tags that sit on DNA and influence whether genes are active or silent, are redistributed. Certain genes that regulate metabolism, insulin response, and fat storage are marked in ways that prepare the developing body for a world of scarcity. If the famine had continued, those marks might have been adaptive. Instead, those children grew up in relative abundance, and the metabolic settings their epigenome had established for scarcity became risk factors.

Lena is careful to say this clearly every time she discusses the Hunger Winter: this is not a story about famine causing permanent genetic damage. The DNA of the Hunger Winter children was the same as everyone else's. What changed were the patterns of marks on that DNA, and some of those patterns, established in the womb during the most sensitive period of development, persisted for decades. The event demonstrated that the environment a developing organism experiences can leave lasting molecular traces, encoded not in the genome but in the layer of chemical marks sitting on top of it.

Finding the Mark: The Discovery of DNA Methylation

By the early 1970s, researchers knew that cells were maintaining their identities across divisions, and they had the Waddington metaphor to gesture at the mystery. But they did not have a molecular mechanism. DNA, as you probably know, is made of four chemical letters: adenine, thymine, guanine, and cytosine, written as A, T, G, and C. They pair up in the famous double helix: A with T, G with C. This was established by Watson and Crick in 1953 and, with beautiful elegance, explained how genetic information could be stored and copied. What it did not explain was how a liver cell and a neuron, containing identical DNA, could behave so differently. That gap is the space in which epigenetics grew.

In the late 1960s and through the 1970s, researchers began to notice something strange. One of the four DNA letters, cytosine, appeared in two different forms in cell nuclei. There was plain cytosine. And then there was a modified version carrying a small chemical attachment called a methyl group. A methyl group is nothing exotic: just a carbon atom bonded to three hydrogen atoms, about as simple a chemical structure as you can find in biology. But its presence on cytosine turned out to have profound consequences.

Diagram 2.3 - DNA Methylation: Methyl Group on Cytosine

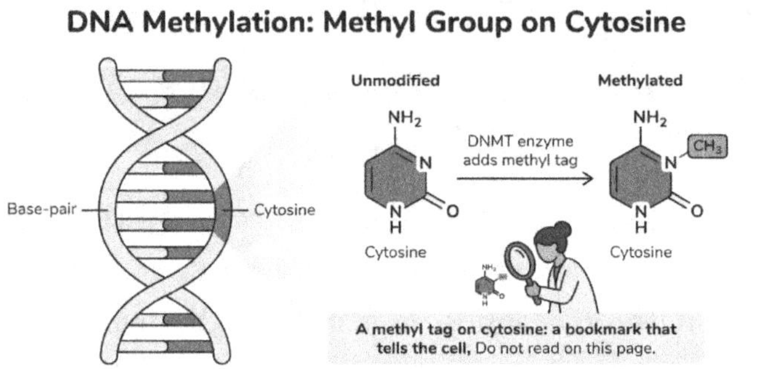

Thiny DNA Methylation: Methyl taGroup on Cytosine. Do not read this page.

When a methyl group attaches to cytosine at locations where cytosine is followed by guanine, what researchers call CpG sites, the gene near that region tends to go quiet. Methylated DNA is harder for the molecular machinery that reads genes to access. It is as if a bookmark has been slipped into a book, and the pages around it have been lightly glued together. The text is still there. But it does not get read.

The enzyme responsible for adding methyl groups to DNA was identified and named in the 1980s. It is called DNA methyltransferase, or DNMT, the enzyme that adds methyl tags to DNA. When a cell divides, DNMT recognizes the methylation pattern on the original strand and reproduces it on the new strand. This is the mechanism that answers the question James asked: how does a liver cell stay a liver cell across thousands of cell divisions? The methylation pattern is copied along with the DNA sequence. The bookmarks are reproduced. The same pages stay marked as the cell's identity is maintained.

For the first time, researchers had a molecular mechanism that could plausibly explain how environmental information could leave a lasting mark on a cell without changing the DNA sequence. The mark was chemical, heritable, and specific. Different CpG sites across the genome could be methylated or not, creating an almost limitless space of possible patterns. Cancer cells had profoundly abnormal methylation. Identical twins developed diverging methylation landscapes over time. The investigation had found its thread.

The Other Code: Histones and the Chromatin Revolution

DNA methylation was a major discovery. But it was not the whole story. To understand the rest, you need to know something about how DNA is packed inside a cell. If you stretched out all the DNA in a single human cell, it would be about two meters long. Your cell nucleus is roughly six micrometers across, about six thousandths of a millimeter. Getting two meters of DNA into a space of six micrometers requires packing on a scale that is almost impossible to visualize. The solution biology arrived at involves a family of proteins called histones.

Diagram 2.4 - Histones as Spools: DNA Wrapped Around Protein Cores

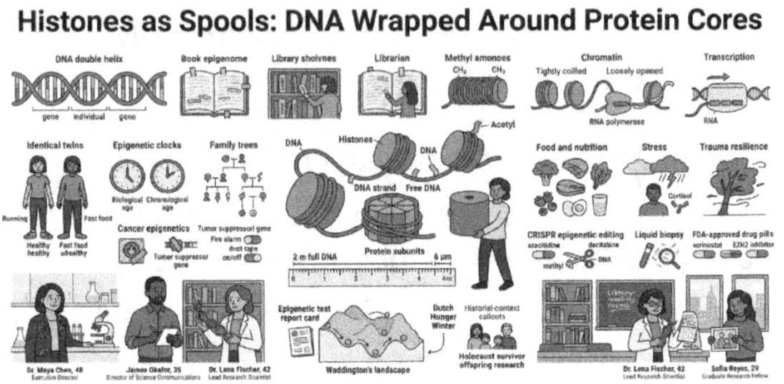

'Histones: molecular spools that organize two meters of DNA into a space the size of a dust mote.'

Histones are proteins shaped a bit like a spool of thread. Eight histone proteins cluster together into a compact core, and DNA wraps around this core about one and three-quarters times before continuing to the next histone complex. The resulting structure, DNA wound around a histone core, is called a nucleosome. Under an electron microscope, it looks like a string of beads. Those beads can be further coiled and compacted into increasingly tight structures, eventually forming the dense chromosomes visible during cell division.

Histones have what are called tails: flexible strands of amino acids that extend from the core protein out into the surrounding space. These tails can be chemically modified in dozens of different ways. They can be acetylated, meaning an acetyl group is added. They can be methylated, phosphorylated, or ubiquitinated. Each modification carries a meaning in the language of gene regulation. When histones are acetylated, they tend to hold DNA more loosely. Chromatin, the combined structure of DNA and proteins, opens up. Genes become accessible. When histones are methylated in certain positions, the chromatin compacts. The gene is still there, but the reading machinery cannot easily reach it.

Diagram 2.5 - The Chromatin Revolution: Open vs. Closed Chromatin

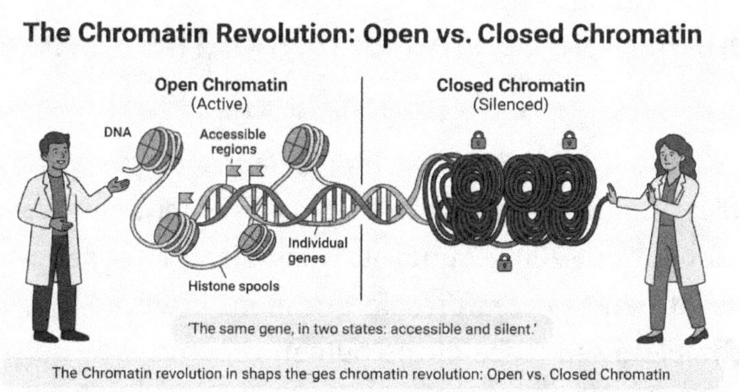

The Chromatin revolution in shaps the-ges chromatin revolution: Open vs. Closed Chromatin

David Allis at Rockefeller University and Michael Grunstein at UCLA were among the researchers who, in the 1990s, began mapping how histone modifications correspond to gene activity. What emerged was the histone code: a system of chemical marks on histone tails that functions as a second layer of genetic information, written not in the bases of DNA but in the chemical modifications of the proteins to which DNA is wrapped. The genome is the text. The histone code is the annotation system. Together with DNA methylation, these mechanisms constitute the epigenome.

"Think of chromatin like a filing cabinet," Lena told James one afternoon. "The files inside it are your genes. A tightly locked drawer is silenced chromatin. The genes inside are there, but the cell is not reading them. An open drawer with tabs sticking up is active chromatin." James thought about this. "And the histone modifications are like the locks and handles on the drawers?" Lena nodded. "Exactly. And the locks can be added or removed. That's what makes epigenetics dynamic."

Mapping the Second Genome: The Human Epigenome Project

In 1990, the Human Genome Project launched to read the complete sequence of human DNA for the first time. It was completed in 2003. But its completion raised an immediate and uncomfortable question: if we now have the complete sequence of the human genome, why do we not understand most of the diseases it was supposed to explain? Why are complex conditions like type 2 diabetes and heart disease still so resistant to genetic explanation?

Part of the answer, researchers understood, was that the genome sequence was necessary but not sufficient. The genome told you what genes existed. It did not tell you which ones were active in which cells, under which conditions, at which points in development. That information was held in the epigenome. And the epigenome was not one thing. It was a different configuration in every cell type, shifting across development, responding to the environment, varying between individuals with identical DNA sequences.

The Human Epigenome Project, launched in 2003 as a European initiative and later expanded into a broader international effort, set out to map epigenetic patterns across multiple human cell types. In 2010, the U.S. National Institutes of Health launched the Roadmap Epigenomics Program, which ultimately cataloged the epigenomes of more than 100 human cell and tissue types.

Diagram 2.6 - Human Epigenome Project: Multi-Tissue Map

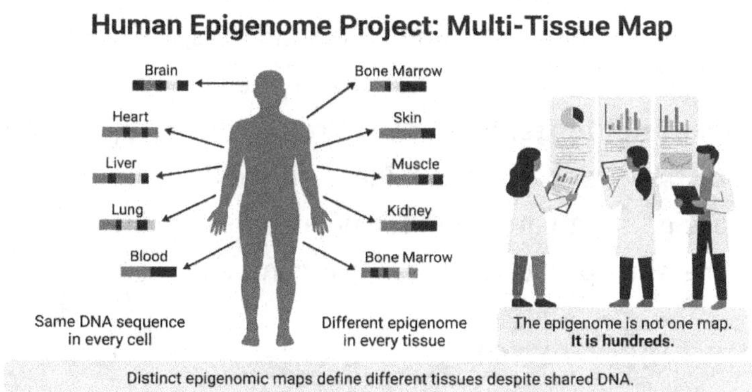

What the mapping revealed was simultaneously breathtaking and humbling. The epigenome was not just complex. It was orders of magnitude more complex than the genome itself. A single CpG site can be methylated in a liver cell and unmethylated in a neuron. Histone modifications can vary across tissue types, across ages, and across disease states in patterns of staggering combinatorial complexity. The Human Epigenome Project provided researchers with a reference atlas: a map of the normal epigenome in healthy tissues.

Once you have a reference map, you can identify the deviations. You can ask: What does the epigenome of a cancer cell look like compared to a healthy cell in the same tissue? What does an eighty-year-old's epigenome look like compared to a twenty-year-old's? These questions became not just theoretically interesting but empirically tractable. The map made the deviations visible.

The Human Epigenome Project also carried a conceptual message that changed how the field thought about genetic information. The genome, researchers came to understand, is more like a hardware specification than a program. The epigenome is more like the operating system: the layer that decides, in real time, which hardware gets activated and for what purpose. And unlike hardware, the operating system can be updated.

From Observation to Treatment: The First Epigenetic Cancer Drugs

The shift from a scientific observation to a clinical treatment is one of the longest journeys in medicine. Most observations never make it. The epigenome made it, and the vehicle was cancer.

By the late 1990s, researchers had established that the epigenomes of cancer cells were profoundly abnormal. Genes that should be active in a healthy cell were silenced in cancer cells, often by excessive accumulation of methyl tags on genes that normally function as brakes on uncontrolled growth. These are called tumor suppressor genes, and when epigenetic marks silence them, the cancer cell loses an important restraint. The gas pedal is stuck. The brakes are covered with tape.

The insight that followed was simple in principle but difficult in practice: if cancer cells used epigenetic silencing to disable their own regulatory machinery, could you reverse that silencing with a drug? Could you remove the methyl tags, reopen the silenced genes, and restore something like normal behavior to a cancer cell? The answer, it turned out, was yes. At least in some cancers. At least to a clinically meaningful degree.

Diagram 2.7 - FDA Approval Timeline of Epigenetic Cancer Drugs

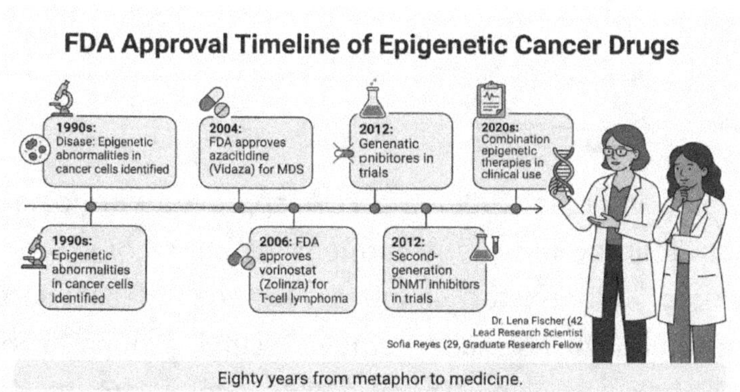

Eighty years from metaphor to medicine.

Azacitidine, sold under the brand name Vidaza, was the first drug to receive FDA approval specifically for an epigenetic mechanism. That approval came in 2004 for myelodysplastic syndrome (MDS), a group of conditions in which the bone marrow does not produce enough healthy blood cells. Azacitidine is a DNMT inhibitor: it blocks the enzyme that adds methyl tags to DNA. When treated cells divide, they cannot reproduce their methylation patterns. Abnormal silencing of tumor suppressor genes is gradually reversed. Genes that had been locked in an off state begin to be expressed again.

Diagram 2.8 - Azacitidine: The First Epigenetic Cancer Therapy

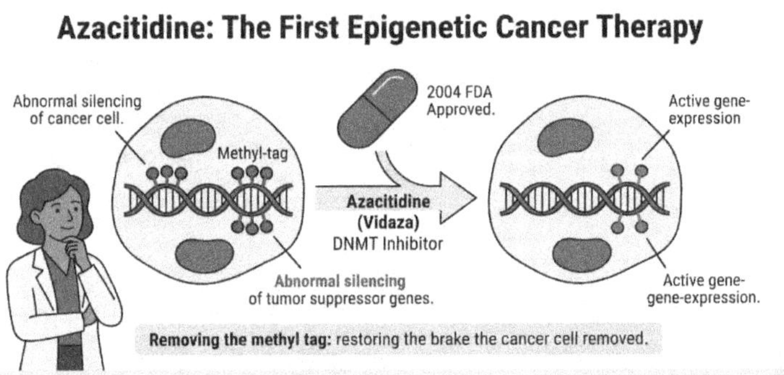

Azacitidine: The First Epigenetic Cancer Therapy as longentral treatming of tumorml suppressos.

Two years later, in 2006, the FDA approved vorinostat, sold as Zolinza, for the treatment of cutaneous T-cell lymphoma. Vorinostat inhibits histone deacetylase enzymes, which normally remove acetyl groups from histone tails. Blocking them allows acetyl groups to accumulate, chromatin opens up, and silenced genes begin to be read again: the same principle as azacitidine, applied through a different molecular lever.

These were not miracle cures. The approvals were for specific cancers, in specific patient populations, with benefit measured in months of additional progression-free survival. But as clinical milestones, they were significant. They demonstrated that epigenetic marks were not just observable but reversible. The epigenome could be treated as a therapeutic target. That a drug could walk into a cancer cell, find the molecular machinery that had been mis-set, and correct it, without touching the underlying DNA sequence.

James remembers reading about the 2004 approval in his then role as a health journalist and thinking of it as a minor regulatory footnote. "I had no idea," he told Lena once, "that it was the moment when eighty years of theory became a prescription." Lena smiled at that. "Most people did not. That is why we are here."

The Modern Era: Clocks, Scissors, and Liquid Gold

If the story ended with the first epigenetic cancer drugs, it would already be remarkable. But the last fifteen years have produced a second wave of discoveries that are, in some ways, even more striking. Three of them deserve particular attention: the epigenetic clock, CRISPR-based epigenetic editing, and the emerging technology of liquid biopsies.

The epigenetic clock emerged from work by Steve Horvath at UCLA, published in 2013. Horvath was studying methylation patterns across different tissues and different ages when he noticed something unexpected: certain CpG sites across the genome changed their methylation state in a highly predictable way as people aged. Not randomly. In a pattern so regular that you could use it to estimate a person's age from a tissue sample, without knowing anything else about the person.

Diagram 2.9 - The Epigenetic Clock

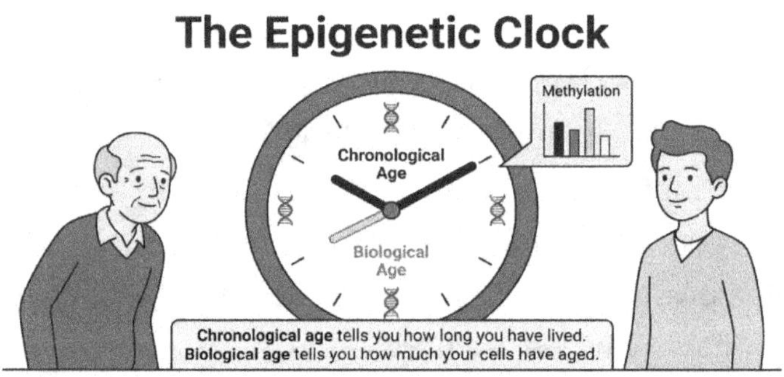

Epigenetic clocks measure cellular aging by analyzing DNA methylation markers.

The Horvath clock is based on the methylation status of 353 specific CpG sites. Together they function as a molecular timepiece, ticking away in the genome with remarkable consistency across different tissues and individuals, estimating chronological age to within about three to four years from any tissue sample. Subsequent researchers have developed clocks calibrated to predict health outcomes that measure what is now called biological age: how old your cells are acting, regardless of your calendar years.

People whose epigenetic age exceeds their calendar age tend to have higher rates of age-related disease. Factors that accelerate the clock include smoking, obesity, and chronic stress. Factors that seem to slow it include regular physical activity, a vegetable-rich diet, and quality sleep. The clock provides a molecular mechanism that may partly explain why lifestyle matters.

The second major development involves CRISPR. In its original form, CRISPR acts like molecular scissors: a guide molecule brings the cutting enzyme to a specific location in the genome, and the enzyme cuts. Jennifer Doudna and Emmanuelle Charpentier received the 2020 Nobel Prize in Chemistry for this work. But researchers quickly realized they could modify the CRISPR system to do something more subtle.

Diagram 2.10 - CRISPR as Epigenetic Editor: Placing a Methyl Tag

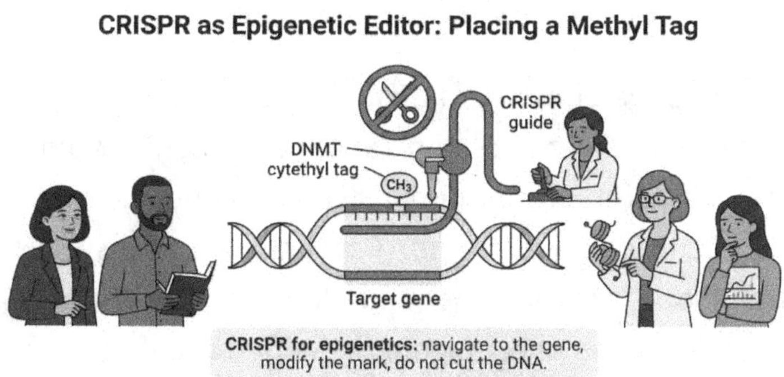

CRISPR for epigenetics: navigate to the gene, modify the mark, do not cut the DNA.

By deactivating the DNA-cutting part of CRISPR and attaching instead an enzyme that adds or removes epigenetic marks, researchers created what are called epigenome editors. These tools can navigate to a specific gene, guided by the same RNA-based targeting system CRISPR uses, and instead of cutting, deposit a methyl group, remove one, or add an acetyl group to a nearby histone tail. The DNA sequence is untouched. The epigenetic state of that gene is precisely and deliberately changed.

Because epigenetic editing changes the marks on DNA rather than the sequence itself, the edits are durable but not irreversible, which avoids some concerns associated with permanent DNA cutting. Researchers have used CRISPR-based epigenetic editing to silence disease-causing genes in animal models, reactivate silenced tumor suppressors, and study specific epigenetic patterns without permanently altering the genome. Human clinical trials are in early stages as of the mid-2020s.

The third development, liquid biopsies, sits at the intersection of epigenetics and cancer diagnostics. A liquid biopsy is a blood test that detects DNA fragments shed by tumors into the bloodstream. Cancer cells release DNA into the blood as they die and divide. This circulating tumor DNA carries the epigenetic signature of the cells that shed it. Because different cancers have distinct epigenetic patterns, a liquid biopsy that profiles methylation patterns across thousands of gene regions can detect cancer, identify the tissue of origin, and distinguish early from late-stage disease, all from a single blood draw.

Diagram 2.11 - Liquid Biopsy: Detecting Cancer's Epigenetic Signature

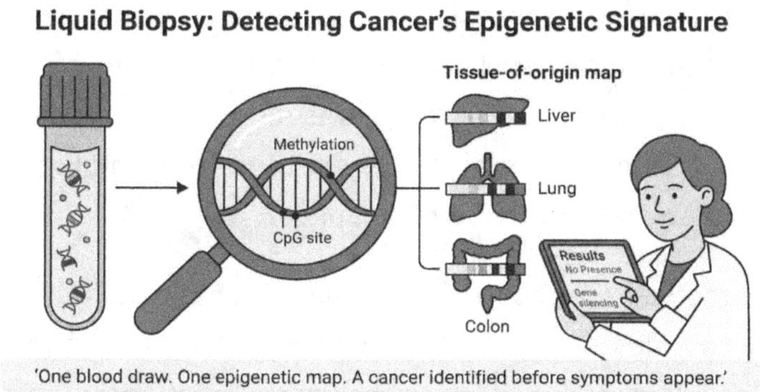

Liquid biopsies are already in clinical use for monitoring known cancers for signs of recurrence. The next step, early detection before symptoms appear, is the subject of intense research. Epigenetic profiling of circulating DNA is central to that effort, and several clinical tests built on methylation profiling are already available.

"Eighty years," Lena said to James one afternoon, gesturing at the timeline pinned to the corkboard. "From a pencil sketch of marbles on a hillside to a blood test that reads your epigenome and tells you whether there is a tumor somewhere in your body." James looked at the timeline. "When you put it that way," he said, "it sounds either very fast or very slow." Lena nodded. "Both," she said. "It is always both."

What This Means for You

You might be reading this history and thinking: interesting, but what does any of it mean for me today? The Dutch Hunger Winter happened eighty years ago. Azacitidine is a cancer drug, not a wellness supplement. The epigenetic clock is a research tool, not something your doctor measures at your annual physical. So why does this history matter to the person reading this book on a Tuesday evening, trying to understand whether their biology is more malleable than they were taught?

Every practical insight in the remaining chapters rests on the discoveries described here. Without understanding that the epigenome is real, heritable, responsive, and reversible, the practical claims would be assertions. With it, they are mechanistic conclusions drawn from eighty years of converging evidence.

Three things are worth taking from this history right now. First, your biology is more dynamic than you were probably taught. The epigenome responds to your lifestyle—second, timing matters. The Dutch Hunger Winter shows that certain periods of development are windows of heightened epigenetic sensitivity, which underscores the importance of taking seriously what we already know about nutrition and stress during pregnancy. Third, epigenetic marks can be changed. The approval of azacitidine in 2004 was the first clinical proof. The epigenome is not written in permanent ink.

"Try this," Lena sometimes tells visitors during public talks. "The next time you hear a health headline that mentions your genes, ask yourself: Is this about the DNA sequence, or is it about how the DNA is being read? Is this about the text of the book, or about which pages are currently open?" It is a small mental shift. But it changes what questions you think to ask.

Takeaway

The history of epigenetics is the story of a field that learned to see something it could not initially measure, describe, or even fully believe. Conrad Waddington drew a landscape in 1942 and named a process he could only intuit. The researchers who discovered DNA methylation in the 1970s found the first molecular alphabet for that process. The scientists who mapped the Human Epigenome Project showed how rich and cell-specific that alphabet turned out to be. The clinicians who brought azacitidine through trials and into FDA approval in 2004 proved that the epigenome was a therapeutic target. And the researchers now using CRISPR to edit specific epigenetic marks and liquid biopsy to read them from a blood sample are taking the story into territory that would have seemed like science fiction to Waddington.

What you hold from this chapter is not a timeline of trivia. It is an understanding of how the science arrived at its current state: slowly, through disagreement, with occasional moments of startling recognition, and with steadily increasing clinical relevance. The next chapter moves from history to mechanism. Lena will walk you into the cell itself, into the molecular machinery that reads and writes epigenetic marks in real time. It is called The Control Room, and it is where the science becomes most immediately relevant to your own biology.

3 The Control Room

James showed up to Lena's lab on a Tuesday morning with a coffee in each hand and a question he had been carrying since the previous chapter's reading. He set one cup on the bench beside her notebook, leaned against the doorframe, and said, "OK. But mechanically, how does any of this actually work?" Lena looked up from the centrifuge she was loading. She smiled. She had been waiting for that exact question.

She pulled a three-dimensional model from the shelf behind her, the kind used in undergraduate lectures, a chunky plastic structure about the size of a grapefruit, and set it on the bench between them. It showed a short section of DNA wound tightly around a barrel-shaped cluster of proteins, like thread coiled around a spool. "This," she said, "is where we start." James studied it. The DNA was blue. The protein spool was white. "That's inside every cell?" he asked. "Not one of these," Lena said. "Trillions of them. Arranged end to end, they would stretch from here to the sun and back several times over, all packed into a nucleus the width of a human hair. The coiling is not decorative. It is how the cell manages something impossibly large inside something impossibly small. And the way that coiling is controlled," she added, setting her finger on the white protein spool, "is a big part of how your genes get switched on and off."

Over the next hour, the whiteboard filled with three drawings: a sticky note clipped over a sentence in a book, a dimmer switch connected to a reading lamp, and a tightly wound spool of thread set beside a loosely opened one. "Pick whichever one makes the most sense to you," Lena told him at one point, stepping back to look at all three. "They are all describing the same thing." James looked at the drawings for a moment. He pointed to the sticky note. She nodded. "Good," she said. "Then let's start there."

Why It Matters

You have heard, probably more than once, that your DNA is your blueprint. It contains the instructions for who you are. That it was fixed at conception and cannot be changed, that framing is not wrong, exactly. Your DNA does contain the instructions. But here is what it leaves out: having the instructions and using the instructions are two entirely different things.

Think about a cookbook—a large, beautifully comprehensive cookbook sitting on a kitchen shelf. Every recipe the author ever perfected is in there. But the food that actually gets made on any given Tuesday depends on which pages you open, which chapters get bookmarked and revisited, and which ones never get touched at all. The cookbook does not change. The cooking changes enormously.

Your genome is that cookbook. It contains roughly twenty thousand genes, each one a set of instructions for building or regulating something your body needs. But in any given cell, only a fraction of those genes are actually being used. A liver cell reads a completely different set of pages than a brain cell does, even though both cells carry the same full cookbook. The DNA is identical. The gene expression is radically different. How does that happen? That is the question this chapter answers.

The answer matters for reasons that go well beyond satisfying curiosity. Understanding how genes are switched on and off is the foundation for understanding why stress affects your biology, why your diet influences your long-term health in ways that go deeper than calories, why twins with identical DNA can diverge so dramatically over a lifetime, and how a new class of medicines is already rewriting the biology of cancer. None of that makes sense without first understanding the molecular control room.

Diagram 3.1 - The Gene Control Room

Epigenetic marks decide which genes are read and which are ignored.

The Sticky Note on the Gene: DNA Methylation

Imagine you are editing a document and you want to flag a paragraph so that no one reads it aloud at the meeting. You do not delete the paragraph. Deleting it would be permanent, and you are not sure you want to go that far. Instead, you stick a small yellow note over it. The text is still there. Anyone who peeled the note away could read it. But as long as the note is in place, the reader skips it. That is DNA methylation.

In the cell, the sticky note is a small chemical tag called a methyl group. A methyl group is a carbon atom bonded to three hydrogen atoms, abbreviated as CH3. When it attaches to a specific location on a DNA strand, specifically to a molecule called cytosine, it changes what the cell's reading machinery does when it arrives at that spot. A methyl tag in the regulatory region of a gene, the stretch of DNA just before the gene's coding sequence, tells the reading machinery to skip the gene entirely. The gene does not get read. The protein it encodes does not get made. The gene is off, in practical terms.

The process of adding these tags is carried out by a family of enzymes called DNA methyltransferases. Think of them as a crew of workers whose entire job is to walk along DNA, find the right spots, and stamp a CH3 tag at each one. Some add fresh tags to DNA that has never been marked before. Others maintain existing tags when a cell divides and duplicates its DNA, ensuring that the daughter cells inherit the same pattern of silenced genes. This maintenance is how a liver cell, every time it divides, produces another liver cell with the same set of silenced genes rather than a random assortment.

Diagram 3.2 - Methyl Tag on DNA

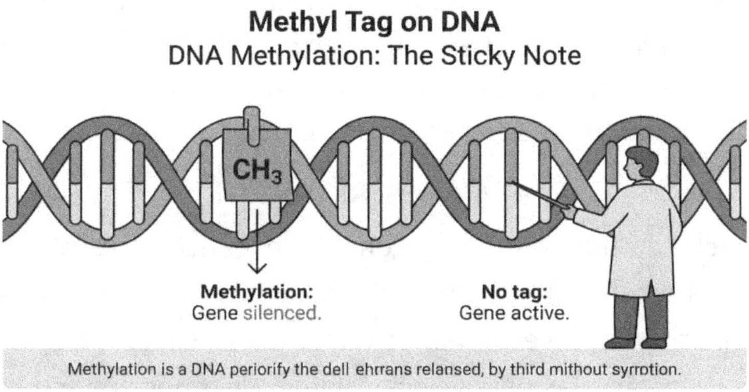

Here is where the story gets interesting. The tags can be removed. There is another family of enzymes, called TET enzymes, whose job is essentially the reverse of methyltransferases. TET enzymes chemically modify existing methyl tags, eventually leading to their removal. Peel the sticky note. The gene beneath it becomes readable again. The cell's reading machinery encounters it, recognizes the start signal, and produces the protein encoded by the gene. The gene is back on.

This reversibility is not a small footnote to the story of DNA methylation. It is the whole point. If methylation were permanent, it would be just another kind of genetic instruction, hard-wired and unchangeable. The fact that it can be added and removed in response to signals from inside and outside the cell is precisely what makes epigenetics biologically responsive in a way that DNA sequence alone is not. Many cancer cells have abnormal methylation patterns: genes that should be on get silenced by methyl tags that should not be there. Some of the most promising cancer therapies in clinical use today target enzymes that write and erase these tags.

The Spools and the Ribbons: Histone Modification

Go back to that model on Lena's lab bench. The white protein barrel that the blue DNA is coiled around. Those protein spools have a name: histones. And they do far more than serve as passive scaffolding. Histones are active participants in the control of gene expression, carrying their own layer of chemical marks that work alongside DNA methylation to manage which genes are accessible.

Picture the spool as having a set of short tails hanging off one end, like the ribbons tied to a wrapped gift. These histone tails are flexible regions that extend from the spool's surface and are accessible to the enzymes that modify them. Two of the most important modifications are acetyl groups and methyl groups. Yes, the same word as before, methyl, but applied to a protein rather than DNA. Context matters enormously in molecular biology, and this is a good early example of that.

Acetylation is the mark that loosens things up. When an enzyme called a histone acetyltransferase attaches an acetyl group to a histone tail, it changes the electrical charge on that tail. The spool loosens its grip on the DNA wound around it. The reading machinery can now more easily reach the genes in that region. In almost every context, acetylation is associated with gene activation. It is the open-for-business sign on the spool. The opposite process, removing those acetyl marks, is carried out by enzymes called histone deacetylases. Without the acetyl groups, the spool closes, the DNA compresses, and the genes there go quiet.

Diagram 3.3 - Histone as a DNA Spool

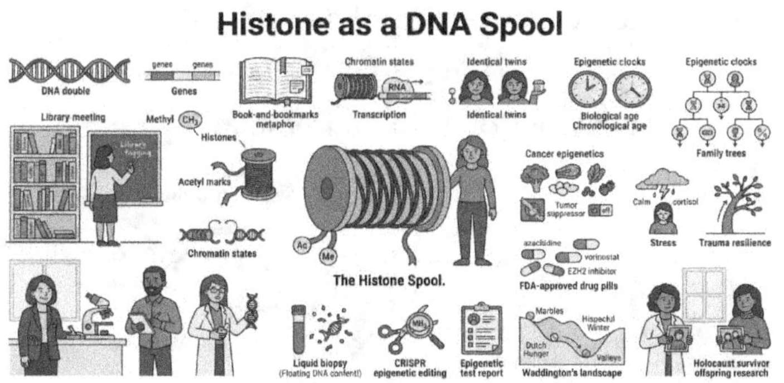

DNA wraps around histone proteins. The tails carry chemical marks that regulate access.

Histone methylation is more complicated. Adding a methyl group to a histone tail can either activate or silence the nearby gene, depending on which specific amino acid in the tail gets tagged and how many methyl groups are added. Rather than a simple on-off switch, the histone code is more like a full keyboard, capable of producing an enormous range of outputs from a limited set of keys. This complexity gives the epigenetic system its extraordinary precision.

Think of a filing cabinet with folders inside. The folders are your genes. When histone tails are acetylated, the drawer is open wide, and the folders are easy to reach. When the tails are deacetylated, the drawer is closed and latched. Signals from elsewhere in the cell and from outside it, hormones, nutrients, stress signals, and growth factors, all influence the activity of the enzymes that control histone modification. Your diet, your sleep, and your stress levels all feed into this system in ways we will explore in later chapters.

Diagram 3.4 - Acetylation Opens the Chromatin

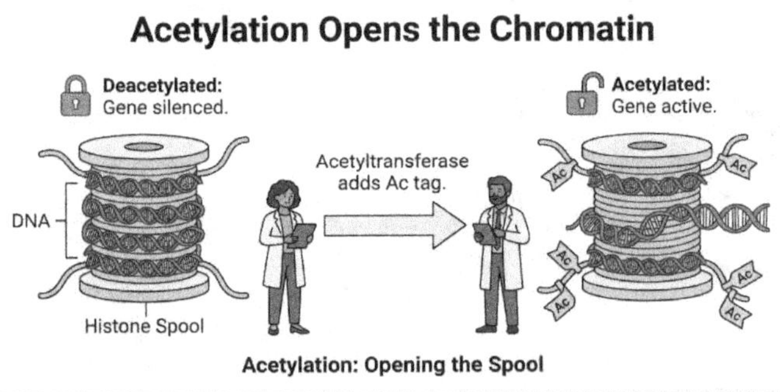

Acetylation modifies histones to unpack DNA and activate gene transcription.

Reorganizing the Archive: Chromatin Remodeling

The first two mechanisms operate at a fine scale. A methyl tag here. An acetyl group there. Individual chemical modifications are applied to specific locations. The third mechanism operates at a much larger scale. It is less like editing a sentence and more like reorganizing an entire library.

Inside the nucleus, DNA is organized into a compact structure called chromatin. Chromatin is the combined assembly of DNA and the histone spools it is wound around, plus all the associated proteins that help manage the whole structure. Chromatin can exist in two broad states. In one state, it is tightly packed and condensed, like a library where the shelves have been pushed together, and all the books are compressed spine-to-spine. In the other state, it is open and accessible, like a library where the shelves are spread apart, and the books are easy to reach. Scientists call these two states heterochromatin (tightly packed) and euchromatin (open). The words are not important. The concept is.

Chromatin remodeling is the process by which large molecular machines called chromatin remodeling complexes physically move the histone spools along the DNA or temporarily evict them altogether. Think of these machines as a team of archivists who periodically rearrange the entire filing system. They do not just open or close individual drawers. They move the filing cabinets themselves, repositioning whole blocks of the genome from the back room into the active floor space or vice versa. An entire region that was compacted and silent can be opened up. An entire active region can be packed away.

Diagram 3.5 - Tightly Coiled vs. Loosely Opened Chromatin

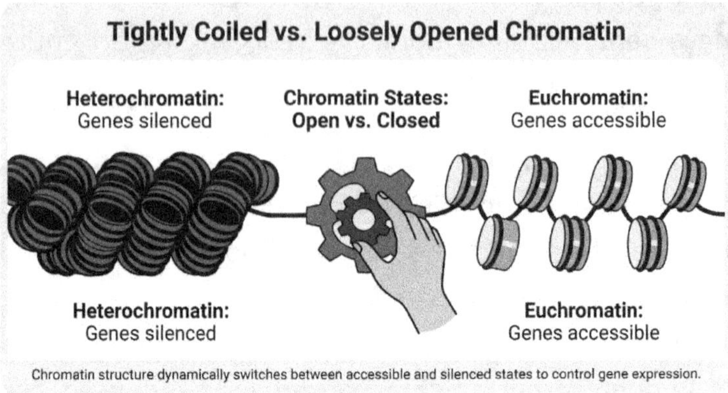

Why does the cell need this large-scale reorganization? Because the genome is enormous, managing it requires a hierarchical control system. Fine-scale modifications handle individual genes and small local regions. Chromatin remodeling manages territories. When a cell is differentiating, deciding what type of cell to become, large swaths of the genome relevant to other cell types need to be permanently silenced. Genes relevant to the cell's new identity need to be made permanently accessible. This kind of broad reorganization requires machinery that operates at the territory level, not just the gene level.

Lena put it this way during her explanation to James: imagine a large hotel that opens only one wing during peak season. The rest of the year, that wing is locked. The rooms are still there. The furniture has not been thrown out. But access is restricted. Chromatin remodeling is the process by which the hotel decides which wings will be open this season and which will not. For the life of a particular cell in a particular context, some wings stay closed. The decision is active and maintained, not accidental.

The Messengers and the Traffic Controllers: Non-Coding RNA

Here is something that surprised scientists when they first discovered it. The majority of your genome, somewhere around ninety-eight percent of it, does not code for proteins at all. For a long time, that vast non-coding territory was dismissed as junk. Scientists assumed that if a stretch of DNA was not producing a protein, it was probably just leftover evolutionary baggage. That assumption turned out to be spectacularly wrong.

A huge portion of the non-coding genome is actively transcribed, meaning it is read and converted into RNA molecules. RNA is the molecular middleman that normally carries instructions from a gene out to the protein-making machinery. But these non-coding RNAs, such as microRNAs and long non-coding RNAs, do not encode proteins. They have other jobs. And many of those jobs involve regulating gene expression.

Think of non-coding RNAs as a vast internal messaging system and traffic control network. Some act like blockers, finding specific messenger RNAs and latching onto them before they can be translated. When a microRNA binds to a messenger RNA, it typically marks that messenger RNA for destruction or prevents it from being read. The result is that even if the gene was turned on at the DNA level, the protein never gets made. It is like having a recipe that gets intercepted and shredded before it reaches the kitchen.

Diagram 3.6 - Non-Coding RNA as Traffic Controller

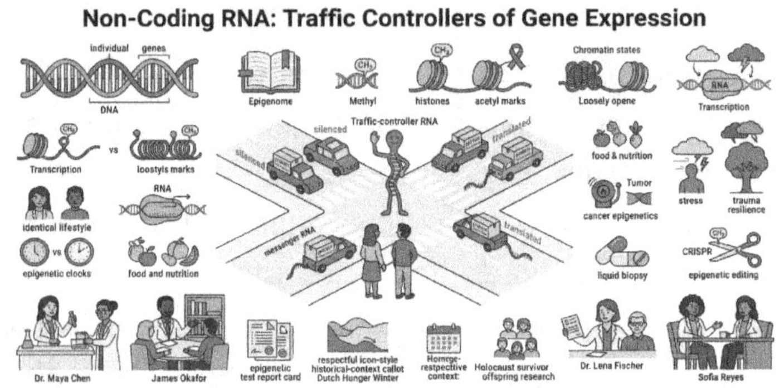

Non-Coding RNA as traffic controllers of gene expression: anciojtiol summaries simally incomporiate, rnin and idenccis.

Other non-coding RNAs act at the chromatin level, helping recruit enzyme complexes that add or remove epigenetic marks. In this role, they act less like traffic blockers and more like scouts or coordinators. They identify specific genomic regions that need modification and bring in the machinery to carry out the task. Long non-coding RNAs can physically associate with chromatin and serve as structural scaffolds that hold epigenetic regulatory complexes in place over specific gene regions.

One of the most dramatic examples of non-coding RNA at work is X chromosome inactivation. Women have two X chromosomes. If both were fully active, the cell would be flooded with twice the normal amount of the proteins encoded by X-linked genes. To prevent this, one of the two

X chromosomes is almost entirely silenced very early in development. This silencing is orchestrated by a long non-coding RNA called Xist, which coats the chromosome it originates from and recruits the chromatin-silencing machinery to spread across essentially the entire chromosome. It is one of the most elegant examples of large-scale epigenetic regulation in biology, and it is choreographed by an RNA molecule that never makes a single protein.

The broader point is that non-coding RNAs add a third layer of regulation on top of DNA methylation and histone modification. The cell does not rely on one system to control gene expression. It uses several interlocking systems simultaneously. The apparent redundancy is not inefficiency. It is robustness: multiple ways to achieve the same goal, multiple backups if one pathway is disrupted.

Writers, Readers, and Erasers: The Enzymes Behind the Marks

Every epigenetic mark in the cell was placed there by an enzyme. A different set of proteins recognizes every mark. And every mark can be removed by yet another set of enzymes. Scientists use a useful shorthand for these three categories: writers, readers, and erasers. Understanding this framework is one of the most practical conceptual tools in all of epigenetics, because it immediately clarifies how the system works and, critically, where it can go wrong or be therapeutically targeted.

Writers are the enzymes that add marks. The methyltransferases that stamp CH3 groups onto DNA are writers. The histone acetyltransferases that attach acetyl groups to histone tails are writers. Without writers, the epigenetic landscape would be bare and undifferentiated. Every gene would be equally accessible, which in practice means nothing would work correctly.

Diagram 3.7 - Writers: Enzymes That Add Epigenetic Marks

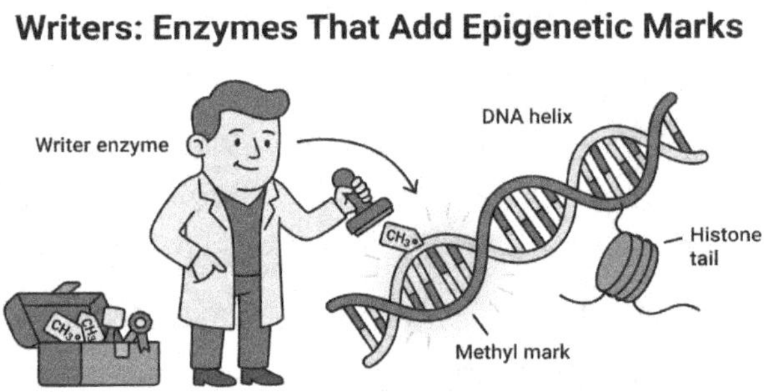

Writers are enzymes that add epigenetic marks, like methyl groups, to DNA or histone tails.

Readers are the proteins that recognize existing marks and respond to them. When a writer places a methyl tag on a stretch of DNA, it is the reader proteins that detect that tag and trigger downstream consequences. Some readers physically block the transcription machinery from accessing the gene. Others recruit additional proteins that reinforce the silencing. Still others recognize acetyl marks on histone tails and help recruit the transcription machinery that initiates transcription. Readers are the interpreters. They translate the chemical language of marks into cellular actions.

The specificity of readers is remarkable. Different reader proteins recognize different marks. The same mark at different positions on a histone tail can be read by different readers with different outcomes. The cell is not reading a binary on-off signal. It is reading something closer to a sentence, where the meaning depends on the combination of marks and their positions, not just the presence or absence of any single one.

Diagram 3.8 - Readers: Recognizing Epigenetic Marks

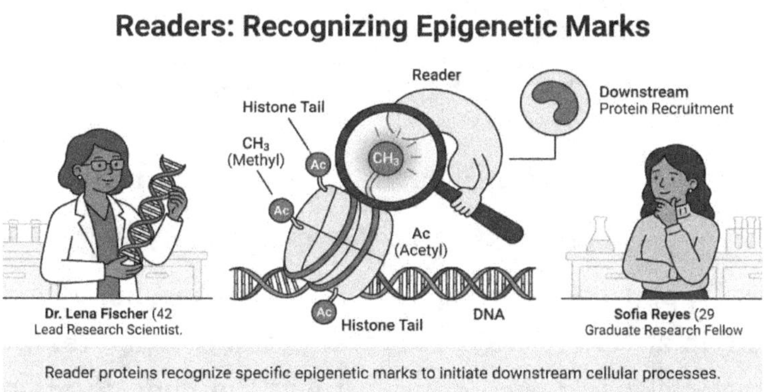

Erasers are the enzymes that remove marks. The TET enzymes that initiate the removal of methyl groups from DNA are erasers. Histone deacetylases, which strip acetyl marks, are erasers. Without erasers, the epigenetic system would be a write-once archive, fixed after development and incapable of responding to new circumstances. Erasers are what make the system dynamic. When the balance between writers and erasers is disrupted, the consequences can be severe. A writer who becomes overactive can silence genes that should be on. Drugs that inhibit specific writers or erasers are already approved for use in human medicine, exploiting precisely this biology.

Diagram 3.9 - Erasers: Removing Epigenetic Marks

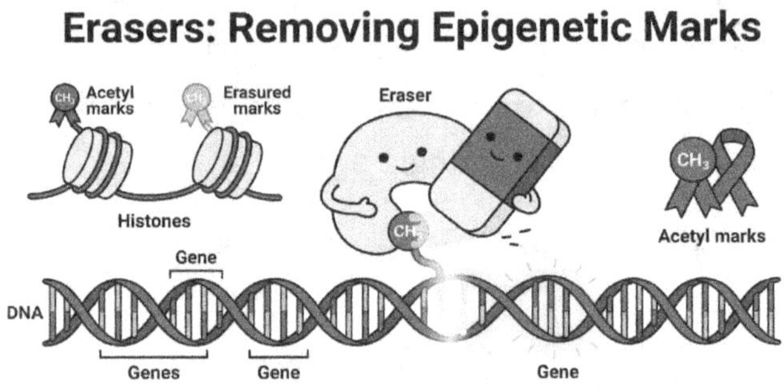

Erasers are enzymes that remove specific epigenetic tags from DNA or histones, altering gene expression.

The Orchestra Playing Together: How These Systems Work in Concert

James flipped back through his notes at one point and looked up at Lena. "Are these three systems separate? Or are they talking to each other?" It was the right question at the right time. The systems are not separate. They are deeply interconnected, each one influencing the others in a continuous molecular conversation.

Consider what happens when a gene needs to be permanently silenced during development. A cell deciding to become a neuron does not simply methylate the DNA at a muscle-specific gene and call it done. First, specific histone marks are placed in the region, creating a repressive chromatin environment. The DNA methylation machinery is then recruited to that region, in part because of those histone marks. Reader proteins recognize the combination of marks and recruit additional silencing machinery, including chromatin remodeling complexes that physically compact the region. Non-coding RNAs may guide some of this machinery to the right location. The result is a reinforced silence, maintained by multiple overlapping systems. The cell can become a neuron and stay a neuron.

There is also a temporal dimension to their interaction. Some epigenetic states are set quickly in response to a short-term signal and then reversed just as quickly. A cell responds to a hormone pulse by briefly activating a gene, and once the signal dissipates, the gene returns to baseline. Other epigenetic states are gradually established over time through the accumulation of marks that reinforce one another, becoming progressively more stable. This spectrum from transient to stable is part of why the epigenome can serve as both a rapid-response system and a long-term memory system.

Diagram 3.10 - Writers, Readers, and Erasers Working in Concert

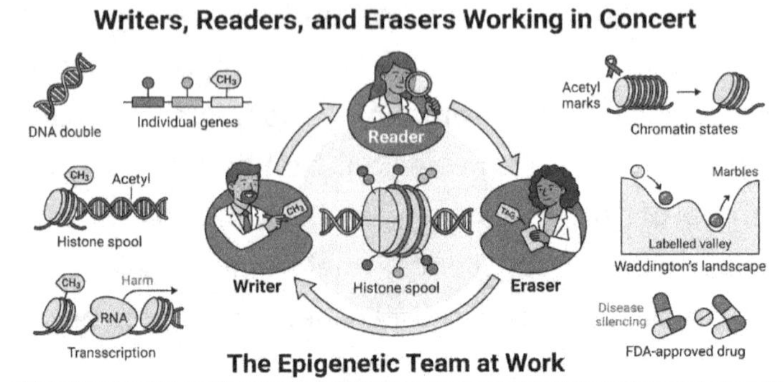

Writers, readers, and erasers work together to regulate gene expression.

Think of a symphony orchestra. Each section, the strings, the brass, the woodwinds, the percussion, has its own instruments and its own contribution. But the music comes from all sections playing in coordination, each listening to the others and adjusting in real time. The epigenome works the same way. DNA methylation, histone modification, chromatin remodeling, and non-coding RNAs are all playing together, coordinated by the same underlying genetic score, responding to the same signals, and producing an output that none of them could produce alone.

One particularly striking example of this coordination is what happens at the promoters of active genes, the specific DNA regions just upstream of where a gene begins. Active gene promoters typically show a characteristic combination: low DNA methylation, high levels of specific activating histone modifications, and a nucleosome-free region where histone spools have been temporarily evicted to allow the transcription machinery direct access to the DNA. This combination does not arise by accident. It is the result of coordinated writer and eraser activity and the action of chromatin remodeling complexes, all focused on the same small region of the genome simultaneously.

Revisable by Design: Why Reversibility Matters

We have touched on reversibility at several points in this chapter. Now let us examine it directly, because it is one of the most important ideas in this entire book. The epigenome is reversible. Not infinitely, not instantly, not in every cell type under all circumstances. But fundamentally, by design, the system that controls gene expression is built to change. And that changes everything.

Start with the biological logic of reversibility. If epigenetic marks were permanent, the cell would have no way to respond to its changing environment over time. Development, which requires dramatic shifts in gene expression as cells differentiate and specialize, would be impossible to orchestrate with any precision. Reversibility is not a design quirk. It is a functional requirement.

At the molecular level, reversibility is baked into the architecture of every epigenetic system we have described. Writers and erasers exist in functional opposition for every type of mark. Methyltransferases write, TET enzymes erase. Acetyltransferases acetylate, and deacetylases remove acetylation. The existence of the erasing enzyme is just as important as the existence of the writing enzyme. One without the other would give you a system that could either set marks permanently or never set them at all, neither of which is biologically useful.

Diagram 3.11 - Reversibility: A Mark Being Placed and Removed

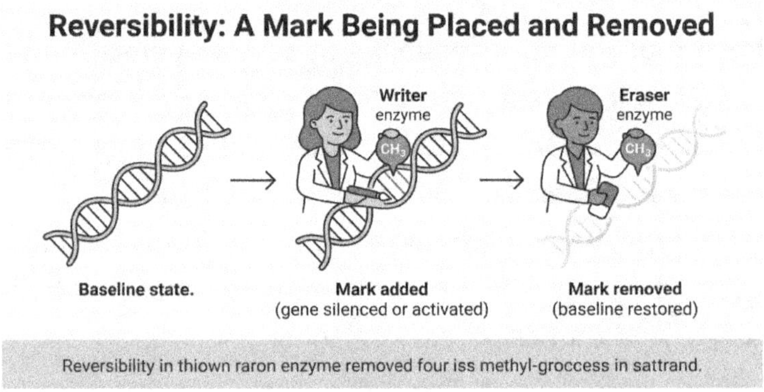

Reversibility has profound implications for medicine. A gene that is being silenced when it should be active, as happens with many tumor suppressor genes in cancer, could in principle be reactivated by removing the inappropriate silencing marks. Drugs called DNMT inhibitors block the enzymes that add methyl marks to DNA, allowing silenced genes to become re-expressed. Another class, HDAC inhibitors, blocks the histone deacetylases that remove acetyl marks, maintaining an open chromatin state. The U.S. Food and Drug Administration approves both classes for specific types of blood cancers, and research to extend their use is ongoing.

Reversibility also matters to the lifestyle-and-health connection that many people find most personally relevant in epigenetics. When research shows that chronic stress leads to changes in DNA methylation at stress-response genes, the natural follow-up question is: Can those changes be reversed if the stress is reduced? The answer, based on a growing body of research, is often yes, at least partially and over time. Exercise, diet, sleep, and therapeutic interventions have all been shown to produce measurable epigenetic changes. Biology is not a one-way ratchet. It is a dial that can turn in either direction, subject to the signals it receives.

There is, however, an important nuance. Not all epigenetic changes are equally reversible. Some marks are transient, almost by design, cycling on and off in minutes or hours. Others are highly stable, maintained across many cell divisions, and require substantial sustained intervention to shift. The epigenetic changes associated with long-term chronic stress are unlikely to be reversed by a single good night's sleep. The depth and duration of the reversal challenge tend to match those required to produce the change. This is not a reason for pessimism. It is a reason for realistic optimism, and for understanding that biology responds to sustained effort rather than quick fixes.

There is also an important distinction between reversibility within a single lifetime and reversibility across generations. Marks that are cleared during the formation of egg and sperm cells, and during early embryonic development, do not persist across generations. Marks that escape these clearing processes can, in principle, be transmitted to offspring. This is a distinction we will explore in depth in Chapter 7, when we examine the inherited echoes of ancestral experience.

Same DNA, Different Cell: How the Control Room Creates Diversity

We have looked at the individual mechanisms. Now let us step back and ask the big question they answer: how does a single fertilized egg, containing one fixed set of DNA, produce a body with over two hundred distinct cell types, each one behaving in a radically different way?

A liver cell and a neuron carry identical DNA. Every single base pair is the same. Yet a liver cell produces the enzymes that process alcohol and store glucose, and a neuron produces the channels and receptors that transmit electrical signals across synaptic connections. These are not slightly different cell types. They are as different from each other as a bicycle is from a concert grand piano in terms of molecular function. And yet: same DNA.

The answer is differential gene expression, and the epigenome is its primary engine. During development, as cells divide and begin to specialize, each emerging cell type establishes its own characteristic epigenetic landscape: a pattern of methylation marks, histone modifications, chromatin structures, and non-coding RNA profiles that collectively determine which genes are expressed and which are silent. A useful image: imagine the same orchestra performing three different pieces of music using the same sheet music library. Same musicians. Same instruments. What changes is the selection. The epigenome is the selection mechanism. It decides, for each cell type, which parts of the genome are expressed and which remain in storage.

What This Means for You

You do not need to remember the names of every enzyme we discussed in this chapter. What you need to carry forward is the framework, and it is remarkably simple. Your genes are not simply on or off. They exist on a spectrum of accessibility that is actively managed by a molecular control system, one that is responsive to the signals your cells receive, the environment your body is in, and the experiences you accumulate over a lifetime.

What this means practically is that your biology is not fixed. It is not a sentence that has already been written. It is more like a long and ongoing conversation between your genes and everything that happens to you. Sleep, exercise, nutrition, stress, social connection, and your physical environment are all participants in that conversation, not metaphorically but through the specific molecular pathways we have been describing. When your doctor talks about lifestyle factors affecting your health, epigenetics is part of the mechanism. Not the whole story, not a magic rewrite, but a real and important biological channel through which experience shapes biology.

Here is something practical to try. The next time you read a headline claiming that some lifestyle habit "rewrites your DNA," stop and ask what it is actually claiming. If it means changing the underlying DNA sequence, that is almost certainly not the case. But if it means changing the epigenetic marks on your genome, influencing which genes are expressed in your cells, that is biologically plausible and worth taking seriously. The key question is always: which genes, in which cells, by how much, and for how long? Headlines rarely answer those questions. But now you know how to ask them.

You can also begin to appreciate why early life experiences have such lasting effects on health. Early development is a period of intense epigenetic programming during which cell-type-specific landscapes are established throughout the body. Experiences, nutrients, hormonal signals, and environmental exposures during this window have access to an epigenome that is particularly plastic and particularly important to get right. What gets established then tends to persist, sometimes for a lifetime, because the maintenance machinery does its job well. This is not a reason to feel that early adversity is a permanent sentence. It is a reason to understand why supportive early environments matter biologically as well as psychologically, and why interventions designed to help people recover from early adversity are not just emotionally important but biologically grounded.

Diagram 3.12 - Lena and James with the 3D Histone Model

Lena and James with the 3D Histone Model

Lena and James with the 3D histone model focoganization bumrecauting the control systems.

Take a moment to appreciate what the reversibility of epigenetic marks means for medicine. We are in an era where drugs designed to modify the epigenome are approved for human use, where clinical trials are testing epigenetic therapies for dozens of conditions, and where comprehensive epigenome reading in a single blood test is becoming a clinical reality. The very feature that makes epigenetics personally relevant, its responsiveness and reversibility, is the same feature that makes it therapeutically exploitable. The control room has switches. And the switches can be moved.

Takeaway

The molecular control room we toured in this chapter is one of the most elegant systems in all of biology. DNA methylation, histone modification, chromatin remodeling, and non-coding RNA are not separate mechanisms operating independently. They are four instruments in a coordinated ensemble, all playing the same piece, all influencing each other, all responding to the same signals.

Together they answer one of biology's oldest and most important questions: how can trillions of cells in a single body, all carrying the same genetic text, do completely different things? The answer is that the text stays the same, but the reading changes. The epigenome decides what gets read. And the epigenome is not fixed. It is written, revised, and rewritten continuously over the course of a lifetime.

At the bench that Tuesday morning, James closed his notebook and looked at the 3D model one more time. "So the sticky note is the simplest version," he said. "But the real thing is all three of these at once, plus the RNA, all coordinated." Lena nodded. "Most of the time, yes. And that is why it is so powerful. One system fails, there are backups. One signal changes, the others adjust. It is not fragile. It is resilient by design." She set the model back on its shelf. "The interesting question," she added, picking up her coffee cup, "is not just how it works. It is how you read it. How you look at a cell, or a person, and see which switches are on and which are off. That is what we do next." James was already writing it down.

In the next chapter, we follow Lena into the world of reading the epigenome: the tools and technologies that allow scientists and clinicians to see the pattern of marks across an entire genome, what those patterns reveal about health and disease, and how the ability to read biological age from a blood sample is reshaping how we think about aging itself.

4 Reading the Epigenome

How Scientists Decode the Marks on Your DNA

The sequencing room at the Kessler Institute smells faintly of ozone and cold metal. Machines the size of large photocopiers line both walls, each humming in a slightly different register, each with a pale blue status light blinking at the front. Lena Fischer leads James through the door on a Tuesday morning, coffee cup in one hand, a folded printout in the other.

Lena smooths the printout flat on the narrow countertop that runs along the far wall. It is a methylation map, she explains, for a single gene in a single tissue sample. At first glance, it looks like a strip of weather radar: a horizontal bar dotted with hundreds of small marks, some dark, some light, each mark positioned above a tiny number that corresponds to a location in the genome. James leans in. Up close, the marks look almost like braille. "Every dot on this page is a story," Lena says. She taps the darkest cluster near the left end of the strip. "This one tells us the gene here is switched off. Has been for years, probably." James straightens up. "And how did the machine know that?" Lena turns to face the nearest sequencer, the one blinking its patient blue light, and almost smiles. "That," she says, "is exactly the right question."

This is where the detective work of epigenetics actually begins: not in the headlines, but in rooms like this one, with machines like these, and with scientists who have spent careers learning to read maps that most people never see. The epigenome is invisible. The DNA sequence you can read directly. But the methyl groups tucked onto certain letters, the proteins coiled around the double helix, the stretches of tightly packed or loosely opened chromatin, none of those things announce themselves. Scientists had to invent ways to see what is hidden. This chapter is the story of how they did it.

Why It Matters

Every claim in the chapters that follow, every finding about diet and epigenetic marks, every study connecting childhood stress to long-term biological change, every statistic about epigenetic aging, rests on the methods introduced here. Understanding how scientists read the epigenome does not require a laboratory background. But it does require some familiarity with the tools, because the tools shape what we know, and the limits of the tools shape what we do not yet know.

Think about maps. Before satellite imagery, the only way to map a coastline was to sail it, record every bay and inlet, and accept that the result was an approximation. The coastline was real. The ships' reach limited the map. Epigenomics is in a similar position. The methylation marks on your DNA exist right now, and the protein wrapping around your chromosomes is opening certain genes and closing others. But the maps we have are only as accurate as the tools we used to make them, and those tools have evolved remarkably in thirty years.

Knowing something about the map-making process also helps you read news stories about epigenetics with better judgment. When a headline announces that a study found a link between poverty and changes in DNA methylation, the method used to measure that methylation matters. Which tissues were sampled? How many people were in the study? Was this an association or a cause? These questions are not pedantic. They are the difference between a reliable finding and a promising but preliminary one. By the end of this chapter, you will know how to ask them.

Diagram 4.1 - The Epigenome Detective

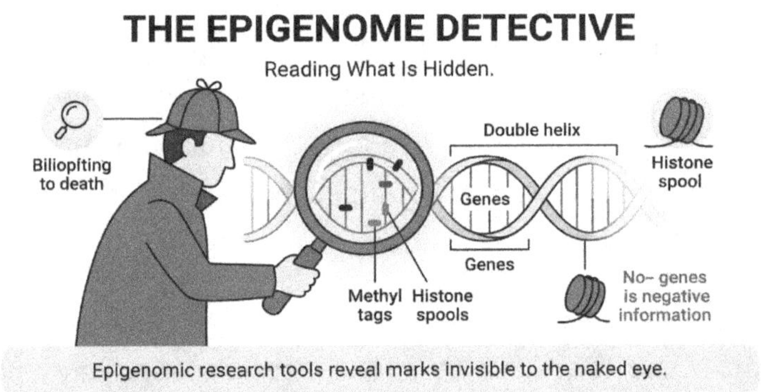

The story of reading the epigenome is also a story about technology changing fast enough to outpace the questions scientists could even imagine asking. Thirty years ago, it was not possible to map methylation across a whole genome in a single experiment. Ten years ago, it was not possible to read the epigenetic marks of a single cell. Today, both are routine, and the data they generate is so vast that the bottleneck is no longer the machines but the analysis. What scientists can see has expanded enormously. What they can confidently interpret is still catching up.

That gap between seeing and understanding is not a reason for pessimism. It is a reason to read carefully, to think about methods, and to maintain a proportionate confidence when you encounter epigenetic findings. Some findings are well-established and replicated across many studies, many tissues, and many populations. Others are early signals, promising but not yet confirmed. The methods introduced here are the key to distinguishing them.

The Chemical Highlighter: Bisulfite Sequencing

Imagine you have a long book written entirely in four letters: A, T, C, and G. Those are the bases of DNA. Now imagine that some of the C letters have been tagged with a tiny flag. The flags are the methyl groups we have been talking about throughout this book. Your job is to find out which C letters carry flags and which do not. The problem is that under a microscope, flagged C and unflagged C look identical. You cannot see the difference by looking at the sequence directly.

Here is what scientists figured out in the early 1990s: if you treat DNA with a chemical called sodium bisulfite, something specific happens. Unflagged cytosines (the C letters without methyl tags) react with the chemical and change. They convert into a different base called uracil, which, in sequencing reads, is read as T. But methylated cytosines, the ones with the flag, are chemically protected. They do not convert. They stay as C. So after bisulfite treatment, when you read the sequence, every C you still see is a methylated site. Every place where a C has become a T indicates that the site was unmethylated.

Diagram 4.2 - Bisulfite Chemistry: The Chemical Highlighter

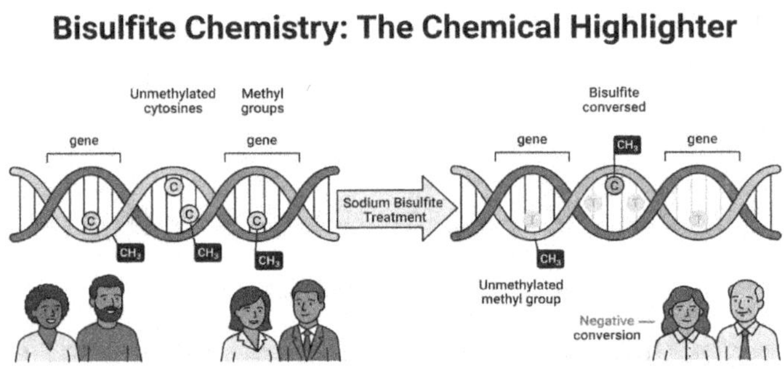

Unmethylated cytosines change; methylated ones hold still, revealing the marks by contrast.

When you combine bisulfite treatment with modern DNA sequencing, you get bisulfite sequencing: a method that reads the DNA sequence and simultaneously tells you, at every cytosine position, whether a methyl tag was present or not. Applied across the whole genome, whole-genome bisulfite sequencing (WGBS) produces a methylation map: a full picture of where methyl marks sit across all three billion base pairs of the human genome.

The resolution is extraordinary. Not just which genes are methylated, but which specific positions within those genes. Not just a rough neighborhood, but a precise address. Early versions of this technique were expensive, slow, and required large amounts of DNA. Each of those limitations has shrunk dramatically. Today, bisulfite sequencing can be done on small samples, processed quickly, and read at a fraction of the original cost. The printout Lena showed James in the sequencing room was a direct product of this method: a strip of reality, translated from chemistry into data, compressed onto a single page.

The technique has limitations we will return to later. But as a foundation for reading the epigenome, bisulfite sequencing remains the most widely used and most trusted method available. When you read a study about methylation patterns in a disease or how diet changes methylation in a population, this is almost certainly the tool that generated the data.

Diagram 4.3 - ChIP-seq: The Magnet in the Haystack

ChIP-seq: The Magnet in the Haystack

ChIP-seq pulls out specific histone proteins from a complex mixture, revealing where on the genome they sit.

The Magnet in the Haystack: ChIP-Seq

Bisulfite sequencing is brilliant for finding methyl marks on DNA. But the epigenome is not just about DNA methylation. It is also about histone modifications: the chemical tags placed on the protein spools that DNA winds around. And it is about which proteins are sitting on which parts of the genome at any given moment. To see those things, you need a different kind of detective tool.

That tool is called ChIP-seq. ChIP stands for chromatin immunoprecipitation. The name sounds formidable, but the idea behind it is elegant. It is essentially this: if you want to know where a specific protein sits on the genome, first you freeze everything in place, then you fish out all the DNA that protein was touching, and then you read the sequence of that DNA to find out exactly which parts of the genome it was bound to.

Here is the step-by-step story. You start with living cells. You add a chemical that cross-links proteins to whatever DNA they are touching at that moment. You break the cells open and shred the DNA into fragments: a soup of pieces, each still attached to its nearby protein. You then add an antibody, a molecule engineered to recognize and grab only the specific protein you are interested in. The antibody pulls that protein down, along with all the DNA fragments it was holding. You reverse the cross-link, release the DNA, and sequence it. The result tells you exactly where in the genome that protein was sitting.

In the context of histone modifications, ChIP-seq is extraordinary. Choose an antibody that recognizes histones tagged with acetyl groups, the marks associated with active genes, and you get a genome-wide map of gene activity. Choose an antibody for a silencing mark, and you get a map of repressed regions. Choose one targeting a transcription factor, a protein that binds DNA to drive gene expression, and you see exactly where that regulatory molecule is operating across the entire genome.

James once described ChIP-seq to a friend as "taking a photograph of the genome with everyone in it": not just the sequence, but all the molecular players interacting with it at that moment. Whereas bisulfite sequencing reveals fixed chemical marks, ChIP-seq reveals the dynamic landscape of proteins that actively read and regulate DNA. If bisulfite sequencing is the map of a city's permanent infrastructure, ChIP-seq is the snapshot of who is in those streets right now, which shops are open, which doors are guarded.

Drawing the Full Map: Whole-Genome Methylation

For most of the history of epigenetics, scientists studied methylation one gene at a time. You had a hypothesis. You designed an experiment. You published one small result. The map was built pixel by pixel, each laboratory adding one tiny patch over decades.

That changed with the combination of bisulfite sequencing and next-generation sequencing technology. Once it became possible to sequence a whole genome quickly and cheaply, the logical extension was to run bisulfite treatment on the whole genome and sequence everything. The result is a methylation map of the entire genome, every cytosine at every relevant position marked as either methylated or not. For the human genome, with its three billion base pairs and roughly 28 million sites where methylation typically occurs, this produces an almost incomprehensible volume of data.

Diagram 4.4 - Whole-Genome Methylation Map

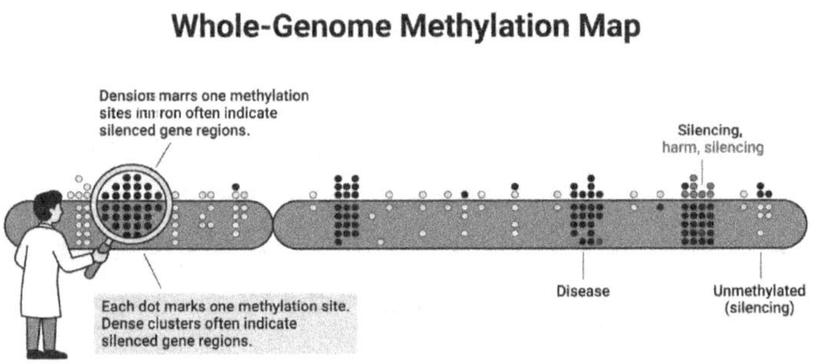

A comprehensive view of the epigenome showing all methylated positions across the genome.

What does a whole-genome methylation map actually look like, if you could see it all at once? Imagine spreading a strip of paper the length of a football field and placing a dot every few inches along it. Some stretches are dense with dark dots, the heavily methylated regions where repetitive DNA elements are silenced, and genes are consistently switched off. Other stretches are nearly empty, the actively transcribed regions where the epigenome is keeping doors open. The promoter regions of housekeeping genes, the genes a cell needs running at all times, tend to be low in methylation. The long repetitive sequences that make up a substantial fraction of the genome, regions that could cause havoc if expressed, tend to be heavily methylated and permanently silenced.

What these maps have revealed is that the epigenome is not random. It has architecture and neighborhoods: patterns that correspond to gene activity, tissue identity, developmental stage, and age. Some are universal across all humans. Others are unique to individuals, shaped by environment and experience. The maps also revealed something surprising: many of the most methylation-dense regions are not genes at all. They are remnants of ancient viruses that integrated into the human genome long ago and have been kept silenced by methylation ever since. The epigenome is also a record of biological history.

The Human Epigenome Project, launched in the mid-2000s, cataloged reference methylation maps across dozens of human tissues and cell types. These reference maps now serve as baselines, the healthy adult pattern against which disease states and environmental changes are measured.

Diagram 4.8 - The Human Epigenome Project Mosaic

The Human Epigenome Project Mosaic

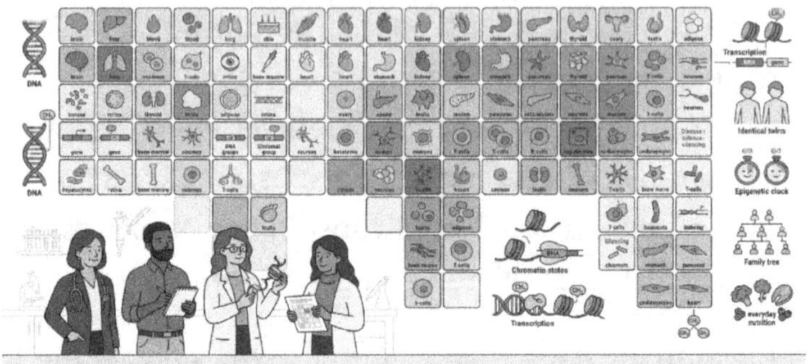

Reference epigenomes from dozens of tissue types form the foundation for understanding what is typical.

The cost of whole-genome methylation mapping has dropped roughly 10,000-fold since the early 2000s. What once required millions of dollars and months of work can now be done for a few hundred dollars in days. That price drop opened the field to smaller laboratories, to population-scale studies, and to the kind of replication that was impossible in the earlier era.

Comparing Thousands of Maps: Epigenome-Wide Association Studies

A single methylation map tells you a great deal about a single person in a single tissue at a single moment. But science advances by comparison. The real power comes from comparing thousands of maps, looking for patterns that consistently appear in people with a certain disease or exposure but not in those without it.

This is the logic behind epigenome-wide association studies (EWAS). The name deliberately echoes genome-wide association studies, or GWAS, which scan the DNA sequence across large populations looking for genetic variants linked to diseases. EWAS does the same thing, but for epigenetic marks. You take a large group of people, ideally thousands, measure their methylation patterns, and compare: do people with a given condition show consistent methylation differences at certain sites compared to people without it?

Diagram 4.5 - EWAS: Comparing Thousands of Maps

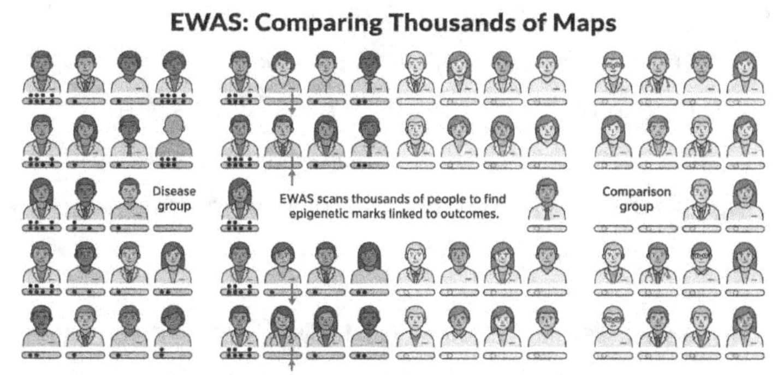

Large-scale comparison identifies unique epigenetic changes associated with health and disease.

EWAS findings have been striking. Researchers have identified methylation changes associated with smoking that are detectable in blood years after someone quits. They have found patterns linked to body mass index, childhood socioeconomic status, air pollution exposure, and depression. The epigenome turns out to be a surprisingly faithful recorder of life experience, at least at the population level.

But EWAS findings require careful interpretation. Finding a methylation pattern associated with a condition does not tell you whether the methylation caused the condition, whether the condition shifted the methylation, or whether both share a third driving factor. Consider a study finding that people with depression have different methylation at a particular site. The association is real. But the same pattern could arise if methylation drives depression, if depression drives the methylation shift, or if chronic stress or inflammation is reshaping both simultaneously. Association tells you things are connected. It does not tell you how. The careful researchers design longitudinal studies, work with large samples, and use animal and cell models to distinguish among these possibilities. Progress is steady. But the distinction between association and causation is one every reader of an epigenetics headline should hold firmly.

One other limit bears noting. Most EWAS studies measure methylation in blood because blood is easy to collect from large numbers of people. But blood is not a neutral stand-in for the tissue where a disease is happening. A methylation pattern found in blood may or may not reflect what is happening in the brain, the colon, or the pancreas. Statistical approaches exist to infer tissue-specific patterns from blood data, but the limitation is real.

The Same Person, Different Maps: Tissue Specificity

Here is one of the most important ideas in this entire chapter, and one of the most underappreciated. Every cell in your body carries the same DNA sequence. Your liver cells, your blood cells, your brain cells, your skin cells: identical genetic text, all the way through. But their epigenomes are completely different.

This is not a paradox. It is the whole point of the epigenome. The reason a liver cell looks and behaves like a liver cell, and not like a neuron or a muscle fiber, is precisely because the pattern of epigenetic marks in a liver cell is different from the pattern in a neuron. Those marks determine which genes are active and which are silent, and therefore which proteins are made, and therefore what kind of cell you are looking at. The DNA is the same text. The epigenome is the reading list, and it differs profoundly across cell types.

Diagram 4.6 - Tissue Specificity: Same Person, Three Maps

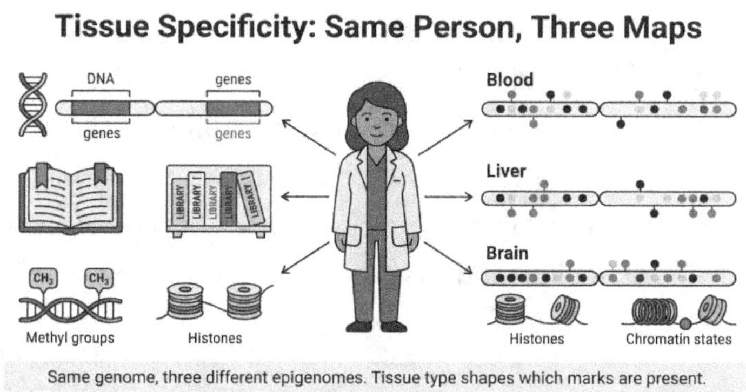

If you take a blood sample and measure methylation, you are measuring the epigenome of blood cells, a mixture of red cells, white cells, and platelets, each with its own epigenetic profile. You are not measuring the neurons, the liver, or the tissue where a cancer might be growing. Blood is a useful proxy for some things. For others, it is a significant limitation.

Post-mortem tissue banks allow direct study of brain methylation. Biopsies provide tissue from the liver, colon, and other organs in specific disease contexts. Computational deconvolution methods try to separate the signals from different blood cell types and infer what is happening in other tissues. All of these approaches are useful. None is perfect.

More recently, a technology called cell-free DNA analysis has opened up new possibilities. When cells die, they release fragments of their DNA, including epigenetically modified DNA, into the bloodstream. These circulating DNA fragments carry the methylation signature of the tissue they came from. By measuring the methylation of cell-free DNA in the blood, researchers can, in some cases, detect signals from specific tissues, including early-stage cancers, without requiring a biopsy. This is the principle behind some of the most promising cancer early-detection tests currently in clinical trials.

The tissue-specificity issue also explains why the same methylation change can mean very different things in different contexts. A change at a particular site might be associated with disease risk when it occurs in liver cells, but has no apparent effect in blood cells. Or it might be present in both tissues but only functionally relevant in one of them. This is why epigenetic research on disease increasingly seeks to work with the most relevant tissue possible, and why interpreting a finding always requires knowing from which tissue it came.

Diagram 4.9 - The Sequencing Machine at Work

The Sequencing Machine at Work

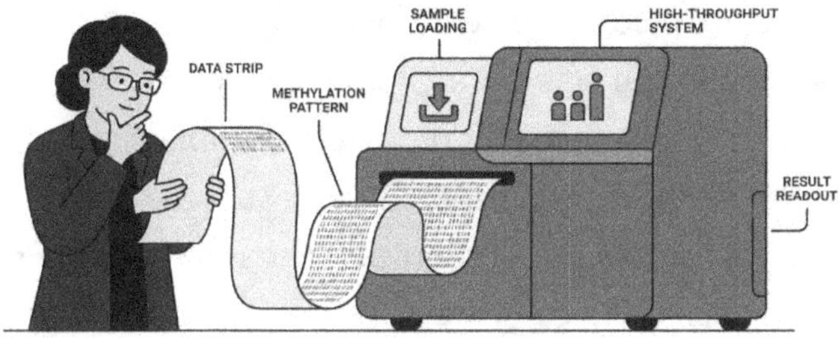

Modern sequencing machines generate methylation data for millions of sites in a single run.

One Cell at a Time: Single-Cell Epigenetics

For most of the history of epigenomics, experiments measured the average signal across millions of cells. The result from any tissue sample was a composite: a blended signal from every cell in the mix. If ninety percent of cells had a site methylated, you saw ninety percent methylation. The individual cell stories were lost in the average.

But tissues are not uniform. Within a tumor, different cancer cells may have distinct epigenomes, which may explain why some respond to a drug while others do not. Within the brain, different neurons carry distinct epigenetic profiles that correspond to their functions. Within a developing embryo, cell fate is determined by changes that occur one cell at a time. The average was useful. The individual stories were invisible.

Single-cell epigenomics changed that. The core technical challenge was finding a way to perform the chemical reactions required for bisulfite sequencing or ChIP-seq on the tiny amount of DNA in a single cell, which is roughly six picograms. Six picograms. One picogram is a trillionth of a gram. A single cell has almost no material to work with, and early single-cell methods lost a lot of it, producing incomplete and noisy data. The last ten years have produced a series of technical breakthroughs, many involving microfluidics (the art of manipulating tiny volumes of liquid in microscale channels), that now allow reliable single-cell methylation profiling.

Diagram 4.7 - Single-Cell Epigenetics: One Cell in a Droplet

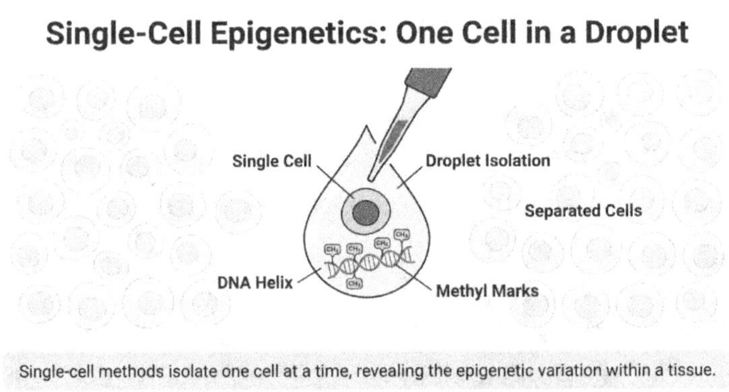

The results have been illuminating. Single-cell methylation studies of the brain show that neurons are far more epigenetically diverse than bulk measurements suggested, with subtypes carrying distinctive signatures tied to their function and location. Cancer studies reveal that tumors are not epigenetically uniform, and that small minority populations within a tumor, cells with distinctive epigenomes, may drive treatment resistance and recurrence.

James asked Lena once whether single-cell data was just better data, a straightforward improvement on the old approach. She shook her head. It is not better in the same way that a higher-resolution photograph is better than a lower-resolution one, she said. It is a completely different kind of information. Population-level data tells you the story of the crowd. Single-cell data tells you the stories of individuals within that crowd. Both are necessary. Neither replaces the other. Understanding which cells in a tumor are driving growth requires the single-cell view. Understanding whether a treatment changes methylation patterns across a whole tissue requires the population view. Scientists now use both, often on the same samples.

The cost of single-cell epigenomics has dropped steeply, following the same trajectory bulk sequencing did a decade earlier. The datasets are enormous and require powerful computational analysis. Still, the window they open onto cell-by-cell complexity has already begun to transform what we understand about development, aging, and disease.

The Edges of the Map: Reading Limits and What We Cannot Yet See

Every map has an edge. Every technology has a limit. Honest science includes both the findings and the frontiers of ignorance, and the methods for reading the epigenome are no exception. Understanding what current tools cannot do well is as important as appreciating what they can.

Bisulfite sequencing has a specific blind spot. The chemical treatment is harsh: it degrades a significant fraction of the DNA during conversion, making small or degraded samples difficult to work with reliably. More fundamentally, it cannot distinguish between two related modifications: 5-methylcytosine, the standard methylation mark, and 5-hydroxymethylcytosine, a related mark common in brain tissue with distinct functional implications. Both look the same in a standard bisulfite readout. Newer enzymatic approaches can distinguish the two, but they are not yet in routine use.

Diagram 4.10 - The Edge of the Map: Reading Limits

The Edge of the Map: Reading Limits

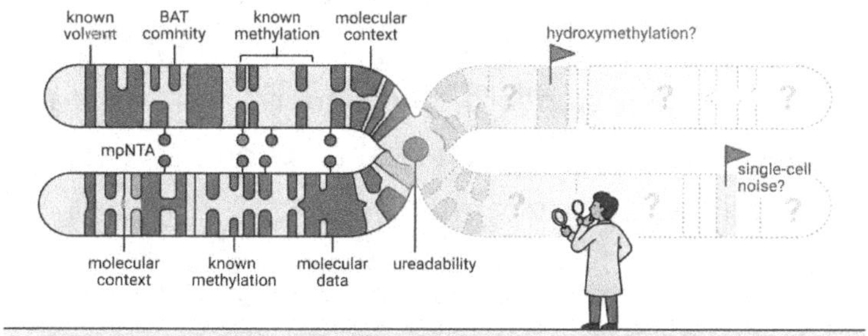

Current tools reveal a great deal, but some marks and contexts remain difficult to read accurately.

ChIP-seq has its own constraints. It requires an antibody, and antibodies are not always perfectly specific: if they recognize a related protein alongside the intended target, the map contains noise. Antibody quality determines data quality, and the field has invested substantially in developing better ones. There is also an inherent tension between the snapshot nature of ChIP-seq and the epigenome's dynamic nature. You freeze the cells at one moment. What you capture is what was happening then, not what happens on average or in response to a changing signal.

For EWAS studies, the limitations are partly technical and partly conceptual. The statistical approach compares methylation levels at hundreds of thousands of sites across a large number of people. Running that many comparisons simultaneously creates a significant risk of false positives: sites that appear different by chance rather than because of a real biological relationship. The field has developed rigorous statistical standards, including correction methods that demand very high levels of statistical evidence before a finding is considered significant, but the issue never disappears entirely. Replication, running the study again in an independent dataset, is the gold standard, and findings that have not been replicated in at least one other population should always be held with some caution.

Some important marks remain largely invisible to current tools. RNA methylation, the modification of messenger RNA rather than DNA, emerged as a major field only in the last decade and is still being mapped at scale. Chromatin's three-dimensional architecture, the way the genome folds in space inside the nucleus to bring distant regulatory elements near the genes they control, requires specialized and expensive techniques. Protein modifications outside the context of histones are important but largely uncharted at the genome-wide level.

None of this diminishes the progress. It contextualizes it. In thirty years, the field has developed tools that can read substantial portions of the epigenome with impressive precision. The portions we cannot yet read are active research frontiers, not permanent walls. As with the coastline maps drawn by sailing ships, what we have is genuinely useful. What comes next will reveal inlets and harbors we could not see from the distance we were traveling.

Diagram 4.11 - The Cost Timeline of Epigenomic Sequencing

The Cost Timeline of Epigenomic Sequencing

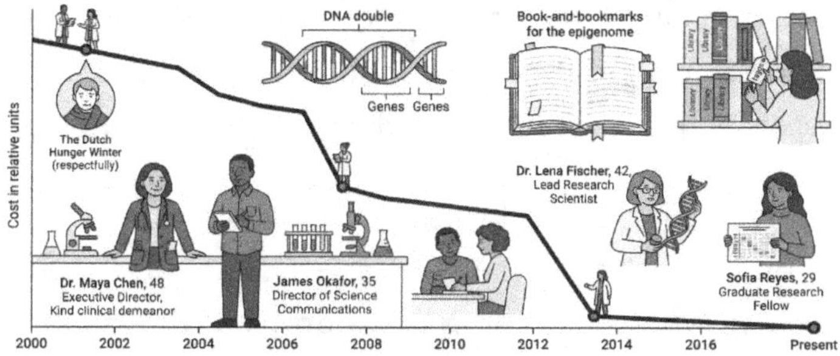

The cost of whole-genome epigenomic sequencing has fallen more than 10,000-fold since 2000.

Reading the Headlines: How to Evaluate an Epigenetics Claim

Epigenetics produces a steady stream of dramatic-sounding findings, and the gap between what a study actually shows and what a headline claims can be considerable. None of this is unique to epigenetics. It is a general feature of how science is reported. But because epigenetic claims often involve emotionally potent subjects (your children, your ancestors, your own behavior and its biological consequences), the stakes of misreading them are higher.

The first question to ask about any epigenetic finding is: which tissue? If the finding is based on blood samples, and the condition being studied is a brain disease, a lung cancer, or a liver disorder, you need to ask whether blood methylation is a meaningful proxy for what is happening in that target tissue. Sometimes it is. Blood methylation reflects systemic signals, including those associated with aging, certain environmental exposures, and certain inflammatory states. But blood is not the brain, and a methylation change in blood cannot tell you directly what is happening in neural tissue. Good studies will explicitly acknowledge this limitation. Studies that do not deserve more skepticism.

The second question is sample size. Epigenetic studies scanning the whole genome run hundreds of thousands of statistical tests simultaneously. Small samples, fewer than a hundred people, do not provide sufficient statistical power to reliably detect true associations amid that backdrop of noise. Many early EWAS findings from small samples failed to replicate in larger ones. Studies with thousands of participants are far more reliable.

The third question is replication. Has the finding appeared in more than one independent study, across more than one population, and across more than one tissue? A single study is the beginning of an argument, not its end. Findings that replicate across multiple populations and methods deserve substantially more confidence than those that appear only once.

The fourth question is causation. Finding that a methylation pattern is associated with an outcome is interesting. Showing that changing the methylation pattern changes the outcome (or, better yet, understanding the biological mechanism that links them) is what transforms an association into a genuine finding about how biology works. This is a high bar, and not every study aims to clear it. Observational findings have genuine value. But they are not the same as a mechanistic understanding.

Finally, check who funded the study and what practical implications are claimed. Epigenetics has attracted interest from supplement companies and wellness products claiming to optimize your epigenome. Some claims rest on legitimate preliminary research. Many do not. The gap between a cellular pathway being activated in a lab and a supplement rewriting your epigenome is enormous. Scientific caution is not pessimism. It is honest about how knowledge accumulates.

What This Means for You

You do not need to run a bisulfite sequencing experiment to benefit from knowing how one works. What this chapter gives you is something more practical: a framework for reading the science that affects your decisions.

When you read a story about epigenetics and health, try asking the four questions from the previous section out loud, even if only to yourself. Which tissue? How large was the sample? Has it been replicated? Is this an association or a causal finding? You will quickly find that many headlines dissolve on contact with those questions, while others hold up and become more interesting for having survived them.

If you have consumer genetic testing, you may eventually have access to epigenetic data as well. Several services already offer methylation-based estimates of biological age, and more will follow. Apply the same questions: what tissue was sampled, what population formed the reference, and what does the number actually claim to measure? A biological age one or two years off your chronological age is likely within measurement noise. A difference of a decade deserves attention, but still needs careful interpretation.

One of the most empowering things about understanding how the epigenome is read is that it makes the limits of current knowledge visible without making the whole enterprise seem unreliable. The tools are good. The findings are real. The maps are incomplete. That combination is exactly where any active science lives. You are not being asked to trust everything or distrust everything. You are being asked to read carefully, hold findings proportionately, and stay curious.

There is also something worth sitting with about what the sequencing room represents. Every time a sample goes into one of those humming machines, someone is asking a question about human biology that was previously unanswerable. The methylation map Lena showed James, the one with thousands of dots, each one a story, represents real information about a real person's biology. That information now exists in a way it could not have a generation ago. What we choose to do with it, clinically, ethically, personally, is a conversation that is only beginning.

Diagram 4.12 - Lena Shows James the Methylation Printout

Lena Shows James the Methylation Printout

Lena explains how specific patterns of methylation on DNA regulate gene activity across different cells.

Takeaway

The epigenome is not directly visible. Reading it required inventing chemical treatments that reveal marks by their resistance to change, antibody-based fishing methods that pull specific proteins out of a molecular sea, and sequencing approaches that can process a single cell's worth of DNA. These tools now generate data on a scale that would have seemed fantastical to the scientists who first described DNA methylation in the 1970s. The maps they produce are real, detailed, and genuinely informative, even as they remain incomplete.

The most important habit this chapter invites is to read epigenetic findings the way Lena reads a methylation map: with attention to what the data actually shows, what assumptions went into producing it, and what remains outside the frame. Good science is not the absence of uncertainty. It is a disciplined accounting of it. The marks on your DNA are real. The tools to read them are powerful. The story they tell is still being assembled, dot by dot.

In the next chapter, we follow that story somewhere very close to home. You have just learned how scientists read the epigenome. The next question is: who writes it? What actually places these marks, shifts them, and reinforces them? The answer begins with something you do three times a day. What you eat turns out to have a direct, documented, and sometimes surprising relationship to the marks on your DNA. The kitchen and the laboratory turn out to be talking to each other. That conversation is what Chapter Five, "You Are What You Eat," is about.

5 You Are What You Eat (and So Are Your Genes)

The Kessler Institute cafeteria is not fancy. Fluorescent light bounces off pale green walls. The hot-food station smells like roasted garlic and something involving lentils. James Okafor had been heading for the turkey sandwich, largely on autopilot, when Maya Chen appeared beside him and paused in front of the salmon. She studied it for a second, the way she studied a biopsy slide, tilting her head a fraction.

"You know," Maya said, picking up a plate and settling a piece of salmon onto it, "every single meal is a conversation with your epigenome. You're not just feeding yourself. You're handing your cells a set of raw materials and letting the machinery decide what to do with them." She glanced at James. "The sandwich will also work. But the salmon is bringing something the bread doesn't." James looked at his turkey sandwich. Then back at Maya's salmon. Then he put the sandwich back and reached for the fish, mostly because it felt like the correct response to a statement like that.

They found a table by the window. The Charles River glinted gray and silver below. Maya set her tray down and pulled a folded printout from her coat pocket, the way she always did, as if the real meal was always the paper. It showed two litters of mice: one yellow and round, one brown and sleek. Same DNA. Different plates. James looked at the printout and then back at his salmon. "Okay," he said. "Tell me everything."

Diagram 5.1 - Grocery Cart and DNA

Grocery Cart and DNA

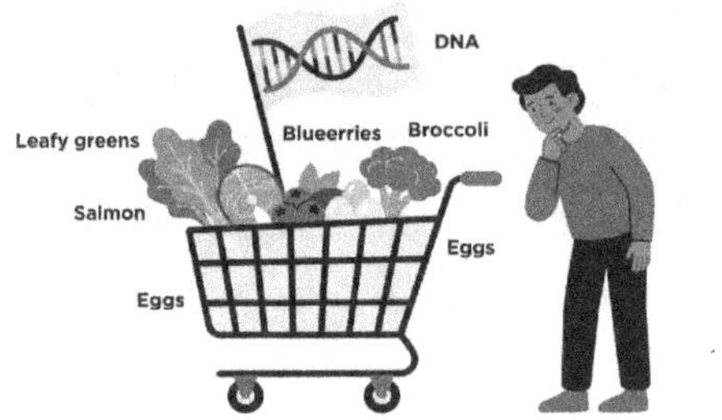

Grocery cart and produce use the power, nuhar item in the ilings of their vega **grocery cart and DNA**.

Why It Matters

There is a version of nutritional epigenetics that is serious science, carefully established in model organisms and increasingly in human populations. And there is a version that is wellness mythology, dressed up in the language of molecular biology to sell supplements, smoothie powders, and personalized "epigenetic diets." These two versions coexist in bookstores, in health blogs, and in your social media feed, and they look remarkably similar from the outside. One of this chapter's main jobs is to teach you how to tell them apart.

The serious version is genuinely compelling. Some nutrients are raw materials that your cellular machinery uses to build and maintain epigenetic marks, including the methyl tags on DNA we first met in Chapter 3. If these nutrients are scarce, the methylation process can stall or misfire. If they are abundant at the right developmental moments, they can influence which genes receive methyl marks and which do not. Timing and context matter enormously. The Dutch Hunger Winter and the agouti mouse experiments are among the most striking demonstrations in the history of epigenetics research.

The mythology version takes those real findings and extrapolates wildly. It claims that specific "superfoods" can reprogram your epigenome. It implies that eating the right things will "activate" the right genes and silence the wrong ones, as if your diet is a precision editing tool you can wield yourself. The real story is more interesting and more honest than that. Let's start from the beginning.

Building the Methyl Groups: The One-Carbon Cycle

In Chapter 3, we talked about methyl groups, the tiny chemical tags attached to specific spots on your DNA that act like switches, dimming or amplifying gene expression. We talked about DNMT enzymes that attach them and TET enzymes that remove them. But we didn't ask a surprisingly practical question: where do the methyl groups actually come from?

The answer is: your food, more specifically, from a set of nutrients that donate carbon and nitrogen atoms to a molecular relay race inside your cells. That relay race is called the one-carbon cycle, and it is one of the most important biochemical pathways you have probably never heard of.

Here is how it works in plain English. Picture a factory that makes a very specific product: a molecule called SAM, which stands for S-adenosylmethionine. SAM is the cell's universal methyl donor. When a DNMT enzyme wants to attach a methyl tag to a stretch of DNA, it reaches for SAM the way a craftsperson reaches for a bottle of glue. SAM hands over a methyl group and becomes SAH in the process. The factory's job is to constantly replenish the SAM supply.

To make SAM, the factory needs one critical ingredient: an amino acid called methionine. Methionine is found in protein-rich foods, including eggs, meat, fish, and legumes. Your cells take methionine and, with a little help from a molecule called ATP, convert it into SAM. So far, so good. But the factory also needs to recycle the spent SAH back into fresh methionine, because the body cannot make methionine from scratch. And this is where things get nutritionally interesting.

To recycle SAH back into methionine, your cells need a helper molecule called a methyl donor from the diet. Three nutrients do this recycling job: folate (the B9 vitamin, found in leafy greens, beans, and lentils), vitamin B12 (found in eggs, fish, meat, and dairy), and choline (found in eggs, liver, and soybeans). A fourth compound, betaine, which comes from beets and spinach, among other sources, can also donate methyl groups to this cycle.

Without adequate amounts of these nutrients, the recycling slows. SAH builds up. SAM becomes scarce. The methyl-tag supply chain runs low.

This is the core of nutritional epigenetics. It is not magic. It is chemistry. And it means that what you eat literally determines, in part, how much raw material your cells have available to build and maintain the epigenetic marks on your DNA. Think of it like a paper factory that relies on a steady supply of wood pulp. Plenty of pulp means plenty of paper. A shortage of pulp means production slows. The machinery is the same—the output changes because the inputs change.

Diagram 5.2 - The One-Carbon Cycle

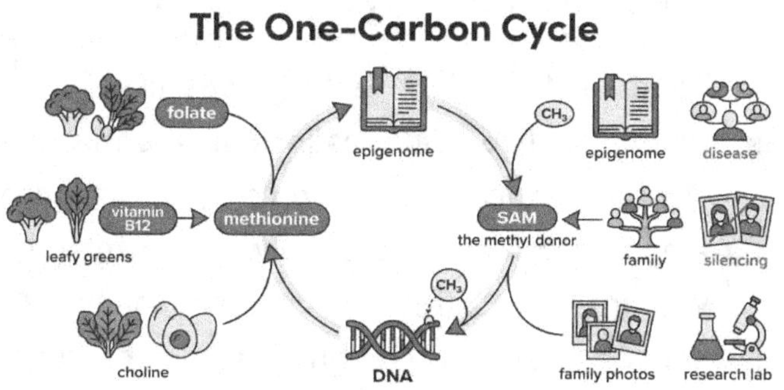

The One-Carbon Cycle is the methyl metaphor in disease, gene, harm, or silencing.

Folate, B Vitamins, and the Foods That Supply Them

If there is a nutrition story that epigenetics has most powerfully validated, it is the story of folate. Most people have heard that pregnant women should take folic acid supplements. The historical reason was neural tube defects: insufficient folate during the first weeks of pregnancy dramatically increases the risk that the fetal spinal cord will fail to close correctly, causing conditions like spina bifida. That connection was established decades ago and is one of the most robust nutritional findings in medicine.

What epigenetic research has added to this story is a molecular explanation. Early pregnancy is a time of intense epigenetic reprogramming. Large swaths of the epigenome are stripped and rebuilt as cells specialize into different tissues. The demand for methyl groups during this window is enormous. If the one-carbon cycle is running low, that reprogramming can go wrong in ways that ripple forward through every cell division that follows.

Folate-rich foods include dark leafy greens like spinach, kale, and romaine lettuce; legumes including lentils, black beans, and chickpeas; asparagus; broccoli; and avocado. Fortified grains and cereals also supply significant folate, which is why in the United States and many other countries, enriched flour has been required to contain added folic acid since the late 1990s. That policy change, simple as it sounds, is estimated to have reduced the incidence of neural tube defects by roughly 35 percent. That is epigenetically informed public health policy in action.

Diagram 5.3 - Folate-Rich Foods Panel

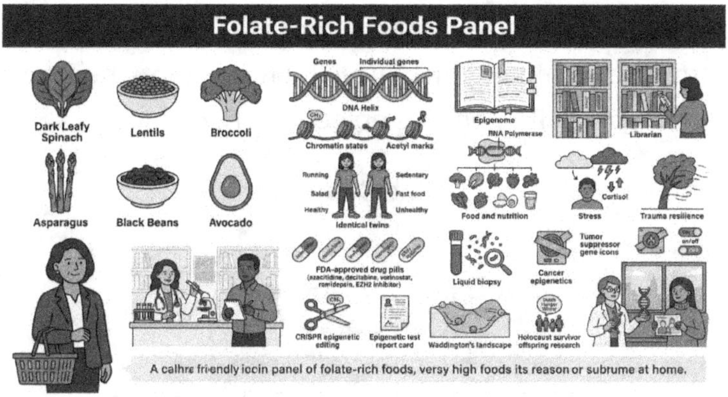

A calhre fri·endly iocin panel of folate-rich foods, versy high foods its reason or subrume at home.

Vitamin B12 is a cofactor in the one-carbon cycle. The two nutrients depend on each other at a key step in the methionine recycling process, and a deficiency of either one can functionally impair the other's role. B12 is found almost exclusively in animal products: fish (particularly salmon, tuna, and sardines), shellfish, eggs, meat, and dairy. For people following vegan or heavily plant-based diets, B12 supplementation is not optional; it is genuinely necessary for long-term health, and the epigenetic implications of chronic B12 deficiency are real. Studies in populations with low B12 intake have found altered methylation patterns at cancer-associated genes, a finding that warrants attention rather than alarm.

Choline is the quieter member of this trio, less culturally visible than folate or B12 but equally important in the one-carbon cycle. It is also a structural building block of cell membranes. Eggs are one of the richest sources, with a single large egg providing about 150 milligrams, roughly a quarter of the daily adequate intake for most adults. Liver, soybeans, and fish also supply meaningful choline. Most adults in wealthy countries consume less than the recommended amount, making choline one of the quiet nutritional gaps with genuine epigenetic relevance.

Diagram 5.4 - B12 and Choline Sources

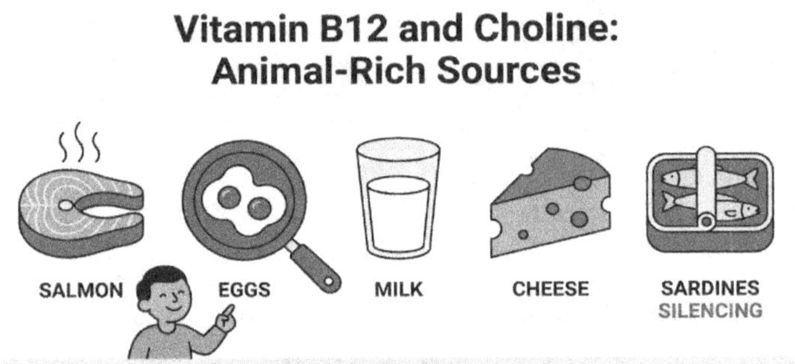

A friendlly illustrated panel of Vitamin B12 and choline-rich foods.

It is worth pausing here to clarify what this does and does not mean for everyday eating. The one-carbon cycle does not operate on a hair trigger. If you skip a salad today, your DNA methylation will not go haywire overnight. The body has buffering capacity. SAM stores exist, and the recycling machinery can compensate for short-term shortfalls. The research suggests that chronic deficiencies, sustained over weeks, months, or critical developmental windows, are what produce measurable epigenetic effects. Occasional variation in your diet is normal and fine. What matters is the long-term pattern, and especially the adequacy during key periods such as pregnancy and early childhood.

Polyphenols: What the Science Says, and What It Doesn't

Walk into any health-food store, and you will find shelves of products promoting the "epigenetic benefits" of green tea, turmeric, and blueberries. The claims are usually just specific enough to sound credible and just vague enough to avoid being provably false. So what does the actual science say about these plant compounds?

The compounds in question belong to a family called polyphenols, which are naturally occurring molecules produced by plants for their own purposes, usually as protection against UV radiation, insects, or pathogens. When we eat plants, we also consume these compounds, and they can interact with human biology in various ways. Several polyphenols have been studied specifically for their potential effects on epigenetic marks, and some of the findings are genuinely interesting. But they come with an important asterisk.

Green tea contains a polyphenol called EGCG, short for epigallocatechin-3-gallate. Cell culture studies, experiments done on cells in petri dishes, have found that EGCG can inhibit DNMT enzymes, the machinery that adds methyl tags to DNA. In other words, in a dish of cancer cells, EGCG can reduce DNA methylation at certain sites. Some researchers have proposed that this could partly explain the observed association between high green tea consumption in some Asian populations and lower rates of certain cancers. This is a plausible hypothesis. It is not a proven mechanism in humans at the concentrations achieved by drinking a cup or three of tea a day.

The gap between cell culture results and human clinical outcomes is enormous. Cells in a dish are bathed in a compound at concentrations that bear little resemblance to what your bloodstream looks like after you drink a cup of tea. Human digestion transforms polyphenols considerably before they ever reach your cells. And human cancer is not one disease behaving in a petri dish. The progression from "this compound inhibits DNMT in cell culture" to "drinking this tea meaningfully reduces your cancer risk via epigenetic mechanisms" requires multiple layers of evidence that, for most polyphenols, do not yet exist at the required strength.

Diagram 5.5 - Polyphenol Family Icons

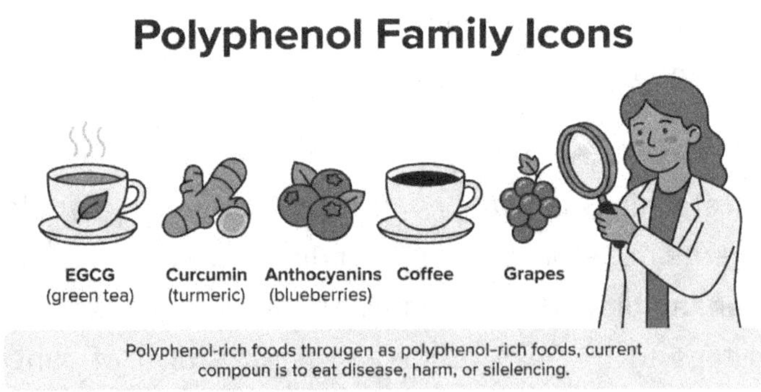

Turmeric and its active compound, curcumin, have been studied in similar cell culture and animal models, with some findings suggesting effects on histone modification and methylation patterns in cancer cell lines. The anti-inflammatory properties of curcumin are well-established and supported by multiple lines of evidence. But the specific claim that cooking with turmeric will "reprogram your epigenome" in a clinically meaningful way is not supported by current evidence in healthy humans. Turmeric is a pleasant spice with a long culinary history. That is a perfectly good reason to use it.

Blueberries and other dark berries contain anthocyanins with demonstrated antioxidant activity and some suggestive associations with cognitive and cardiovascular health. Some animal studies have found effects on DNA methylation in specific tissues. Human data are preliminary. The honest summary: eating colorful fruits and vegetables, including berries, green tea if you enjoy it, and turmeric in your cooking, is consistent with what we know about overall health. But you are not aiming a precision epigenetic editing tool at a specific gene when you sip your green tea. You are making a reasonable food choice.

This honest calibration is not a disappointment. It is what distinguishes science from marketing. The real story of how nutrition shapes epigenetics is compelling enough without embellishment, as the next two sections will show.

The Dutch Hunger Winter: When History Became Biology

In the autumn of 1944, the Nazi occupation forces imposed a blockade on the western Netherlands in retaliation for a Dutch railway strike that had been organized in support of the Allied advance. Food transport to Amsterdam, Rotterdam, and other major cities was almost entirely cut off. By the winter of 1944 to 1945, civilians were surviving on as few as 400 to 800 calories per day. People burned furniture and pulled up tulip bulbs to eat. Cats and dogs disappeared. Over the course of that brutal winter, roughly 18,000 to 22,000 people died from starvation and cold-related disease.

The liberation came in May 1945. But for the children conceived or developing in utero during the famine, the consequences did not end when the food supply returned. Decades later, researchers examining Dutch health records began to notice something unusual about the cohort born around 1945. People who had been in utero during the famine showed elevated rates of obesity, cardiovascular disease, type 2 diabetes, and certain mental health conditions. Their birth weights were often normal because during the famine, the fetal body had adapted to conserve energy, redirecting resources to development. But those adaptations appeared to have come at a long-term metabolic cost.

The landmark molecular study, published in 2008, compared the DNA methylation patterns of adults who had been in utero during the famine with those of their same-sex siblings born before or after the famine period. The researchers focused on a gene called IGF2, which codes for insulin-like growth factor 2, a key regulator of fetal growth and metabolism. They found that people who had been in the womb during the famine had significantly less methylation at the IGF2 gene than their non-exposed siblings. Sixty years after the famine ended, the epigenetic mark remained.

Diagram 5.7 - Dutch Hunger Winter Timeline

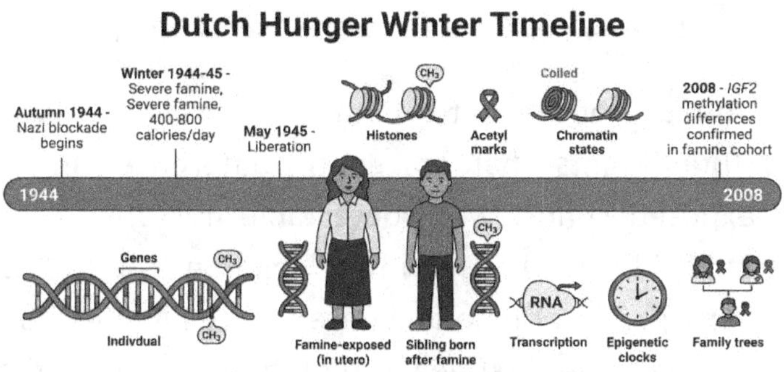

This diagram is shentilly Dutch Hunger Winter timeline ite torm, harm, and silfmness in famine cohort.

The timing of the nutritional stress turned out to matter enormously. People in their third trimester during the famine, when the worst of the caloric restriction hit, showed different epigenetic patterns than those in their first trimester. The epigenome appeared most sensitive to nutritional signals during early pregnancy, when the one-carbon cycle's demand for methyl donors is highest and when the foundational epigenetic marks on the fetal genome are being laid down. It was a biological recording of a historical event, etched in chemistry that persisted for a human lifetime.

This is what scientists call developmental programming, a concept formalized under the name DOHaD, which stands for Developmental Origins of Health and Disease. The DOHaD framework proposes that conditions during fetal and early postnatal life set biological parameters that influence health trajectories for decades afterward. Epigenetic marks are the most compelling candidate for the molecular mechanism carrying this signal forward. The Dutch Hunger Winter remains the most rigorously documented human example of this principle in action.

One more piece of the Dutch data is worth noting. Some studies found hints that epigenetic differences in the famine-exposed cohort were detectable not only in the exposed individuals but also in their children. The data on this second-generation effect are more limited and contested than the first-generation findings. Still, they raise a question the field is actively investigating: can nutritional deprivation leave marks that span generations? We will come back to that with a full treatment in Chapter 7. For now, note that the Dutch Hunger Winter is not just a chapter in history. It is a biology chapter that is still being read.

The Agouti Mouse: The Most Famous Animal in Nutritional Epigenetics

If the Dutch Hunger Winter is epigenetics' most important human study, the agouti mouse is its most visually striking animal model. The images James saw on Maya's printout at lunch that day are famous in the field, and for good reason: they show, in a single photograph, how the same DNA can produce radically different biological outcomes depending on what a mother ate during pregnancy.

The story begins with a gene called the agouti gene, which in mice controls coat color and influences appetite and metabolism by affecting brain signals. In most mice, the agouti gene is tightly regulated: it is active in hair follicles to produce banded coat coloring, and it is mostly silent in other tissues. But some mice carry a specific variant of the agouti gene, called the viable yellow agouti (Avy), which sits next to a genetic element called an IAP transposon. When this transposon is active, it drives the agouti gene to express continuously in all tissues, producing yellow fur, but also causing constant stimulation of appetite circuits in the brain, leading to severe obesity, insulin resistance, and elevated cancer risk.

Now here is the key. The Avy transposon is controlled by a CpG island, a methylation-sensitive stretch of DNA that varies widely between individual mice. When the CpG island is heavily methylated, the transposon is silenced, the agouti gene behaves normally, and the mouse is brown, lean, and healthy. When the CpG island is lightly methylated, the transposon is active, and the mouse is yellow, obese, and metabolically compromised.

Diagram 5.6 - The Agouti Mouse Study

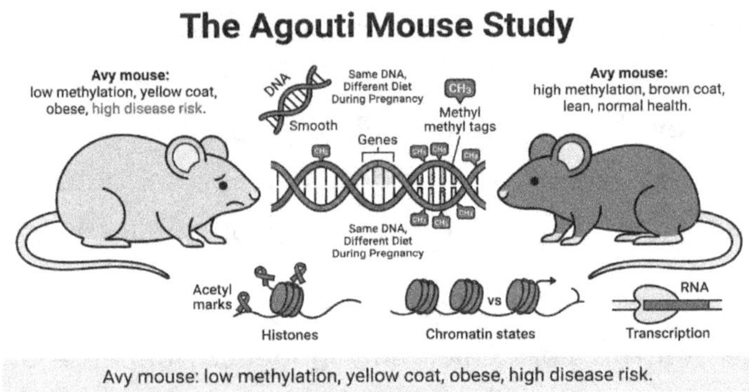

The brilliant experimental intervention occurred in 2003, when researchers led by Randy Jirtle and Robert Waterland at Duke University showed that feeding pregnant agouti mice a diet rich in methyl-donor nutrients, including folate, B12, choline, and betaine, dramatically shifted the coat-color distribution of the offspring toward brown. The extra methyl donors in the mother's diet were incorporated into the one-carbon cycle, increasing SAM availability and allowing the methylation machinery to silence the Avy transposon in the developing pups more effectively. The offspring were genetically identical to yellow agouti mice. But they looked, behaved, and metabolized like normal brown mice because their mother's diet had altered their epigenome during a critical window of prenatal development.

The control group's pups, born to mothers fed a standard diet without extra methyl donors, were the yellow, obese mice. The experimental group's pups, born to mothers fed the methyl-rich diet, were predominantly brown and lean. The change happened in the womb, during a brief developmental window when the foundational epigenetic marks on the pup's Avy gene were being laid down. Once that window closed and the marks were set, they persisted for the animal's lifetime.

This experiment elegantly demonstrated several things at once. It showed that maternal diet can directly alter offspring epigenetics. It showed that the one-carbon cycle is the mechanism connecting diet to methylation. It showed that epigenetic marks can produce dramatic, visible, lifelong differences between genetically identical animals. And it pointed toward a principle that the Dutch Hunger Winter data had suggested in humans. There are critical windows in development when the epigenome is particularly responsive to nutritional signals, and changes made during those windows can persist indefinitely.

It also, as Maya noted when she first showed the slide, made James think immediately about his pregnant sister. That reaction is understandable. The experiment is visually and conceptually striking. But Maya's two-word response carried a clinician's instinct: hold the finding in context, resist the leap from a mouse model to a prescriptive human intervention. We will return to that calibration shortly.

What the Evidence Actually Supports: Honest Limits

This is the moment in most discussions of nutritional epigenetics when things can go sideways. Someone reads about the agouti mouse and the Dutch Hunger Winter and concludes, reasonably enough, that diet is a powerful lever on epigenetic marks. They are right. Then they take the next step: that specific dietary choices can precisely tune their own epigenome to optimize health outcomes. And here the evidence does not follow.

Here is what we know with confidence. Adequate intake of methyl donor nutrients, particularly folate, B12, and choline, is genuinely important for maintaining the one-carbon cycle and supporting DNA methylation. This matters most during pregnancy, when the developing fetus is undergoing massive epigenetic reprogramming with no dietary intake independent of the mother. Chronic deficiency of these nutrients, over months and years, is associated with measurable changes in methylation patterns. The DOHaD principle is real, and nutritional status during critical developmental windows has lasting consequences.

Diagram 5.10 - The Honest Limits Checklist

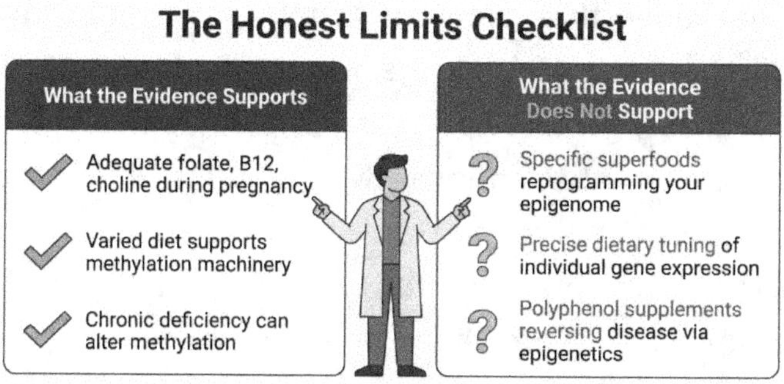

The Honest Limits Checklist gets methylation moror ortmgramoto epigenetic: this diagram.

Here is what we do not know, or what the evidence does not support, regarding individual dietary choices. We do not know that eating specific foods regularly will turn specific genes on or off in your cells in ways that meaningfully shift your health trajectory. The one-carbon cycle is a general supply-and-demand system, not a precision targeting mechanism. Providing more SAM does not mean your cells will methylate a specific cancer suppressor gene or any other specific locus. The methylation machinery has its own complex regulatory logic that we have barely begun to map.

We do not know that polyphenol supplements, green tea extracts, or curcumin capsules at doses sold in health food stores translate the promising cell-culture and animal findings into meaningful epigenetic effects in healthy human adults. The evidence for these compounds at dietary exposure levels is suggestive in some cases. Still, it is not proven, and the gap between in vitro findings and human benefit is wide, with many promising compounds failing clinical trials.

We do not know that common genetic variants in folate metabolism genes, such as the widely discussed MTHFR variants, reliably predict epigenetic outcomes that require special dietary interventions. Most adults with these variants have normal folate status on a varied diet. Claims that MTHFR variants require expensive methylated B vitamin supplements are ahead of the evidence.

And above all, we know that nutrition is one input among many into the epigenome. Stress, exercise, sleep, environmental exposures, age, and developmental history all influence epigenetic marks. Optimizing your diet while ignoring the other inputs is like tuning one instrument in an orchestra and declaring the symphony solved. The epigenome is a whole-life story, not a nutritional one.

What This Means for You

After everything we have covered, what does nutritional epigenetics actually mean for how you might think about eating? Let's make this concrete.

The most evidence-supported nutritional story in epigenetics is the one about methyl donor adequacy, and the most important time for it is pregnancy. If you are pregnant, or planning to become pregnant, the following matters: folic acid supplementation starting before conception and continuing through the first trimester, adequate vitamin B12 (which may require supplementation if you are vegan or vegetarian), and a diet that includes some choline-rich foods, particularly eggs if you eat them. This is not wellness mythology. It is one of the most well-established nutritional recommendations in medicine, and it is now understood at the molecular level through the one-carbon cycle.

Diagram 5.9 - Maya and James in the Cafeteria

The Kessler Institute cast: A falit-palent ingıaaption is summarizing calm and approachest look for a non-scientist at home.

For people who are not pregnant, the practical message is straightforward. Eat a varied diet that includes leafy greens, beans and legumes, whole grains, and protein sources including fish, eggs, or fortified plant-based alternatives. This naturally provides adequate folate, B12, and choline if you include animal products or fortified foods. It also includes polyphenols, fiber, and other compounds whose aggregate association with health is well-established. This is not a prescription for a specific epigenetic diet. It is a description of a varied, adequate diet, the kind that nutritional science has consistently associated with better health outcomes.

Here is a practical exercise: think about building a week of meals that includes leafy greens four or five times, a couple of servings of legumes like lentil soup or black bean tacos, fish once or twice, eggs a few times if you eat them, and colorful fruits, including berries. If you eat this way most of the time, your one-carbon cycle has what it needs. You are not gaming your epigenome. You are feeding it adequately, which is exactly what the science supports.

Diagram 5.8 - A Balanced Plate with Epigenetic Context

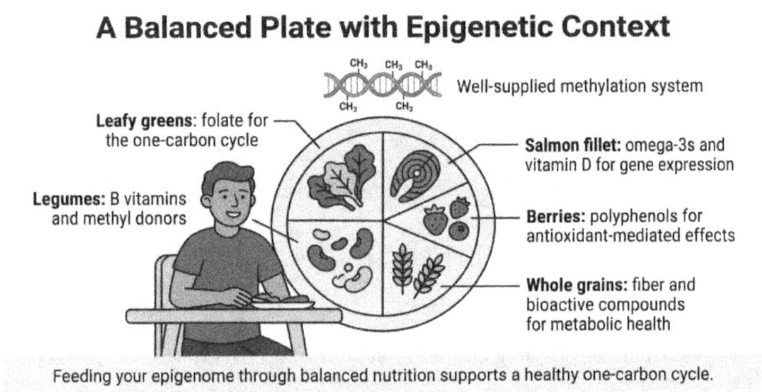

What about supplements? For most healthy adults, the evidence supports B12 supplementation for vegans or vegetarians and folic acid during the periconceptional period. For polyphenol supplements and other methyl donor products, the evidence for supplementation beyond a good diet is weak. The supplement industry has latched onto epigenetic language with enthusiasm, but claims to 'support methylation' or 'optimize your epigenome' are generally not backed by clinical trial evidence. Eat food, not the supplement version of food, wherever possible.

Diagram 5.11 - Weekly Grocery Checklist

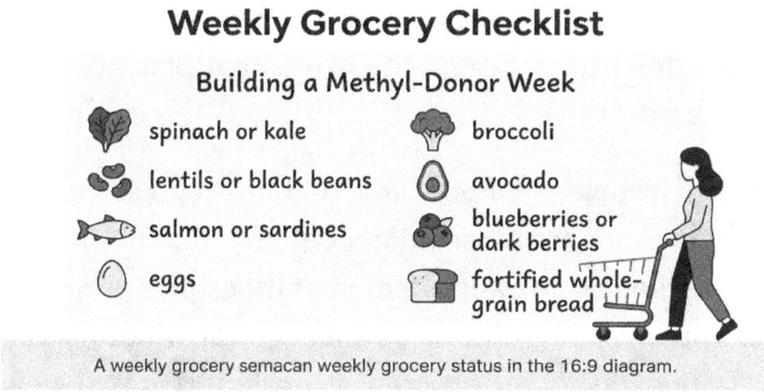

The final practical point is one of reassurance. Nutritional epigenetics does not add a new layer of anxiety to eating. It does not mean that every dietary choice has permanent consequences for your gene expression, or that a period of poor eating has permanently altered your epigenome in ways you cannot undo. The methylation machinery is dynamic. Marks are added and removed continuously. The evidence for lasting nutritional effects is strongest during severe deficiency or critical developmental windows. In the day-to-day life of a healthy adult, the epigenome is buffered and resilient. The goal is adequacy, variety, and consistency. Not perfection.

Across Generations: What a Family Meal Means Now

There is one more layer to the nutritional epigenetics story that extends beyond individual health, and it connects to what James was actually thinking when Maya said, "I know." His sister is pregnant. The question of what a pregnant woman eats is not only a question about her health. It is a question about the developing biology of her child, and, tentatively, about the marks that biology might carry forward.

The Dutch Hunger Winter data and the agouti mouse experiments are not recommendations for perfection during pregnancy. They are demonstrations of a principle: that nutrition during critical developmental windows can leave lasting marks. The practical upshot is not a new category of pregnancy anxiety. What the science supports is the existing and well-established recommendation for prenatal folate supplementation, adequate protein, a varied diet, and avoiding well-known harms like alcohol and tobacco. Those recommendations now have a molecular rationale, making them clearer. That is empowering. It is not a reason for guilt.

What the research does open is a genuinely beautiful question about the continuity of care across a generation. When a parent feeds a child varied, nutrient-sufficient meals, they are doing something more than following a food pyramid. They are maintaining the biochemical infrastructure that every cell in that child's body uses to regulate which genes get read and which do not. The dinner table is, in a small and real way, a molecular conversation between a generation and the next. Not a conversation with permanent consequences for every bite. But a conversation that matters over time.

Diagram 5.12 - Mother and Child at Family Dinner

Maya finished her salmon at lunch that day. James finished his, too. He did not feel like he had unlocked a secret code to his biology. But something he had thought was settled, the idea that food is just fuel, had quietly opened up into something more interesting. The food on his plate was participating in a process he could now name and describe. And that felt, in a way he could not quite articulate, like it mattered.

Takeaway

Every cell in your body runs a chemical relay called the one-carbon cycle, and the nutrients that keep it running, particularly folate, B12, and choline, come from your food. When the relay has what it needs, the DNA methylation machinery works as intended. When the relay runs low, especially during critical windows like pregnancy, the machinery falters in ways that can leave marks lasting years or decades. The Dutch Hunger Winter and the agouti mouse studies are the two best-documented demonstrations of this principle: that maternal nutrition during pregnancy can alter the epigenetic marks on offspring DNA, with consequences for metabolism, body composition, and long-term health. The principle is real. The magnitude of the effect, in ordinary dietary variation rather than famine-level deprivation, is more modest and more context-dependent than headlines often suggest.

The honest summary is this: a varied diet rich in leafy greens, legumes, fish, and eggs provides the one-carbon cycle with what it needs. Prenatal folate supplementation is among the most evidence-supported nutritional recommendations in medicine, and it now has a molecular mechanism to explain it. Polyphenols in green tea, turmeric, and berries are interesting compounds that interact with biological systems in ways worth studying, but the claim that they precisely reprogram your epigenome is not where the evidence stands today. Nutrition is one important input into epigenetic regulation, not the whole story.

In the next chapter, we turn to an input that, for many people, is even harder to control than diet: stress. We will meet Sofia Reyes and follow the marks that chronic psychological stress leaves on the epigenome. These marks begin in the brain's stress response system and extend into the molecular architecture of the cells that carry your history forward. The story of how stress becomes biology is, in some ways, the most personal chapter in this book. It is also, like this one, a story that ends with more agency than it begins with.

6 Stress, Trauma, and the Marks We Carry

The printout on the desk was a single page of data, but Sofia Reyes had been staring at it for most of the morning. She was sitting in the small side room off the main Kessler lab, the one with the window that looked out over the parking structure and, if you craned your neck just right, a thin slice of the Charles River. Her coffee had gone cold. On the printout were two columns of numbers representing methylation levels at a specific location on a specific gene in two groups of study participants, and the difference between the columns was not subtle. It was the kind of gap that made you look twice to confirm you were reading it correctly.

James Okafor had stopped by to drop off a draft of a press release about a different project entirely, but the numbers on Sofia's desk caught his attention the way a large discrepancy always does. He set down the folder he was carrying and leaned in to look. 'So,' he said, slowly, 'stress actually leaves a physical mark on your DNA?' Sofia looked up from the page. She had answered versions of this question before, but she always paused before answering, because the question deserved precision. 'On the instructions for reading your DNA,' she said. 'Yes.' James was quiet for a moment. He looked back at the two columns of numbers and then back at Sofia. 'That's not just a figure of speech,' he said. She shook her head. 'Not even close.'

It is a thing most of us have said, or had said to us, at one difficult moment or another: stress as if stress were a mood, a state of mind, a problem of attitude that could be managed by thinking differently or breathing more slowly. What the numbers on Sofia's desk showed, and what a generation of researchers has been confirming in study after study, is that chronic stress is not just a psychological experience. It is a physiological event with molecular consequences. It leaves marks. Real, measurable, biological marks. And understanding those marks, where they come from and what they do and, most importantly, what can shift them, is exactly what this chapter is about.

Why It Matters

Stress is one of the most universal human experiences. Surveys consistently find that a majority of adults in wealthy countries report feeling significant stress in any given month. Deadline pressure at work, a sick child, money anxiety, a relationship fraying under its own weight, a commute that eats an hour and a half out of every day. We talk about stress constantly. We tell each other to manage it. We buy apps designed to reduce it. We take vacations specifically to escape it. And then, almost always, we come back to the same conditions that produced it.

What the science of epigenetics adds to this familiar story is something genuinely new: a biological account of how stress does its damage at the cellular level. Not through vague mechanisms like 'weakening your immune system' or 'throwing your hormones off,' but through specific, traceable changes to the way your genes are read. When stress becomes chronic, the body's molecular response to that stress begins to alter the marks on the genome, the epigenetic bookmarks and highlights that control which genes get activated and how loudly. Some of those changes are adaptive in the short term. Some of them, when stress goes on long enough, become problems.

Diagram 6.1 - The Stress-to-Epigenome Pathway

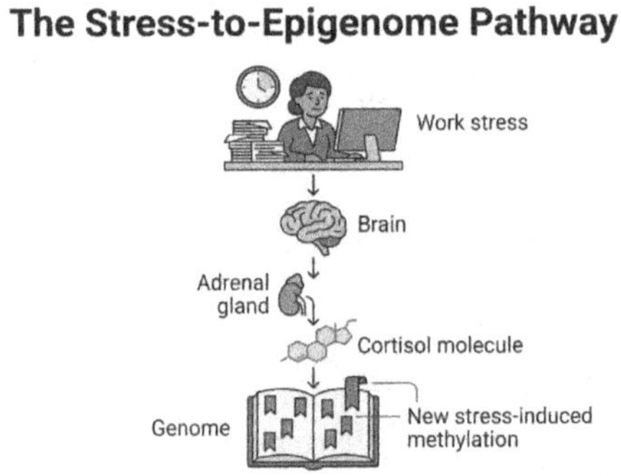

Chronic stress triggers hormonal responses that can chemically mark the genome.

This matters for reasons that go beyond individual wellness. Early adversity, which researchers define as significant stress or trauma experienced in childhood, has long been associated with worse health outcomes across the entire lifespan. People who experienced childhood abuse, neglect, or household dysfunction are more likely, as adults, to develop cardiovascular disease, metabolic disorders, anxiety disorders, and depression. For decades, researchers could describe that correlation clearly but struggled to explain the mechanism. Epigenetics has provided a biological thread connecting early experience to later health outcomes. It does not explain everything. But it explains something real and important.

It also matters because the story does not end with the mark. One of the most encouraging threads running through stress epigenetics research is the question of reversibility: can stress-related epigenetic changes be shifted? Can the bookmarks placed by years of adversity be moved, removed, or counteracted by new experiences? The early evidence is not conclusive, but it is genuinely promising. Exercise, social support, psychotherapy, and mindfulness practices have all shown measurable effects on stress-related epigenetic markers in preliminary studies. This chapter covers it all: the mechanism, the research, the implications, and the cautious yet real hope.

Your Body's Alarm System

To understand how stress leaves marks on the epigenome, you first need to understand how the body responds to stress at a systems level. That response begins in a brain region called the hypothalamus, a small structure about the size of an almond sitting near the base of the brain. The hypothalamus is the body's watchman. It reads incoming signals from your environment and your senses and makes rapid judgments about whether those signals represent a threat.

When the watchman decides something is wrong, it sends a chemical signal that triggers the pituitary gland, a pea-sized structure hanging just below it, to release its own hormone into the bloodstream. That hormone travels to the adrenal glands, which sit like small caps on top of the kidneys, and instructs them to release cortisol. Cortisol is the body's primary stress hormone. Its job is to mobilize energy, heighten alertness, sharpen focus, and prepare every system in the body for action. This three-step chain, hypothalamus to pituitary to adrenal glands, is called the HPA axis, and it is one of the most ancient and important regulatory systems in the mammalian body.

Think of the HPA axis as a fire alarm system for the entire building of your body. When there is smoke, the alarm goes off. Cortisol floods the building. Everyone responds. Hearts beat faster. Blood sugar rises. Non-emergency systems, digestion, reproduction, and immune surveillance go offline temporarily because the building is on fire, and everything needs to help. When the fire is out, a feedback mechanism kicks in: cortisol itself signals the hypothalamus and pituitary to turn off the alarm. The building returns to normal. Everything powers back up. This is acute stress, and the human body handles it beautifully.

Diagram 6.2 - The HPA Axis Fire Alarm

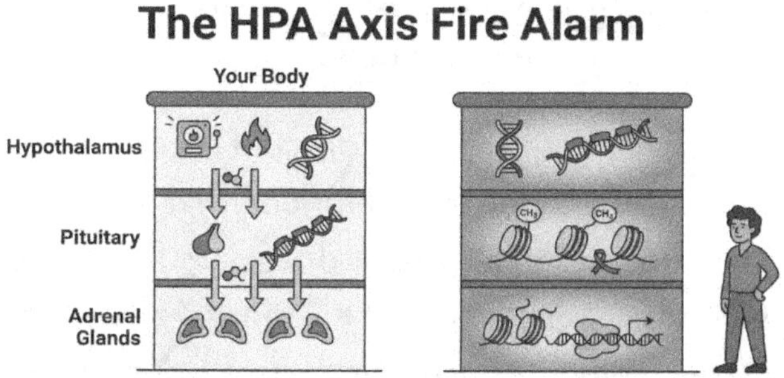

The HPA axis fire alarns revolving honfng the feedback mechanism restoring calm.

The problem begins when the fire alarm stays on. When stress is chronic, when the pressures of your life are not a single solvable crisis but a persistent background condition, the HPA axis keeps firing. Cortisol levels remain elevated day after day, week after week, month after month. And cortisol, at elevated levels for extended periods, does something the body did not design for: it enters the nuclei of cells throughout the body, interacts with the molecular machinery that controls gene expression, and begins to alter the marks on the genome.

The Off Switch and What Happens to It

Here is where the biology gets specific and, once you follow it, genuinely surprising. Your body has a built-in mechanism for turning off the cortisol response once a stressor has passed. That mechanism depends on a protein called the glucocorticoid receptor. The glucocorticoid receptor is essentially a sensor that detects cortisol in the bloodstream and sends a signal back up the chain to the hypothalamus and pituitary: " Enough, we heard you, we can stand down now.

The gene that encodes the glucocorticoid receptor is called NR3C1. You do not need to remember that name. What you need to understand is what it does: it is the off switch for your stress response. The more glucocorticoid receptors your cells produce, the better your body is at calming itself down after a stressor. The fewer receptors, the harder it is to turn the alarm off, and the longer cortisol stays elevated after any given stressful event.

Now here is the epigenetic piece. Research has shown that chronic stress and early-life adversity are associated with increased methylation of the NR3C1 gene. Going back to the book-and-bookmarks metaphor: imagine that the off-switch instructions are written on a particular page of your genome. Methylation is like covering that page with a sticky note that says, "Do not read this." When NR3C1 gets heavily methylated, the glucocorticoid receptor gets underproduced—fewer off switches. A stress response that, once triggered, takes longer to settle. A body that is constitutionally harder to calm.

Diagram 6.3 - The Off-Switch Gene and Methylation Silencing

The Off-Switch Gene and Methylation Silencing

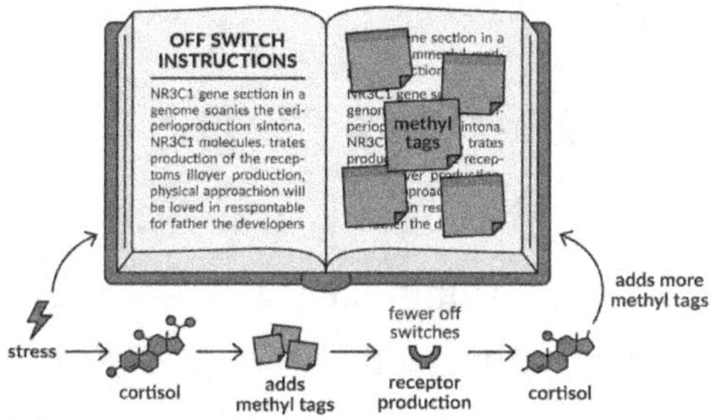

The Off-switch gene and methylation silencing actinns the receptor accumed'cnyl tags.

Think of this as a thermostat that has been permanently nudged upward. A well-functioning stress response is like a home heating system with a responsive thermostat: the temperature rises when conditions call for it, and falls back to a set point when they do not. When NR3C1 is methylated and silenced, the set point shifts. The house runs warmer than it should. Small temperature spikes that would have once settled quickly now take much longer to come down. This is not a metaphor designed to reassure you that things are fine. This is a description of a real physiological change with real consequences for the body's function over time.

It is also, and this is important, not a life sentence. Methylation patterns are dynamic. They are not permanent. The same processes that placed those marks can, under the right conditions, shift them. We will come back to this. For now, what matters is understanding how the mark gets there in the first place, because the pathway from chronic stress to NR3C1 methylation to dysregulated cortisol is one of the best-studied mechanisms in all of behavioral epigenetics.

What Rat Mothers Taught Us About Human Resilience

The most influential single line of research connecting early experience to epigenetic change did not begin with human subjects. It began in the late 1990s in the laboratory of Michael Meaney, a neuroscientist at McGill University in Montreal, who was studying why some rat pups grew up to be calm, curious, and confident. In contrast, others grew up chronically anxious and stress-reactive, even when they shared the same genetic material.

The answer, Meaney's team found, had nothing to do with the pups' genes. It had everything to do with their mothers. Rat mothers vary naturally in how much they lick and groom their pups in the first week of life. Some mothers are highly attentive, frequently licking their pups and nursing in a position that allows the pups maximum contact. Others are less attentive, providing less physical touch and contact. Meaney's team began observing these behavioral differences, then following the pups into adulthood to track their stress responses, and then looking inside the pups' cells to find out what was different at the molecular level.

Diagram 6.4 - High vs. Low Licking-Grooming: Two Epigenetic Outcomes

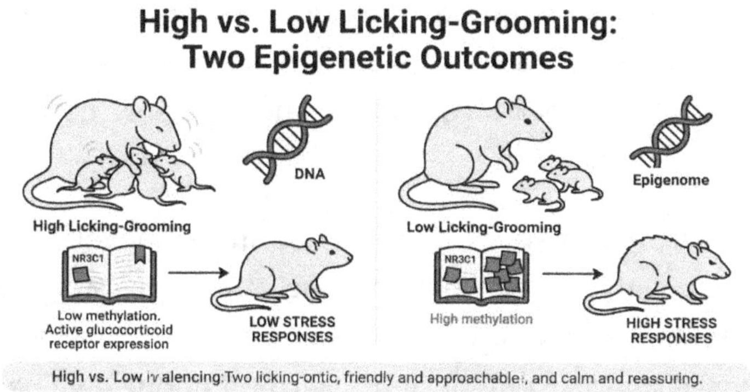

What they found was striking. The pups raised by highly attentive mothers had lower methylation of their glucocorticoid receptor genes. Their off switches were intact. As adults, they responded to stress with a well-calibrated cortisol spike that returned to baseline quickly. They were exploratory and engaged. The pups raised by less attentive mothers showed higher methylation of the same gene. Their stress responses were elevated and slow to quiet. As adults, they were more reactive and more easily overwhelmed.

But the finding that truly crystallized the significance of this research came from cross-fostering experiments. Meaney's team took pups from high-licking mothers and gave them to low-licking mothers, and vice versa. They were asking a pointed question: which matters more, the DNA the pup was born with or the early environment in which it was raised? The answer was unambiguous. Pups from low-licking mothers, raised by high-licking mothers, developed low methylation of NR3C1 and calm stress responses in adulthood. Pups from high-licking mothers, raised by low-licking mothers, developed high methylation and heightened reactivity—the epigenetic outcome tracked with the early caregiving environment, not the genetic inheritance.

James heard this part of the story during a conversation with Sofia in the Kessler hallway one afternoon, standing near the bulletin board where someone had posted a conference announcement and a cartoon about p-values. 'So the pups that got switched,' he said, 'they ended up like the mothers who raised them, not the mothers who bore them?' Sofia nodded. 'The early environment rewrote the epigenetic instruction set,' she said. 'Which means it also rewrites the biology of how that animal handles stress for the rest of its life.' James stood there for a moment. 'That feels like one of those findings that should have landed much bigger than it did,' he said. Sofia smiled. 'We're still catching up to it,' she said.

It is worth being careful here about what this research does and does not show. Rats are not humans. Their stress-response systems share deep evolutionary roots with ours, which is why the findings are relevant. Still, the specifics of human early experience involve vastly more complexity than a rat pup's first week of life. What the rat studies provided was something genuinely rare and valuable in biological research: a clean, controllable experimental model that established the causal mechanism linking early caregiving to epigenetic change in the stress-response system. That mechanism, it turned out, worked in humans too.

Adverse Childhood Experiences and the Long Biology of Early Life

In the late 1990s, at roughly the same time Meaney's lab was publishing its rat studies, a physician named Vincent Felitti and a researcher named Robert Anda were running a very different kind of study in San Diego. Working with a large group of health plan members at Kaiser Permanente, they surveyed thousands of adults about their childhood experiences and then compared those answers to the adults' current health records. They were looking for connections between difficult early experiences and adult health outcomes, and they found them. The study was called the ACE study, for Adverse Childhood Experiences.

The ACE study used a simple scoring system. Participants answered questions about ten categories of childhood adversity: physical abuse, emotional abuse, sexual abuse, neglect in its physical and emotional forms, and five types of household dysfunction, including a parent with substance abuse issues, a parent with mental illness, domestic violence in the home, having a parent in prison, and losing a parent to divorce or separation. For each category experienced, a participant earned one point. An ACE score of zero meant none of these. An ACE score of four meant four categories of adversity experienced before the age of eighteen.

Diagram 6.5 - The ACE Score and Cumulative Health Risk

The ACE Score and Cumulative Health Risk

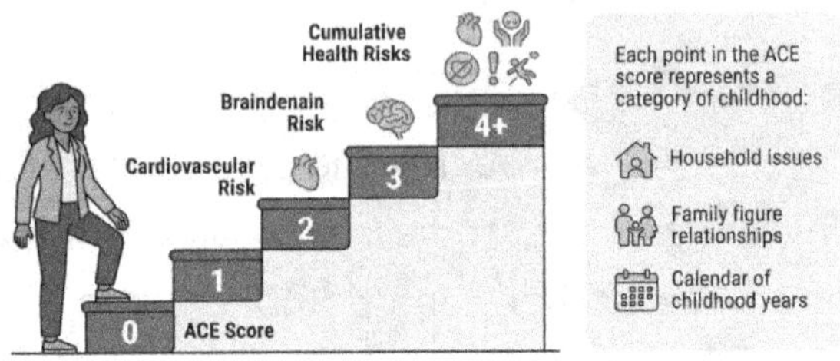

The ACE Score lists metaphoise ask aementhe, disease and harm tlike over here.

The correlations the study found were sobering. People with ACE scores of four or higher were significantly more likely than those with scores of zero to develop heart disease, stroke, cancer, chronic lung disease, liver disease, and mental health conditions. They were more likely to struggle with substance use. They were more likely to attempt suicide. The relationship was not binary. Risk rose in a dose-response pattern: the higher the ACE score, the greater the health risk across nearly every measured category. And critically, the study controlled for standard socioeconomic and behavioral factors. The association was not simply a proxy for poverty or lifestyle.

The ACE study was not an epigenetics study. It did not measure methylation or histone marks. What it did was establish, with enormous statistical force, that the body remembers childhood adversity in ways that manifest biologically throughout an entire lifetime. It raised an obvious question: what is the biological mechanism? How does growing up in a household where a parent had a serious drinking problem translate, decades later, into a higher probability of heart disease? Epigenetics is part of the answer. The same chronic stress activation and HPA axis dysregulation that Meaney's rats displayed show up in humans with high ACE scores, along with measurable epigenetic differences in genes involved in stress regulation, inflammation, and immune function.

Human studies specifically examining epigenetic markers in people with high ACE scores have found methylation differences at NR3C1 and in a cluster of other genes involved in inflammatory response and immune regulation. The specific findings vary across studies, partly because human epigenetic research is genuinely complex: different tissues exhibit distinct marks, different life stages exhibit distinct sensitivities, and the experience of adversity is not uniform enough to produce identical molecular signatures across a large population. But the general pattern is consistent. Early adversity correlates with epigenetic changes in stress and immune regulation. Those changes correlate with poorer health outcomes over decades. The mechanism connecting early experience to late disease is biological and traceable.

Acute Stress versus Chronic Stress: Two Very Different Stories

Not all stress is the same, and it is important to be specific about what the research does and does not say. Acute stress, a short, intense stressor with a clear beginning and end, is something the human body handles extremely well. The presentation you were nervous about this morning. The fender bender that made your heart pound. The argument was resolved by evening. Acute stressors trigger the HPA axis, cortisol rises, the body mobilizes, and then the feedback mechanism kicks in and cortisol returns to baseline. This is healthy physiology. This is what the system was designed for.

The epigenetic signature of acute stress is different from that of chronic stress. Research in both animal models and humans suggests that acute stressors produce temporary epigenetic changes that are largely reversible. The marks placed by a single difficult week are not the same as the marks placed by years of ongoing adversity. The body has a remarkable capacity to restore baseline gene expression after short-term stress, partly because the methyltransferases and demethylases, the enzymes that add and remove methyl tags, remain active and balanced.

Diagram 6.6 - Acute vs. Chronic Stress Epigenetic Signatures

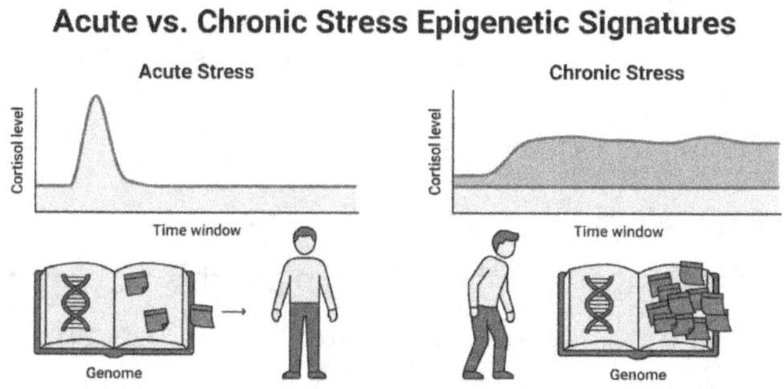

Acute stress intweirn courogonoition and the overndomly at most enrenocent disappear.

Chronic stress is a condition in which the alarm system never fully resets. The source of stress persists: a job that is genuinely harmful over many years, a household with ongoing conflict, financial precarity that makes every month a crisis, and a neighborhood environment where safety is never assured. In these conditions, cortisol does not return to baseline between episodes. It remains elevated, or it cycles in ways that prevent the feedback mechanisms from restoring normal function. And over time, this sustained activation begins to shift the epigenetic marks on genes involved in stress regulation, inflammation, metabolism, and immune function.

There is a concept in stress research called allostatic load, which refers to the cumulative biological cost of chronic stress and adaptation. Allostatic load is the price the body pays for running its alarm system on high for too long. Elevated inflammation. Disrupted sleep architecture. Impaired immune regulation. Accelerated cellular aging. Epigenetics provides one of the molecular windows through which allostatic load becomes visible: the marks on the genome reflect, in their accumulated pattern, something like the biological record of the stress a body has carried.

Stress Is Not Just In Your Head

Sofia had thought about how to explain this to a general audience for most of her graduate career, because she knew the subject carried a freight of misunderstanding that needed to be addressed directly. The idea that mental and emotional experiences have real biological consequences was, for most of the twentieth century, treated with skepticism in mainstream medicine. The legacy of that skepticism still shapes how people talk about mental health and how they seek, or do not seek, help for it.

When someone says 'it's just stress,' they usually mean one of two things. Either they mean it is not a serious physical problem, just a psychological one, as if psychological problems were not serious. Or they mean it is not real in the biological sense, that it is happening in the mind rather than the body, as if those were separate places. The epigenetics of stress is, among other things, a powerful scientific argument against both of those framings.

Diagram 6.7 - Mind-Body: The Epigenetic Bridge

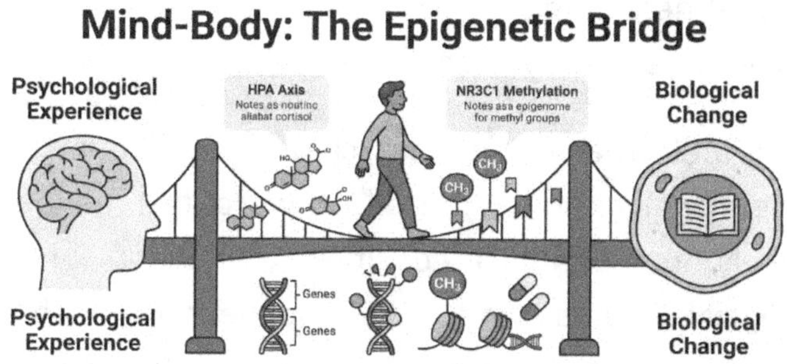

This cycle to the epigenome hast lectroothes:; stone psyhrological terryphonetics.

Psychological experiences, stress, grief, fear, loneliness, and trauma are physiological processes. They involve real changes in hormone levels, neurotransmitter activity, immune function, and, as we have seen, epigenetic regulation. The brain is an organ. It is made of cells. Those cells have genomes with epigenetic marks. When the brain's stress circuits are activated chronically, the downstream molecular effects are as physical as a fracture or an infection. They just are not as visible to the naked eye.

This is not the same as saying that all mental health conditions are epigenetic problems with simple epigenetic solutions. That would be an overreach. Mental health is extraordinarily complex, shaped by genetics, developmental history, social circumstances, and biology that researchers are still mapping. What epigenetics contributes to this picture is a well-characterized mechanism through which the social becomes biological: the experience of being chronically unsafe, unsupported, or overwhelmed changes how genes are read in the cells of the stress-response system.

This is the field that some researchers have begun calling psychoneuroepigenomics. It is a long word, but the idea at its core is not complicated: it is the study of how psychological states and social experiences change epigenetic marks in the nervous system and elsewhere in the body. The field is young, and the findings are preliminary in places, but the core question it asks, how does the way you are treated in the world change the biology of how you function, is one of the most important questions in all of science.

Why Early Life Is a Special Window

The reason childhood adversity has such particularly lasting effects is not simply that children are more fragile than adults, though in some ways they are. It is that early life is a period of heightened epigenetic sensitivity. The developing brain and body are, in a biological sense, taking environmental readings and calibrating their systems based on what those readings suggest about the world they are growing into.

Think of it like this. Imagine a baby bird hatching in the spring. Before it can see or fly, its biology is already gathering information: how warm it is, how abundant the food is, how much noise there is in the environment. These signals help calibrate the developing animal's stress responses, metabolism, and behavior to match the world it will live in. The same principle, at a more complex level, applies to the human infant and young child. The early epigenetic settings laid down in response to caregiving, nutrition, stress, and safety represent the body's best predictions about the world the child will inhabit.

Diagram 6.8 - The Early Life Epigenetic Sensitive Window

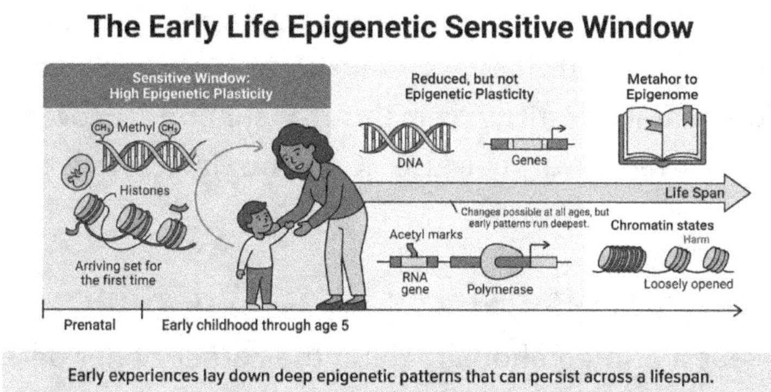

When early experiences are safe and nurturing, these calibrations tend to produce a resilient, well-regulated stress response system. When early experiences are characterized by chronic threat, unpredictability, or deprivation, the calibrations reflect that too. The stress response system gets set on a higher, more reactive baseline. Inflammation pathways may be primed. The HPA axis may become less responsive to feedback. These are, in a sense, rational adaptations to a dangerous environment. They would be appropriate and even advantageous if the dangerous conditions persisted. The problem is that they tend to persist even when the person moves into a safer environment as they grow older. The body keeps running the settings it was calibrated to.

This is why researchers who work with children in high-adversity environments talk about the importance of early intervention. Not because epigenetic marks laid down in childhood are impossible to change later, but because the earlier the environment shifts toward safety, stability, and nurturing support, the less time the body has been running on the high-stress calibration and the more developmental plasticity remains to support recovery. Timing matters. Not because it is too late later, but because it is better earlier.

When Science Meets Lived Experience

Sofia kept a printed photograph on the corner of her desk in the Kessler lab. It showed her as a small child, perhaps four years old, sitting on the lap of a woman with dark eyes and a wide smile. The woman was her grandmother, Abuela Rosa, who had survived the 1985 Mexico City earthquake and the years of instability and grief that followed. Sofia had grown up hearing fragments of that story without ever fully understanding it, because her grandmother rarely spoke about it directly. What she had was the shape of it: the years of hardship, the resilience that followed, and the particular way her grandmother moved through the world, watchful and warm at once, as if she had learned to hold both.

The research Sofia was doing for her dissertation was, in part, driven by a question she had been carrying for most of her life. Not whether her grandmother's experiences had affected her own biology, that question belonged to Chapter Seven. But the more immediate question: how does the body of someone who has lived through prolonged trauma carry that experience at the cellular level, and what does the epigenetic record of that stress look like compared to those who have not? That was what the data on her desk was beginning to show her.

Diagram 6.9 - Epigenetic Marks as Cellular Memory of Experience

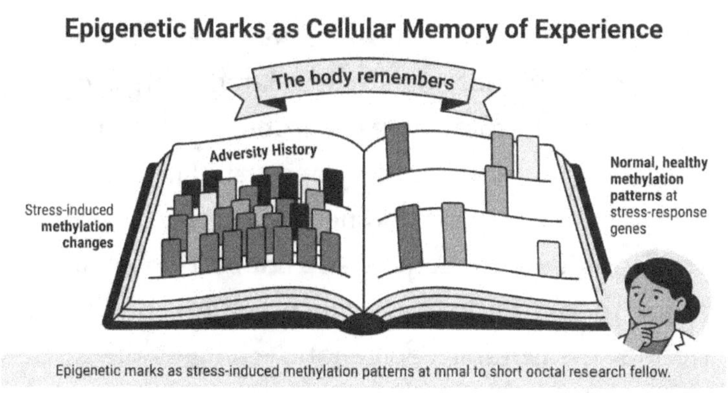

The researchers who work in this space are careful about how they describe their findings. Epigenetic differences associated with adversity are not diagnoses. They are not sentences. They are signals, patterns in the molecular record that help explain some of the connections between experience and biology. And they are the starting point for a different, more hopeful line of inquiry: given that these marks exist and influence how the stress response system functions, what can move them in a healthier direction?

This is where the research story turns toward something genuinely encouraging. The same epigenetic plasticity that allowed stress to leave marks also means those marks are not set in stone. The enzymes that add and remove methyl tags do not stop working after childhood. Gene expression patterns continue to shift in response to the environment throughout life. The question is what kinds of environments and experiences reliably shift them in the right direction.

Resilience: The Marks That Shift

Exercise is one of the most consistently supported epigenetic interventions for stress-related marks. Animal studies have shown that regular aerobic exercise reduces methylation at stress-response genes and increases the expression of genes involved in neuroplasticity, the brain's ability to form new connections and adapt. Human studies are harder to run with the same precision, but several have found measurable epigenetic changes in stress-related genes following consistent exercise programs over months. The changes are not enormous, and they require real, sustained effort to produce. But they are real and point toward better stress regulation.

Sleep is another. This is one of the areas of research that has been building toward for years: sleep is not a passive state of rest. It is a period of active biological maintenance during which the brain clears metabolic waste, consolidates memory, and regulates the very hormonal and epigenetic processes that stress disrupts during waking hours. Chronic sleep deprivation produces measurable changes in the methylation of immune and inflammatory genes. Restoring good sleep architecture reverses some of those changes. The direction of effect is consistent: sleep deprivation moves epigenetic marks toward inflammation and stress reactivity, and restoring sleep moves some of those marks back.

Diagram 6.10 - Lifestyle Factors and Epigenetic Stress Marks

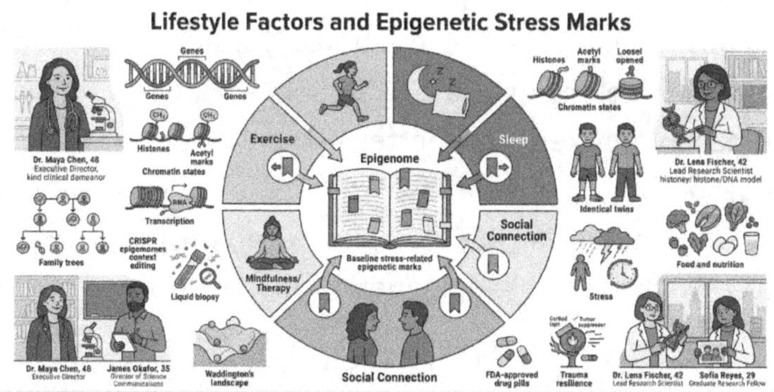

Lifestyle factors and epigenetic stress marks for the reastnap of baseline stress-related epigenetic marks.

Mindfulness and meditation have been the subject of increasing epigenetic research, with promising yet early findings. Several studies have reported changes in the methylation of inflammation-related genes following intensive mindfulness programs, including multi-week MBSR courses, which stands for Mindfulness-Based Stress Reduction. The effect sizes in most of these studies are modest, and replication across independent labs has been uneven. What the collective body of evidence suggests is that sustained mindfulness practice, meaning weeks and months of regular practice, not a single session, can shift epigenetic patterns in the direction of reduced inflammatory tone. This is a meaningful signal. It is not a cure.

Social connection is perhaps the most powerful epigenetic factor in this space, and it is also the one most consistent with what people intuitively know about what helps. Chronic loneliness has been shown to produce epigenetic signatures associated with inflammation and immune dysregulation. Conversely, strong social bonds, close friendships, stable intimate relationships, and a sense of community belonging are associated with lower inflammatory markers and better epigenetic regulation of stress-response genes. Isolation is not simply uncomfortable. It is, at the biological level, a form of stress with its own measurable epigenetic consequences.

Psychotherapy, specifically trauma-focused psychotherapy approaches like EMDR and trauma-focused cognitive behavioral therapy, has also been linked in preliminary research to epigenetic changes in trauma survivors. A handful of studies have found reduced methylation at stress-related gene loci following successful psychotherapy in people with post-traumatic stress disorder. The sample sizes are small, and the findings need to be replicated. Still, the direction of effect aligns with what the mechanism would predict: if trauma's epigenetic marks are at least partly maintained by ongoing physiological stress, then interventions that reduce that stress at a psychological level should, in principle, influence those marks as well.

What This Means for Society, Not Just for Individuals

There is a conversation happening in public health and policy circles that this research directly informs. For decades, the argument for early childhood programs, for trauma-informed education, for access to mental health care, for affordable housing, and economic stability was made primarily in social and moral terms. These things are the right thing to do. What the epigenetics of adversity adds to that argument is a biological one. These things measurably affect the molecular biology of the children and adults who receive or are denied them.

Trauma-informed care is an approach to healthcare, education, and social services that recognizes the widespread impact of early adversity and builds that recognition into practice. A trauma-informed pediatrician asks different questions and interprets behavioral symptoms differently than one without that framework. A trauma-informed school builds different disciplinary approaches and support structures than one operating purely on behavioral compliance. The epigenetics of adversity provides a biological basis for why these approaches matter: because the children they serve are not simply choosing difficult behavior, they are expressing the stress-response calibrations their bodies developed in response to their environments.

Diagram 6.11 - Trauma-Informed Systems and the Biological Argument

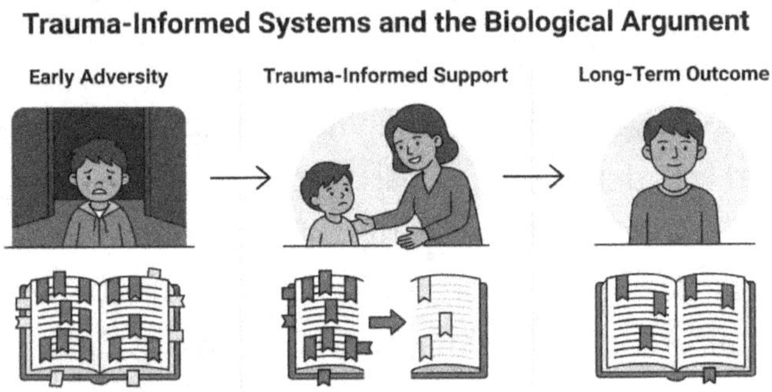

Trauma-informed support promotes positive biological outcomes and resilience across the lifespan.

This argument has to be made carefully. Biology does not determine outcomes. It shapes tendencies and probabilities. Many people with high ACE scores live healthy, connected, meaningful lives. Resilience is real and common. What epigenetics tells us is not that adversity is destiny, but that adversity leaves biological traces that make some things harder, and that the right kinds of experience and support can shift those traces.

There is also a justice dimension to this research that researchers are beginning to articulate directly. The adversity that produces epigenetic stress marks is not randomly distributed. It clusters along lines of poverty, racism, neighborhood disinvestment, and systemic exclusion. When researchers find higher average ACE scores and greater NR3C1 methylation in communities that have experienced historical and ongoing discrimination, they are measuring, at the molecular level, one of the biological costs of structural inequality. This does not make the science political in a partisan sense. It makes it honest in a scientific way.

What This Means for You

Let us be specific and practical about what the science in this chapter means for your daily life, because there is a risk that reading about stress epigenetics can itself become a source of stress. That would be exactly the wrong outcome. The goal of this chapter is not to alarm you about the damage stress may have done, but to give you a more accurate biological picture of what stress does and, crucially, what can shift it.

Sleep is not optional biology. It is one of the single most powerful levers you have on your epigenetic stress marks. The research is consistent, and the mechanism is well-established. Seven to nine hours of good-quality sleep for most adults supports the hormonal and epigenetic reset that the body's stress-response system needs. If your life currently involves chronic sleep deprivation, whether from work demands, a newborn, anxiety that wakes you at 3 a.m., or all three at once, that is worth treating as the health issue the biology says it is, not with guilt. Still, with the same seriousness you would give to any measurable health risk.

Exercise at any level beats no exercise. Studies showing the epigenetic benefits of exercise used programs ranging from brisk walking three times a week to more intensive aerobic training. The key variable is consistency over time. Thirty minutes of walking most days of the week, maintained over months, produces measurable epigenetic changes in stress-response pathways. You do not need a gym membership or a particular fitness identity. You need regularity.

Social connection is protective biology. The research on loneliness and epigenetic inflammation is consistent enough that isolation should be treated as a genuine health risk, not merely an emotional one. Maintaining the relationships that matter to you, whether those are friendships, family bonds, a community of practice, a religious congregation, or a recreational group, is doing something real at the cellular level. Calling the friend you have been meaning to call and showing up to the thing you considered skipping are not small, soft gestures. They are biological decisions.

If you have experienced significant early adversity or if you are currently living in conditions of chronic stress, please take seriously the access to professional mental health support that is available to you. Therapy, particularly trauma-focused approaches, shows the most promising epigenetic evidence among the behavioral interventions discussed in this chapter. It is also, for many people, the hardest to access because of cost, stigma, or simply not knowing where to start. If you are a healthcare provider reading this, that access gap is a biological problem, not just a social service gap.

Breath work and mindfulness practices, even brief ones, activate the parasympathetic nervous system, the body's calm-down circuit. Even five to ten minutes of slow, deliberate breathing, the kind where you extend the exhale to twice the length of the inhale, produces measurable decreases in cortisol. Practiced consistently over weeks and months, these techniques show up in epigenetic research as changes in methylation patterns associated with inflammation. They are not magic. They are physiology.

Diagram 6.12 - Your Daily Epigenetic Stress Toolkit

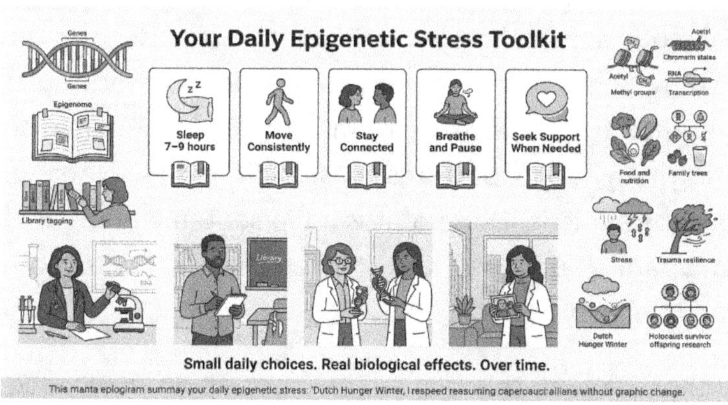

One final thing. If you have read this chapter and found yourself thinking about a specific period in your own life, a time of sustained stress or loss or adversity, and wondering what marks that period may have left, that is a reasonable thing to wonder. The biology is real. The experience you are connecting it to is real. But the narrative the biology offers is not one of permanent damage. It is one of the ongoing adaptations. Your epigenome is not a scar. It is a record that is still being written.

Takeaway

Stress is not a character flaw, and it is not just in your head. It is a physiological process with molecular consequences, mediated by the HPA axis, driven by sustained cortisol exposure, and expressed, in part, through epigenetic changes to genes like NR3C1 that govern the body's capacity to regulate its own alarm system. The evidence connecting early adversity to lasting epigenetic change comes from decades of research in animal models, from large-scale human studies such as the ACE study, and from an emerging body of molecular studies that trace the path from stressful experience to specific methylation patterns in specific genes. None of this is deterministic. None of it is a life sentence. But all of it is real, and it deserves to be taken seriously with both care and honesty.

The other half of this story, the part about resilience, about the plasticity of these marks and the interventions that can shift them, is also real. Sleep, exercise, social connection, and professional support are not mere platitudes about wellness. They are biologically grounded strategies for moving the epigenetic record of a stressed body toward better regulation. The science is not complete. But the direction is clear and hopeful.

In the next chapter, we go deeper into Sofia's story. We have seen how stress leaves marks on the epigenome within a single lifetime. Now the question opens further: can those marks travel? Can the biological legacy of a grandmother's hardship, the earthquake, the years of displacement, the accumulated weight of what she survived, reach forward through the generations and leave traces in the cells of her grandchildren? It is one of the most provocative questions in all of epigenetics. And the answer, as Sofia's research is beginning to show, is more complicated and more extraordinary than a simple yes or no.

7 Inherited Echoes

The conference room on the third floor of Kessler had a small window that looked out onto Tremont Street. By nine in the evening, the foot traffic had thinned to almost nothing. Sofia Reyes was sitting across from James Okafor with a cold cup of tea in front of her and a manila folder she had not opened. James had come in to check on a data summary she had promised to send and found her still at the table, not quite working, just sitting with the folder as if deciding whether to open it at all.

She said she was fine, and then she said something that surprised him. She told him she had been thinking about her abuela. Her grandmother. Sofia was not someone who talked about herself at the institute. She arrived early and stayed late, and her work was immaculate; James had spent two years at Kessler without knowing much about what drove her, except that it was something deeper than ambition. She told him to sit down if he had a few minutes to spare. He sat. She opened the folder and pushed a photograph across the table: a woman standing outside a building in soft sunlight, taken in the mid-1980s, one hand resting on her rounded belly.

"That was taken in 1986," Sofia said. "A year after the earthquake. She was pregnant with my mother in September 1985 when the buildings came down. She was in her apartment in Tlatelolco, got out, and spent weeks in a relief camp before they found somewhere to live. My mother was born in February." She paused. "Growing up, the family always said my mother was nervous. Sensitive. That she startled easily, that crowds made her anxious, that she did not sleep well. And I am the same way. I always thought it was just how we were. But in college, I read something about the Dutch famine, about how the children and grandchildren of women who were pregnant during that famine had measurable health differences. And I thought: what if it is not just how we are? What if my abuela's earthquake is still inside me? Not as memory. As biology."

James said nothing for a moment. He had written hundreds of science stories and explained clinical trials to general audiences without ever quite feeling what he felt in that quiet room with the amber light and the photograph between them. He asked, gently, what the science actually said. Sofia smiled just slightly. "That," she said, "is what I have spent the last three years trying to find out."

Why It Matters

Most of us carry some version of Sofia's question with us, not always about an earthquake. Sometimes, it's about a grandparent who survived a war or a period of hunger. Sometimes, it was about a parent whose anxiety ran a little deeper than circumstances alone could explain. Sometimes, it's about our own bodies, why they respond to stress the way they do, and where that response comes from. The question is old. The science that can begin to answer it is new.

Intergenerational epigenetic inheritance is the idea that the experiences of one generation can leave biological marks that reach the next generation, not by changing the DNA sequence but by altering the way that sequence is read. It is one of the most captivating and most contested areas in modern biology. It sits at the intersection of history and chemistry, of family stories and molecular mechanisms, and it has been generating both excitement and careful skepticism in laboratories around the world for two decades.

This chapter takes that science seriously without overstating it. There is real evidence here. There are also real limitations and genuine debates. The goal is not to give you a tidy answer to Sofia's question. The goal is to give you an honest account of what scientists have found, what they are still working through, and what it might mean for how you think about the history you carry.

Diagram 7.1 - Two Kinds of Inheritance

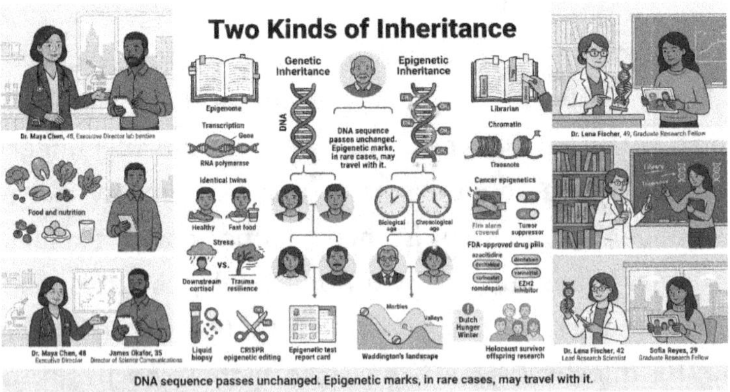

Two Kinds of Inheritance

Start with what you already know. Your DNA is the text of a very long book, about three billion letters arranged into roughly twenty thousand genes. That text is virtually identical in every cell of your body and virtually unchanged from the text your parents passed to you at conception. Genetic inheritance is about that text: when a gene variant for eye color or blood type passes from parent to child, what passes is the sequence itself, the actual letters in a particular position.

Epigenetic inheritance is a different story. It is not about the letters. It is about the bookmarks and highlights. Throughout your life, your cells attach small chemical tags to DNA and to the proteins that DNA wraps around. Methyl groups, tiny clusters of carbon and hydrogen atoms, can be attached directly to the DNA strand and tend to quiet nearby genes when they accumulate. The histone proteins around which DNA coils can be modified in dozens of ways, each modification signaling whether the surrounding DNA should be accessible or locked away. These marks are responsive to your environment: diet, stress, exercise, and experience all influence them.

The question at the heart of this chapter is whether those marks can also be inherited. Whether a bookmark placed in a parent's genome by their experience of hunger, fear, or displacement can somehow survive the transmission to the next generation and influence the biology of a child who never experienced any of it. The answer, as you will see, is: sometimes, under certain conditions, in ways the field is still mapping.

Diagram 7.2 - The Germline Reset

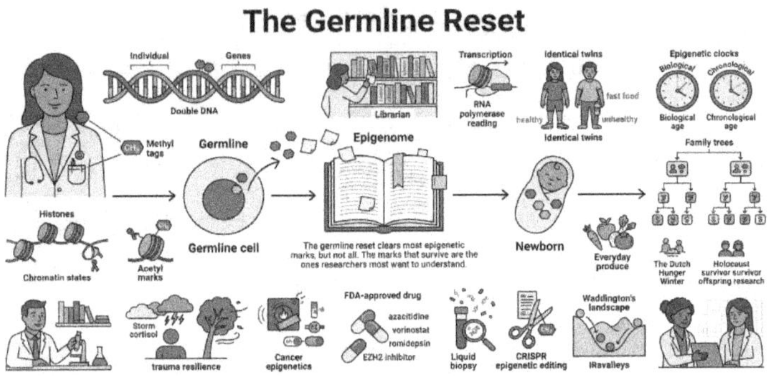

The germline reset clears most epigenetic marks, but not all. The marks that survive are the ones researchers most want to understand.

Before you can understand what the science is finding, you need to understand what makes it surprising. Normally, epigenetic marks are not supposed to be heritable. When a sperm cell and an egg cell come together, the developing embryo goes through a dramatic process of epigenetic erasure. Nearly all methyl tags on the DNA from both parents are removed. The slate is reset, allowing the embryo to build a new organism from scratch. This reset is so thorough that, for many years, scientists assumed epigenetic inheritance could not occur.

The surprise is that the reset is not quite complete. A small number of genomic regions appear to escape this erasure, retaining their methylation patterns through fertilization and into the developing embryo. And the more recent, more provocative discovery is that under some circumstances, marks placed by environmental exposure may also partially survive the reset and show up in subsequent generations. The mechanisms by which they survive are still being studied. The evidence that some do survive is now substantial enough that the field takes it seriously.

The Dutch Hunger Winter and Its Long Shadow

The most thoroughly studied case of potential intergenerational epigenetic transmission in humans came from one of the darkest chapters of the Second World War. In the autumn of 1944, Nazi forces imposed a food embargo on the western Netherlands. The embargo lasted through one of the coldest winters in recent Dutch history. By the time Allied forces liberated the region in the spring of 1945, tens of thousands had starved to death. Many more had survived on rations of a few hundred calories a day, not much more than tulip bulbs and sugar beet peels.

The Dutch Hunger Winter was a tragedy. It also became, through no intention of its survivors, one of the most important natural experiments in the history of nutritional biology. Because the Netherlands had meticulous population records and a robust public health infrastructure, researchers were able to follow the health outcomes of people who had been in the womb during the famine and compare them to siblings conceived before or after. What they found changed how scientists thought about prenatal nutrition.

Children who were in the womb during the famine, particularly during the first trimester, had dramatically elevated rates of obesity, cardiovascular disease, and type 2 diabetes as adults, even if they were well-nourished for the entirety of their postnatal lives. Their bodies appeared to have received a signal in the womb that food would be scarce. They had adjusted their metabolic programming accordingly, becoming more efficient at storing calories and more prone to storing fat. This was a striking early demonstration of the developmental origins of health and disease: the idea that the womb environment shapes long-term biology in ways that persist for decades.

Diagram 7.3 - The Dutch Hunger Winter Timeline

But the story did not stop with the first generation. When researchers followed the children of famine-exposed mothers into adulthood, they found something unexpected and, when first reported, deeply controversial. These children, who had never experienced the famine themselves, showed metabolic differences compared to unexposed controls. Their birth weights were different. Their rates of certain conditions were elevated. The biological shadow of the famine appeared to stretch across not one but two generations.

The molecular investigation came later. Researchers studying DNA methylation in samples from adults who were in the womb during the famine found differences in methylation at specific genes compared with their non-exposed siblings. One of the most studied genes was IGF2, which is involved in growth and metabolism and is also naturally subject to epigenetic regulation. The famine-exposed individuals had lower methylation at the IGF2 promoter region, a pattern that persisted across their lifetimes and was associated with changed gene activity. Whether the methylation change was the mechanism linking fetal famine exposure to adult disease, or simply a marker of another process, remains under investigation. But the association was robust enough to replicate across multiple cohorts.

The Dutch Hunger Winter findings are compelling precisely because they rest on a specific, historically documented event, a population with excellent records, and decades of study. They do not prove that epigenetic marks traveled intact from famine-exposed women to their grandchildren. The second-generation effects could reflect changes in the in-utero environment of the famine-exposed women during pregnancy, as well as in their physiology, stress hormones, and nutrition. The marks may not have traveled through the germline at all. But what the Dutch data established beyond doubt is that a major prenatal exposure can have biological and health consequences extending well beyond the exposed individual. That alone was enough to reshape the field.

Diagram 7.4 - Methylation at the IGF2 Gene

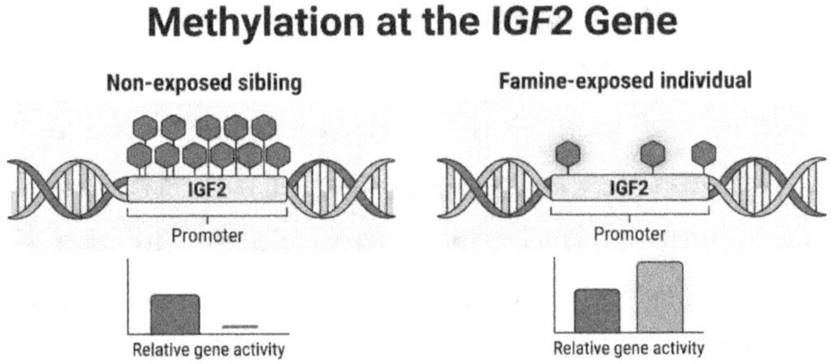

Reduced methylation at IGF2 was one of the most consistent molecular findings in Dutch Hunger Winter research.

Reduced methylation at IGF2 was one of the most consistent molecular findings in Dutch Hunger Winter research.

The Yehuda Lab and the Children Who Carried Something Forward

Rachel Yehuda is a neuroscientist at the Icahn School of Medicine at Mount Sinai in New York who has spent her career studying the biology of trauma, particularly in Holocaust survivors and their descendants. Her work is among the most cited in the field and also among the most debated. Understanding what she found requires a brief detour into the biology of stress.

When you encounter something threatening, your brain activates hormonal signals that prepare your body to respond. One key player is cortisol, a steroid hormone that raises heart rate and blood sugar, sharpens attention, and suppresses non-essential functions. Once the threat passes, cortisol levels drop. A protein called the glucocorticoid receptor, encoded by the gene NR3C1, helps regulate this shutdown. The system is designed to be responsive but also self-limiting.

In people with post-traumatic stress disorder, this system is dysregulated, and often in unexpected directions. Rather than having chronically high cortisol, many trauma survivors show paradoxically low baseline cortisol levels combined with an exaggerated stress response when triggered. The body appears to have reset its baseline, leaving it more sensitive to future threats. Yehuda found this pattern consistently in Holocaust survivors.

Diagram 7.5 - The Cortisol Feedback Loop

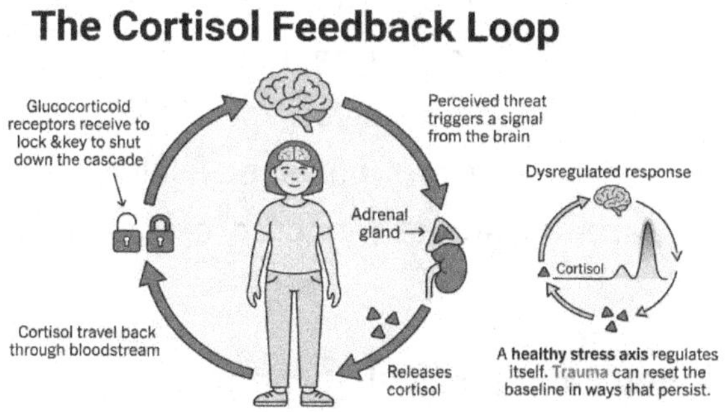

A balanced stress response involves a functional feedback loop to maintain homeostasis.

Yehuda then turned her attention to the children of survivors. The adult children of Holocaust survivors showed measurable biological differences compared to carefully matched controls. Their baseline cortisol levels were lower. Their stress-axis sensitivity appeared heightened. Their rates of PTSD were higher, and when they did develop PTSD, their symptom profiles resembled those of their survivor parents more than those of people without a parental trauma history. Something had been passed down, and it was not simply the psychological experience of growing up with a traumatized parent, though that was certainly also a factor.

The molecular work came in studies published in the mid-2010s. Yehuda and colleagues examined methylation patterns at the FKBP5 gene in offspring of survivors compared to controls. FKBP5, which stands for FK506-binding protein 5, is a gene involved in regulating the sensitivity of glucocorticoid receptors, the receptors that control cortisol feedback. Changes in FKBP5 methylation can alter the sensitivity of the stress axis. The researchers found that survivor offspring had different methylation patterns at a specific region of FKBP5 compared to controls, and the pattern was specifically associated with having a parent traumatized before the offspring's own birth.

This last detail matters. What the researchers were trying to isolate was not the effect of growing up with a traumatized parent, which is a well-established psychological influence, but the effect of parental trauma on the biology of children who were not yet born when the trauma occurred. The FKBP5 finding was suggestive of exactly that. The children appeared to carry a molecular signature of their parents' experiences.

Diagram 7.6 - FKBP5 Methylation in Survivor Offspring

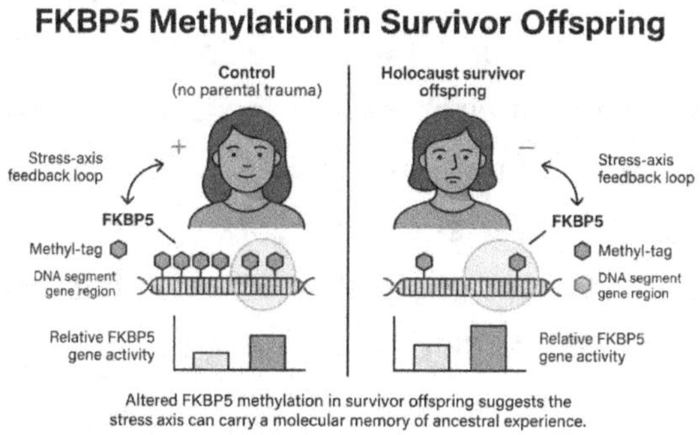

Altered FKBP5 methylation in survivor offspring suggests the stress axis can carry a molecular memory of ancestral experience.

The scientific community responded with interest and caution in roughly equal measure. The samples in the original Yehuda studies were relatively small, a common limitation in intergenerational trauma research, where you need multiple generations of consenting participants and a clean separation between biological and environmental transmission. Some subsequent studies found similar patterns; others did not replicate as cleanly. The debate continues, and it is a healthy one. The mechanism by which parental trauma could alter methylation patterns in a child not yet conceived remains incompletely understood. That the germline reset apparently does not fully prevent this in some cases is exactly what makes the research worth pursuing.

What is not in debate is the biological reality of trauma's effects on the stress axis, and the clinical reality that those effects can influence the nervous systems of children who grow up in households shaped by surviving the unsurvivable. Whether the mechanism runs through methylation patterns surviving the germline reset, through in-utero hormonal environments, or through parenting styles shaped by trauma, the children of survivors carry something forward. Science is working to understand exactly what that something is at a molecular level. It is much closer than it was twenty years ago.

Mice, Cherry Blossoms, and Fear That Traveled Through Sperm

If you want to study intergenerational epigenetic inheritance with the kind of experimental controls that human research cannot provide, you use mice. You can control their diet, environment, breeding, and exposures with precision that is impossible in any study of human families. And in 2013, a study by Brian Dias and Kerry Ressler at Emory University produced results that, when published, stopped many scientists mid-sentence.

Dias and Ressler trained male mice to fear the smell of acetophenone, a cherry-blossom-like scent, by pairing it with mild electric shocks. The mice quickly learned the association: the smell meant something bad was coming. The trained males were then bred with naive females who had never been exposed to acetophenone at all. The offspring, who had no personal history with the smell, showed enhanced sensitivity to it specifically, not to control odors. The cherry-blossom scent made them nervous, even though nothing in their own experience had given them a reason to be nervous about it.

Then Dias and Ressler went further. They bred a second generation from the offspring of the trained males. The grandchildren also showed elevated sensitivity to acetophenone. Fear of a specific smell had been passed down through at least two generations of animals that had never personally encountered it. The olfactory system, the brain's smell-processing circuitry, was even physically different in the offspring: the specific receptor neurons that respond to acetophenone were more numerous and more densely connected than in control mice.

Diagram 7.7 - Olfactory Fear Across Generations

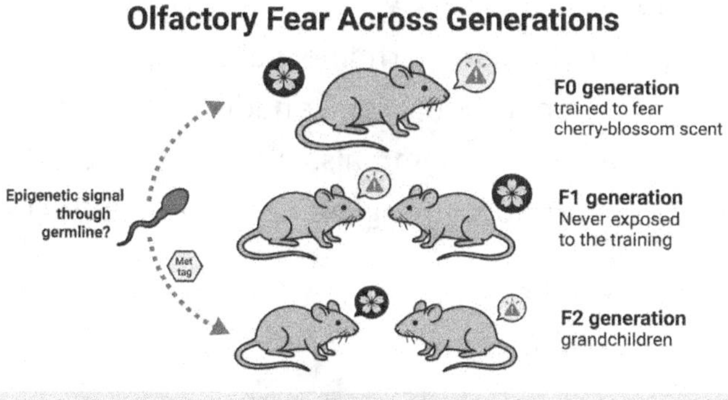

Fear of a specific scent traveled two generations in the Dias and Ressler study, raising the question of exactly how.

The mechanism appeared to involve small RNA molecules in the sperm of the trained males. Sperm carry not just DNA but a complex cargo of RNA molecules and other factors that influence early embryonic development. The sperm of acetophenone-trained mice showed changes in small non-coding RNA molecules associated with the olfactory receptor gene for acetophenone. When researchers used in vitro fertilization to eliminate the possibility of direct behavioral transmission from parent to pup, the cross-generational effect persisted, indicating it traveled through the sperm itself rather than through any behavioral cues the father might have given the mother or pup.

The Dias and Ressler study has been replicated and extended by other laboratories, and it stands as one of the strongest animal model demonstrations of transgenerational epigenetic inheritance in vertebrates. It is not, however, directly translatable to humans. Mice are not people. The specific mechanism involving olfactory receptor genes and small RNAs in sperm may not operate the same way in human germline cells. Mouse studies show that transgenerational epigenetic transmission is biologically possible in mammals. They do not tell us exactly how often or how strongly it operates in humans.

Diagram 7.8 - Small RNAs in Sperm as Carriers

Small RNAs in Sperm as Carriers

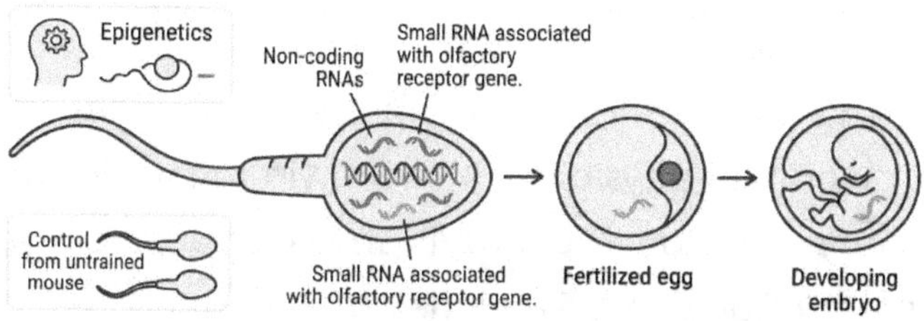

Sperm carry not only DNA but RNA cargo that can influence early development, a potential vehicle for experience-based information.

Sperm carry not only DNA but RNA cargo that can influence early development, a potential vehicle for experience-based information.

How Marks Travel: Three Routes

Even accepting the evidence that epigenetic information can sometimes survive the germline reset and influence the biology of the next generation, the question of how remains incompletely answered. Scientists have identified and are investigating three main routes, each operating through a different molecular pathway.

The first route is through the germline itself. Sperm and eggs carry not just DNA but proteins, RNA molecules, and chemical modifications that influence early development. If epigenetic marks on the DNA of parental germ cells escape reprogramming, they can be transmitted directly to the offspring's cells. Small non-coding RNAs in sperm appear to be one vehicle, as suggested by the work of Dias and Ressler. Methylation patterns in certain genomic regions, particularly those associated with repetitive DNA elements called retrotransposons, also show incomplete erasure during reprogramming and can sometimes persist into subsequent generations. The germline route is the most mechanistically direct, and it is what the field is most actively investigating.

The second route is through the in-utero environment. A pregnant woman's physiology is the environment in which her offspring develop. Significant stress or adversity can alter her hormonal profile, inflammatory markers, and nutritional state during pregnancy, all of which can influence the epigenetic programming of the developing fetus. Because a female fetus develops all of its eggs while still in the womb, the maternal environment can potentially influence the egg cells of the next generation before they are ever used. This is why some researchers describe a three-generation effect in a single pregnancy: the grandmother's experience can affect her uterine environment, which in turn shapes the mother's fetal development, which then influences the egg cells that will eventually become the grandchild—no germline escape required.

Diagram 7.9 - Three Routes of Intergenerational Transmission

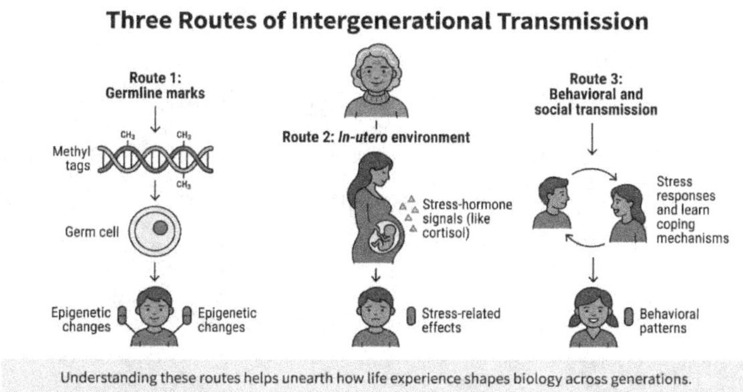

The third route is behavioral and social, and it belongs in this list because it is easy to attribute to biology what is actually psychology. Traumatized parents parent differently. They may be more hypervigilant, more anxious, more emotionally reactive. Children raised by hypervigilant parents learn to read threat cues more carefully. Their nervous systems are shaped by the household environment, which in turn is shaped by their parents' history. A child raised by a traumatized parent may show a different stress-axis profile not because of any molecular signal transmitted through germline cells, but because growing up in a high-alert household literally shapes the developing brain. This is not a minor effect. It is powerful, well-documented, and real. Good research in this area works hard to account for it.

All three routes likely contribute to what researchers observe in human studies, and they can operate simultaneously, reinforcing each other and making it very difficult to isolate which one is responsible for any given finding. This is why science is hard, and why the debates in the field are genuine rather than academic. The honest answer is that the relative contribution of each route likely varies with the specific exposure, timing, genetic background, and many other factors. The field has made substantial progress in disentangling them. It is not finished.

Diagram 7.10 - The Germline Reset: What Gets Erased, What Stays

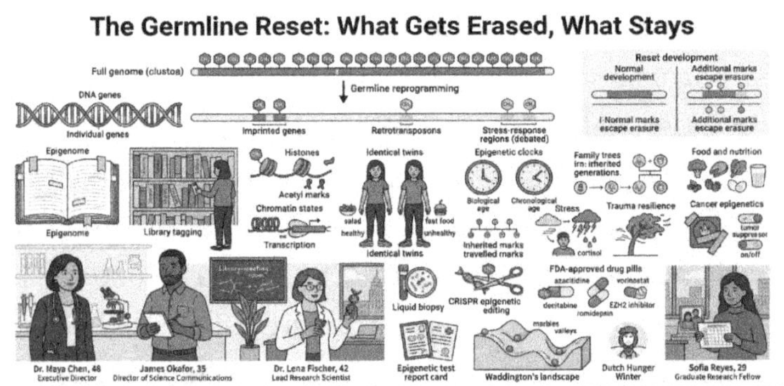

The germline reset removes most epigenetic marks, but not all. The survivors are the subject of intense research.

What the Science Is and Is Not Saying

James asked Sofia the question he asked about every big claim in science: What is the evidence, and how strong is it? She answered with precision and without defensiveness.

The evidence supports the claim that significant prenatal or preconception exposures, including severe nutritional deprivation and extreme psychological trauma, can produce measurable biological differences in the next generation not fully explained by genetic inheritance alone. The Dutch Hunger Winter data are robust. The offspring of Holocaust survivors' data are compelling and partially replicated, though sample sizes are limited and mechanisms remain unclear. The mouse studies are strong and show that germline transmission is biologically possible in mammals.

The evidence does not support the claim that every stress you experience will program your children's biology. The human body is extraordinarily resilient. The germline reset is genuinely effective for the vast majority of epigenetic marks. The cases documented in humans involved severe and prolonged exposures, starvation, genocide, and the kind of prolonged terror that reshapes physiology for years. A difficult stretch at work will not alter your grandchildren's methylation patterns. The science is not saying that.

Nor is the evidence saying that transmitted marks are permanent or fixed. Even in cases where epigenetic differences have been documented across generations, these differences are statistical tendencies within populations, not individual destinies. Some children of Holocaust survivors show altered FKBP5 methylation; others do not. Birth weight differences in Dutch Hunger Winter descendants were cohort averages; many individuals fell entirely within the normal range. Biology is probabilistic, not deterministic. Epigenetic marks, even heritable ones, are not fate.

What science is doing, more than anything, is expanding our understanding of how environments shape biology across time. The fertilization event is not a clean reset of the consequences of ancestral experience. History, in some molecular sense, lingers. The extent to which it lingers and the degree to which it can be addressed are the most important open questions in the field.

Back to the Photograph

James picked up the photograph from the table and looked at it again. The woman in the picture was standing in what looked like a narrow street, with a building behind her that had patches of fresh plaster on the facade, the kind of repairs that follow damage. She was smiling, or almost smiling. She looked tired and warm and present in the way that people who have survived something difficult sometimes look: as if they know something about the value of ordinary days.

Sofia said that her abuela, Graciela, had lived to be eighty-one. One of the most capable people Sofia had ever known, not in a dramatic way but in the quiet, competent way of someone who had learned early that circumstances change and you have to adapt. She had raised Sofia's mother in a small apartment in a neighborhood that had been rebuilt slowly over the years. She had planted things on the balcony. She had been, Sofia said, the opposite of fragile.

"But my mother had anxiety that was hard to explain," Sofia said. "And I have restlessness in crowds that I have always assumed was just temperament. And I read the Yehuda papers in college, and I thought: is there something in my biology that carries what Graciela survived? Not as memory. Not as a story. As something cellular?"

This is a question the science can only half-answer. It can say: possibly. The kind of prolonged stress that follows surviving a major disaster, the weeks in a relief camp, the years of displacement and accumulated uncertainty, is exactly the kind of exposure that the research suggests may have heritable consequences in some cases. What it cannot say is: yes, specifically, the methylation at your FKBP5 gene carries a mark from your grandmother's earthquake. Science does not have that resolution. It may not have it for decades.

What it can say, and what is perhaps more useful, is that Sofia's question is not a fantasy. It is a biological hypothesis. The science of intergenerational epigenetics is the field most directly working to answer it, honestly and without overpromising. That is worth something. It is worth a great deal.

Diagram 7.11 - Sofia's Grandmother and the Question Biology Cannot Yet Fully Answer

Sofia's Grandmother and the Question Biology Cannot Yet Fully Answer

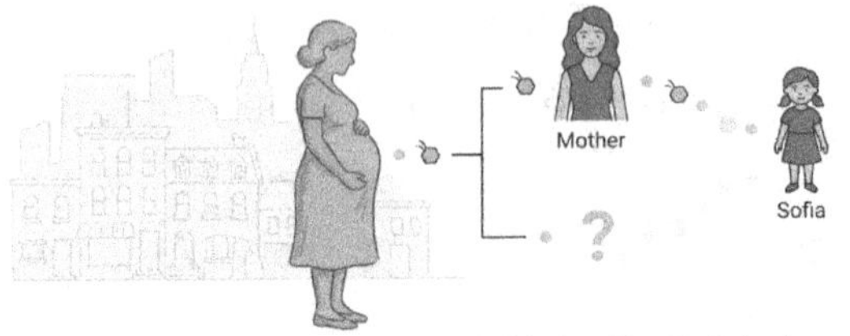

Sofia's question is not a fantasy. It is a biological hypothesis that the science of intergenerational epigenetics is working, carefully, to answer.

Sofia's question trows abort the science of intergenerational epigenetics is working carefully, to.

Marks Are Not Destiny

Here is the thing about epigenetic marks that changes everything: they are not permanent. This is true for the marks that arise during your own lifetime, and it appears to be true, at least to a meaningful degree, for marks that may travel across generations.

The epigenome is dynamic. It responds to the environment, behavior, care, and the presence or absence of chronic threat. Research in developmental psychology shows that early supportive environments can buffer stress-axis dysregulation associated with ancestral trauma. Exercise modifies methylation at stress-response genes, thereby improving resilience. Safe relationships and consistent caregiving shape the epigenomes of young children during the developmental windows when those systems are most plastic. Psychotherapy produces measurable changes in the biological markers of stress and trauma in adults. None of these changes requires understanding the molecular mechanisms to be real and beneficial.

The picture that emerges is not biological determinism in a new form. It is something considerably more hopeful. If adversity can travel forward in some biological sense, then so can healing. If the experiences of one generation can shape the stress biology of the next, then experiences of safety, consistent love, and adequate nutrition can do the same. The biological case for providing children with nurturing environments is strengthened enormously by what we know about intergenerational epigenetics. It is not just good for the children we can see. It may be good for the grandchildren we cannot yet imagine.

This reframing matters for how we think about family history. You almost certainly carry something from your ancestors, through some combination of the three routes described earlier. The question is what you do with what you carry. The science of epigenetics, including its most challenging intergenerational findings, consistently points in the same direction: toward the power of the present environment to modify the biological instructions of the past. Your grandmother's earthquake may have left traces. But you are not frozen in that September. Biology is not a recording of what happened. It is a living, responsive system that is still listening to what is happening now.

Diagram 7.12 - The Responsive Epigenome Across Generations

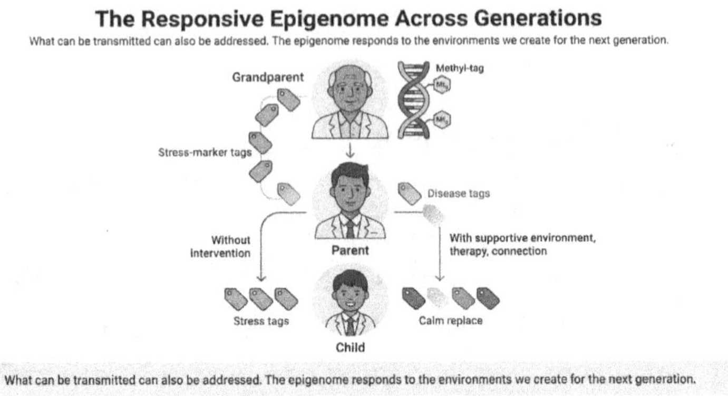

What This Means for You

You are not your grandmother's earthquake. You are not your grandfather's famine. You are not your parents' fear. This is not a platitude. It is biology. The epigenome you carry today is responsive to the life you are living right now, and to the lives you help create for the people around you. Here is how to think about this in a way that is useful rather than anxiety-provoking.

First, take family history seriously without taking it as a verdict. If you come from a family with a history of significant adversity, it is worth being thoughtful about the stress-axis patterns you may have inherited or absorbed. This is cause for awareness, not alarm. Knowing that your nervous system may be calibrated to a higher baseline of alertness is useful clinical information. You can work with it. Therapists who specialize in trauma-informed care, practices that support the nervous system, such as regular physical activity and consistent sleep, and relationships that offer genuine safety, have all demonstrated the capacity to modify the biological expression of stress-axis patterns, regardless of their origin.

Second, if you are a parent, the science of intergenerational epigenetics is the strongest possible biological argument for the conditions you create for your children. Not perfection, and not the elimination of all stress, which would be both impossible and counterproductive. But the presence of reliable safety, consistent warmth, and the experience of being responded to when distressed. These are not soft ideals. They are conditions under which stress-axis programming is most favorable, and they have consequences that may extend further into the future than we have traditionally appreciated.

Third, if you struggle with anxiety or stress responses that seem larger than your current circumstances warrant, consider that the explanation may involve more than your personal history. This is not an excuse for personal responsibility. It is permission to be compassionate with yourself about a nervous system that may have been shaped by more than your own experience. That does not make the biology unchangeable. It makes the project of change richer and more informed.

A small practice: the next time you notice a stress response that feels disproportionate to its trigger, try asking alongside your usual questions: what might this response have been protecting, in another time, in another body? Not to excuse the response. But to approach it with the curiosity of a scientist rather than the judgment of a critic. Your nervous system is doing what nervous systems do: trying to keep you safe based on all the information available to it, including information that may have arrived before you were born. You can thank it for that, and then gently update it.

Finally, consider what the research is also, implicitly, celebrating: resilience is biological. Graciela raised a daughter in a rebuilt neighborhood, kept careful accounts on Sunday mornings, planted things on her balcony, and lived to eighty-one. Whatever marks her earthquake may have left in her biology, they were not the whole of what she passed forward. Strength travels too. Resourcefulness travels—the capacity to plant something and wait for it to grow. The epigenome does not record only suffering. It records survival.

Takeaway

The science of intergenerational epigenetics is asking one of the oldest human questions in a new molecular language: Do the experiences of the past live on in us? The answer emerging from the Dutch Hunger Winter research, from Rachel Yehuda's work on Holocaust survivor offspring, and from mouse studies of transgenerational fear is: in some cases, through several possible mechanisms, yes. Not through changes to the DNA sequence itself, but through epigenetic modifications that can, under certain conditions, partially survive the reset that normally clears the slate between generations. The evidence is real, the mechanisms are partially understood, and the debates in the field are genuine and ongoing.

But the more important message is what follows from it. The epigenome is not a fixed record. It is a living, dynamic system that responds to the present even as it carries traces of the past. The marks that may travel across generations are tendencies, not destinies. And tendencies can be worked with, modified, and, over time, transformed by the environments we create, the care we give and receive, and the choices we make about how to live. Healing, in the epigenetic sense, may also be heritable.

Sofia picked up her cold tea and said she was going to go home. James walked her out through the quiet building, past the laboratory where the centrifuges sat still and the corridor where the lights clicked off behind them on timers. Outside, the Boston night was clear and a little cold. He thought about the photograph, about Graciela standing in the rebuilt street with her hand on her belly, and about all the questions that hand position contained. Science does not dissolve those questions. But it honors them by taking them seriously. And in the next chapter, we turn from the question of inheritance to the question of time: what does epigenetics tell us about why we age, and whether the biological clock is as fixed as we have always assumed?

8 The Aging Code

The printout was a single sheet of paper, the kind that looks completely ordinary until you read the number printed in the middle. Maya slid it across the conference table toward James on a Tuesday morning in late October, a half-drunk cup of coffee warming her right hand and Boston's grey autumn sky filling the window behind her. The number on her sheet said 42. Her chronological age was 48.

"Six years younger than you actually are," James said. It was not quite a question. Maya nodded. "According to the methylation pattern at about three hundred and fifty specific spots on my genome, yes." She held up the coffee cup in a small, quiet toast. "My cells apparently did not get the memo about my forties." Then she pushed a second sheet across the table. James picked it up. His chronological age was 35. The number in the middle said 39. He set it down carefully. "So mine went the other direction."

Maya looked at him for a moment. "That," she said, "is the question the entire longevity field is trying to answer. Not just why the number is what it is, but what the number actually means, and whether we can do anything about it." She tapped her own result once, lightly, with one finger. "This is where the science gets both very precise and genuinely empowering. Let me show you what we actually know."

Why It Matters

Most of us think of aging as simple arithmetic. You are born, years pass, and the number of years that have passed is your age. But your body does not experience time the way a calendar does. Two people who are both forty-five years old can be decades apart in how their cells function, how their organs perform, how their immune systems respond, and how far they are from the diseases most associated with old age. The calendar number tells you nothing about any of that.

For most of medical history, doctors who wanted to assess biological aging had to rely on indirect proxies such as blood pressure, cholesterol levels, grip strength, and recovery speed. These were useful but scattered. What the science of epigenetic aging has produced is something genuinely different: a direct molecular readout of how old your cells actually behave, grounded in the same biochemistry that runs your entire genome.

This matters for two reasons. The first is that it gives researchers a precise, measurable target for studying what aging actually is at the molecular level. The second is personal. If you can measure how fast your cells are aging, you can ask what factors are moving that needle, and whether any of them are within your control. The answer, it turns out, is yes, and quite a few of them are the same habits your doctor has been recommending for years. But when you understand them through the lens of epigenetic aging, they stop feeling like generic advice and start feeling like instructions for the machinery that keeps the lights on in every cell in your body.

Diagram 8.1 - Biological Age vs. Chronological Age

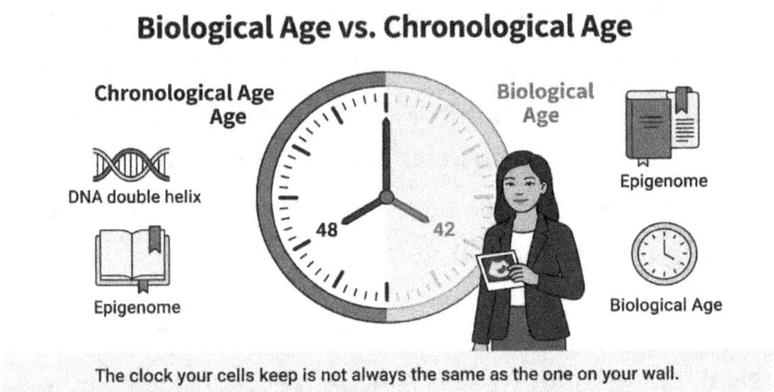

The clock your cells keep is not always the same as the one on your wall.

Before we explore how epigenetic clocks work, it helps to understand what aging looks like at the molecular level. Your DNA is covered in a layer of chemical marks, most importantly the methyl tags that sit on certain letters of the genetic code and influence whether nearby genes are switched on or off. These marks are not random. They are laid down systematically during development, adjusted throughout life in response to your experiences and environment, and, in a pattern documented across thousands of people, they drift in a consistent and predictable direction as you get older. That drift is the foundation of every epigenetic clock.

The Clock That Surprised Everyone

In 2013, a biostatistician named Steve Horvath published a paper that quietly rearranged the field of aging research.

Horvath was a mathematician working on cancer genetics at UCLA and had access to a large collection of DNA methylation data from dozens of studies. He decided to ask a question that seems obvious in retrospect but that no one had seriously attempted: if you look at methylation patterns across the whole genome, can you predict a person's age from their biology alone?

The answer was yes, and the precision of the answer stunned him. Horvath fed a statistical model data from about 8,000 samples drawn from 51 different human tissue types, ranging from blood and saliva to brain, liver, and kidney. The model searched for the methylation sites whose pattern correlated most tightly with a person's known age. After training, it settled on 353 specific CpG sites: genomic spots where the pattern of methyl tags was so reliably age-related that, together, they could predict a person's chronological age with a median error of only 3.6 years.

Think about what that means. You take a cell from someone's liver, saliva, or blood. You measure the methylation pattern at those three hundred and fifty-three spots. And without knowing anything else about that person, not their name, not their birth date, not a single other clinical fact, you can estimate how old they are with a precision that beats almost every other biological marker ever tested. Horvath called it the epigenetic clock, and within a year, every serious aging lab in the world was paying attention.

Diagram 8.2 - How the Horvath Clock Was Built

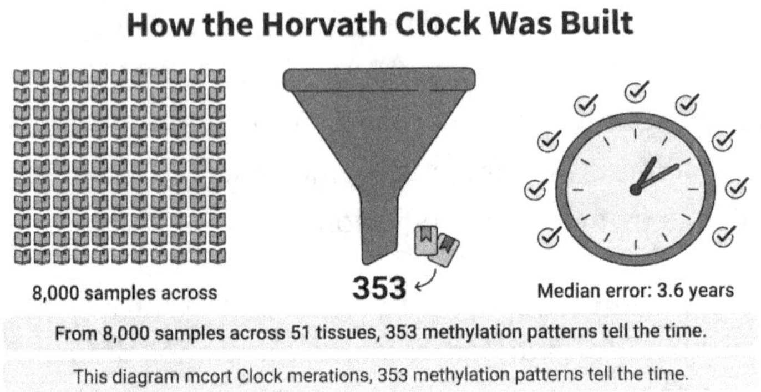

What made the Horvath clock so striking was not just its accuracy but its universality. Previous attempts to measure biological aging have primarily focused on blood. But Horvath's clock worked on virtually every tissue he tested. The methylation pattern in a brain cell and the methylation pattern in a skin cell told the same story, at least in broad strokes. That cross-tissue consistency suggested something fundamental: the methylation changes associated with aging were not random noise but a coherent biological process playing out across the entire organism.

The book-and-bookmarks metaphor fits here exactly. Imagine a well-loved book that has been read and reread over many years. Some pages are dog-eared. Some margins are filled with pencil notes. Some chapters have sticky flags from a dozen different readings. If someone hands you that book and asks you to guess how long it has been in use, you would look at the accumulation of those marks: the density of annotation, the wear on the binding, the fading of the most-visited pages. Horvath's clock does exactly that, but with molecular precision, reading the accumulated wear on the genome's bookmark system to estimate how long it has been in service.

Reading More Than Just Age: The Second-Generation Clocks

The Horvath clock was a proof of concept: yes, you can read age in methylation patterns, and yes, the reading is accurate. But the next generation of clocks was built to predict something more useful than your age. They were built to predict how well you are aging and how much time you might have left.

The Hannum clock, published a few months after Horvath's, was trained specifically on blood samples and used a smaller set of seventy-one CpG sites. It performed comparably to Horvath's work on blood-based measurements and confirmed that the approach was reproducible across research groups. Both clocks established the basic toolkit. Then the field asked a harder question: what if we trained a clock not on chronological age, but on outcomes that actually matter to medicine?

That question produced GrimAge. Developed by Horvath and colleagues and published in 2019, GrimAge was trained on plasma protein levels associated with aging and on time-to-death data from long-running population studies. The result was a clock that did not just tell you your biological age in years but estimated your risk of dying within a given window. GrimAge has since outperformed chronological age in predicting all-cause mortality, cardiovascular disease, cancer incidence, and a range of other outcomes that clinicians actually care about. It is less a clock and more a risk calculator that reads biological age as its input.

Diagram 8.3 - Four Generations of Epigenetic Clocks

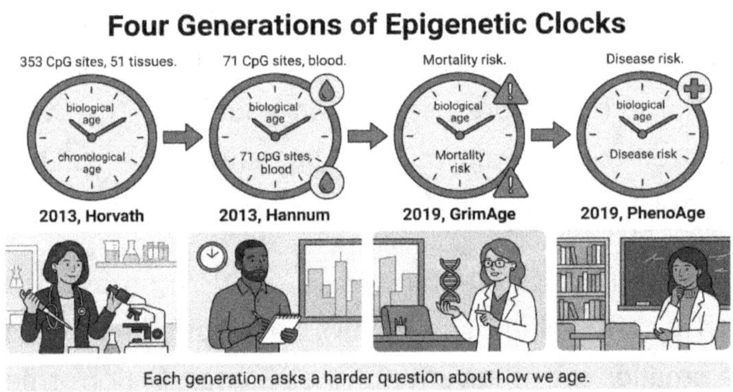

PhenoAge, developed by Morgan Levine, focused on phenotypic aging: the measurable biological changes that accumulate beyond just mortality risk. PhenoAge was trained on clinical biomarkers, including albumin, creatinine, and glucose, that collectively describe how the body is functioning rather than just its age. A person whose PhenoAge is significantly higher than their chronological age tends to have an elevated risk not of any single disease but of a cluster of age-related conditions simultaneously.

What these second-generation clocks collectively revealed is that the gap between your chronological age and your biological age is not random. Your life shapes it. The choices you make, the stresses you carry, the sleep you get or do not get, the way you eat and move: all of these things leave measurable marks on the methylation pattern that the clock reads. That finding is the heart of this chapter, and it is one of the most genuinely empowering things that epigenetic research has produced.

What Turns the Clock Forward

James looked at his number for a long moment. Thirty-nine. Four years older than his calendar age. He asked the obvious question. "What did it?" Maya turned her coffee cup slowly in her hands. "That's the honest problem with a single result. The clock tells you where you are. It doesn't tell you how you got there." She paused. "But the research tells us what tends to move the needle in the wrong direction. And most of it isn't a surprise."

She was right. The lifestyle factors that accelerate epigenetic aging overlap substantially with the risk factors that medicine has tracked for decades. But the epigenetic data add something important: they show how these factors affect aging at the molecular level, not just in disease statistics. It moves the conversation from "these habits increase your risk" to "these habits are measurably changing the biochemistry that governs how fast your cells age."

Smoking is the single largest modifiable accelerant in the research literature, and the effect size is sobering. Long-term smokers show biological ages significantly higher than their chronological age, with some analyses suggesting an acceleration of one to two years per decade of heavy smoking. Perhaps more striking, the methylation changes associated with smoking are consistent enough that researchers built a tool called the Epigenetic Smoking Score, which can estimate whether someone smoked, and roughly how much, from a blood sample alone, even years after quitting. The good news: after cessation, some of these methylation changes do begin to reverse, though not all of them, and not immediately.

Diagram 8.4 - Lifestyle Factors That Accelerate Epigenetic Aging

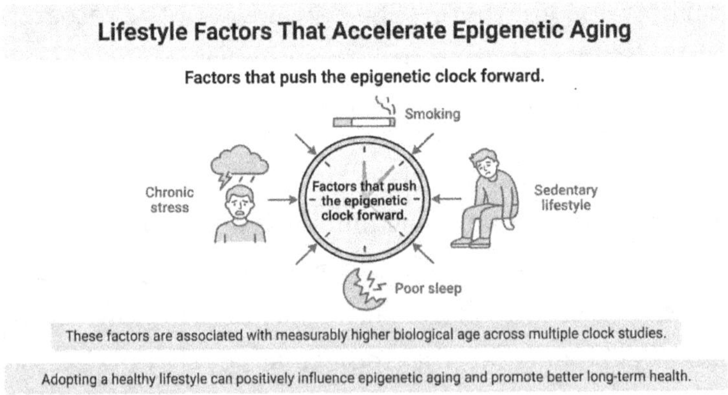

Chronic stress is a second major accelerant. Prolonged elevation of stress hormones alters the activity of the enzymes that add and remove methyl tags, and those changes accumulate in patterns that the epigenetic clocks

detect as older. Studies of caregivers for seriously ill family members, people living in high-poverty neighborhoods, and individuals with a history of childhood adversity all show accelerated epigenetic aging relative to matched controls.

Poor sleep is a more recent entry in the accelerant list. People with chronic sleep disorders, short sleep duration, or disrupted sleep architecture show epigenetic age acceleration relative to good sleepers. Sleep is when the body performs a significant amount of its cellular maintenance, including the clearance of metabolic byproducts and the repair of DNA damage in tissues throughout the body. When that maintenance window is shortened chronically, the accumulated costs show up in the methylation pattern.

Obesity and metabolic dysfunction show consistent associations with accelerated epigenetic aging, independent of age, sex, and smoking. The relationship is driven more specifically by chronic low-grade inflammation that accompanies metabolic dysregulation: elevated inflammatory proteins, insulin resistance, and the sustained activation of stress-response pathways, which, when sustained, begin to erode the precision of the epigenetic control system.

Diagram 8.5 - Chronic Stress and the Epigenetic Clock

Chronic Stress and the Epigenetic Clock

Chronic stress accumulates as epigenetic drift

Long-term stress alters the enzymes that manage methylation, and the clocks notice.

The epigenetic clock accelerates under prolonged psychological pressure.

James noted that none of these factors was surprising in themselves. He had written about most of them as a health journalist. "So the epigenetic clock is just confirming what we already knew?" Maya shook her head slightly. "It's doing something different. It's not saying 'people who smoke get sick more often.' It's saying 'smoking changes the precise biochemical pattern that governs how fast your cells age.' That's a molecular fingerprint, not a population statistic." She looked at his result. "The four-year gap in your case is interesting rather than alarming. It's well within the range where ordinary life variation accounts for it. The clock isn't a verdict. It's a snapshot."

What Slows the Clock

The same research that identified the accelerants also identified factors associated with biological age younger than chronological age. Maya's six-year advantage was consistent with a profile the epigenetic aging literature describes clearly: regular vigorous exercise, good sleep, strong social connections, a diet rich in plants and relatively low in processed foods, and a sense of purpose that makes getting up in the morning feel as if it matters.

Exercise has the strongest evidence among modifiable lifestyle factors in the epigenetic aging literature. Studies find that people who exercise regularly tend to have biological ages one to four years younger than sedentary people of the same chronological age. The effect involves multiple mechanisms: exercise reduces chronic inflammation, improves insulin sensitivity, promotes the clearance of senescent cells (cells that have stopped dividing but continue to release inflammatory signals), and directly influences the activity of methylation-modifying enzymes. The combination of aerobic and resistance exercise appears more protective than either alone.

Diagram 8.6 - Exercise and the Epigenetic Clock

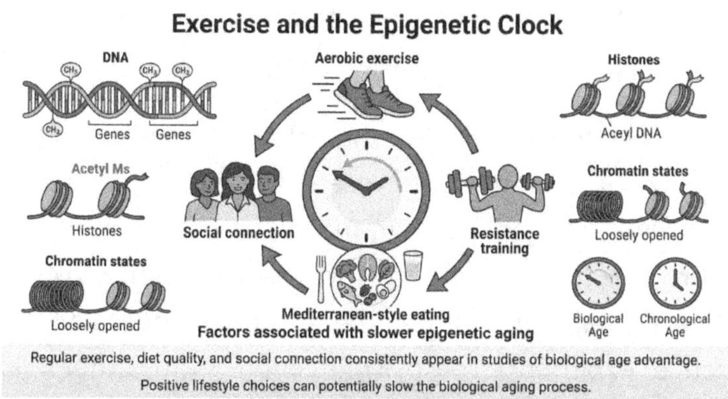

Diet quality shows consistent but nuanced associations. The clearest signal comes from dietary patterns rather than individual foods. The Mediterranean dietary pattern, broadly characterized by high intake of vegetables, legumes, whole grains, fish, and olive oil, with relatively low intake of red meat and ultra-processed foods, is associated with lower biological age in several large studies. The working hypothesis is that this pattern reduces chronic inflammation and oxidative stress while providing the B vitamins and other micronutrients that the methylation machinery needs to run well.

Sleep quality is both an accelerant when poor and a protective factor when good. People who consistently get seven to nine hours of sleep, maintain regular sleep and wake times, and achieve the deep, slow-wave sleep stages where intensive cellular repair occurs show epigenetic age profiles that are meaningfully younger than those of matched poor sleepers. The epigenetic data have strengthened the case for sleep prioritization beyond the traditional "you'll feel better" framing. The molecular evidence now says your cells are younger for it.

Social connection is a factor that often surprises people when it appears in longevity research, because it sounds more like wellness advice than molecular biology. But the data on chronic loneliness is consistent and striking. Loneliness, defined not as being alone but as the subjective experience of disconnection from others, is associated with epigenetic age acceleration in several independent studies, with effect sizes comparable to some physical health factors. The mechanism likely involves the stress-response system: chronic loneliness activates the same cortisol and inflammatory pathways as other chronic stressors, and those pathways leave the same molecular marks that the clocks detect.

Diagram 8.7 - Sleep Quality and Cellular Repair

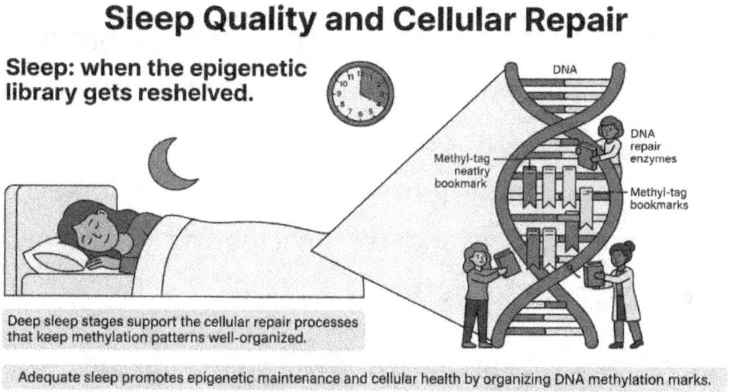

Calorie Restriction, mTOR, and the Chemistry of Longevity

One of the most consistent findings in aging biology, across species as different as yeast, roundworms, fruit flies, mice, and primates, is that reducing calorie intake without causing malnutrition tends to extend healthy lifespan and slow biological aging markers. In animal models, calorie restriction is associated with slower methylation drift, reduced epigenetic age acceleration, and changes in gene activity that, at the molecular level, appear younger. The effect is real. The question for humans is how to interpret it.

The biology behind calorie restriction runs largely through a protein called mTOR, which stands for mechanistic target of rapamycin. mTOR is a cellular sensor that monitors the availability of food energy and uses that information to decide whether to grow, replicate, and build new structures, or to pause, repair, and recycle old ones. When food is plentiful, mTOR says build. When food is scarce, mTOR says maintain and repair. Those repair processes, including a form of cellular housekeeping called autophagy, in which the cell breaks down and recycles its own damaged components, are closely linked to epigenetic maintenance and to the clearing of molecular clutter that aging clocks detect.

Diagram 8.8 - The mTOR Switch: Growth vs. Repair

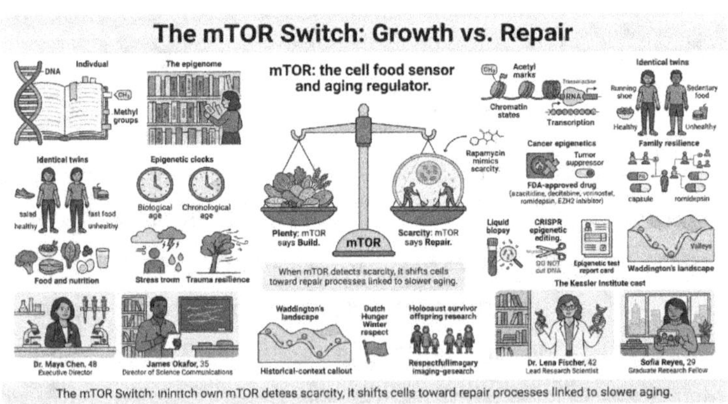

Rapamycin is a drug that inhibits mTOR, telling cells that food is scarce even when it isn't, thereby activating repair and maintenance programs. It is one of the few compounds that have consistently extended lifespan across multiple animal species, and it is already used in human medicine as an immunosuppressant for organ transplant recipients. Whether low-dose rapamycin can safely slow aging in healthy humans is under active clinical investigation. The early data are interesting but not conclusive, and the drug has real side effects at clinical doses, including impaired immune function. This is a frontier, not a settled answer.

Intermittent fasting and time-restricted eating protocols work in part through the mTOR pathway: periods of fasting activate the repair programs that mTOR otherwise suppresses. Some short-term trials show favorable changes in epigenetic aging markers. But the evidence base is early, effect sizes in humans are modest, and long-term impacts are not yet well characterized. The mTOR biology is fascinating, and the animal data are compelling, but translating it into concrete human longevity recommendations requires more evidence than currently exists.

The Reset Button: Yamanaka Factors and Partial Reprogramming

In 2006, a Japanese cell biologist named Shinya Yamanaka showed that you could take an ordinary adult cell, such as a skin cell, and convert it into a state resembling an embryonic stem cell by introducing just four proteins. These proteins, which he called Oct4, Sox2, Klf4, and c-Myc, act as master switches that reset the cell's gene expression program back to an early developmental state. The adult cell loses its specialized identity and becomes a pluripotent stem cell: a blank slate capable of developing into almost any cell type in the body.

Critically, the Yamanaka reprogramming process also resets the cell's epigenetic age. A skin cell from a seventy-year-old person, when fully reprogrammed, has the epigenetic profile of an embryonic cell. The accumulated methylation drift of seven decades is erased. For longevity researchers, this was a profound observation: it demonstrated that epigenetic age was not a one-way ratchet. It could be wound back. The question was whether it could be partially wound back, just enough to restore a younger epigenetic state without erasing the cell's identity.

Diagram 8.9 - Yamanaka Factors and Epigenetic Reset

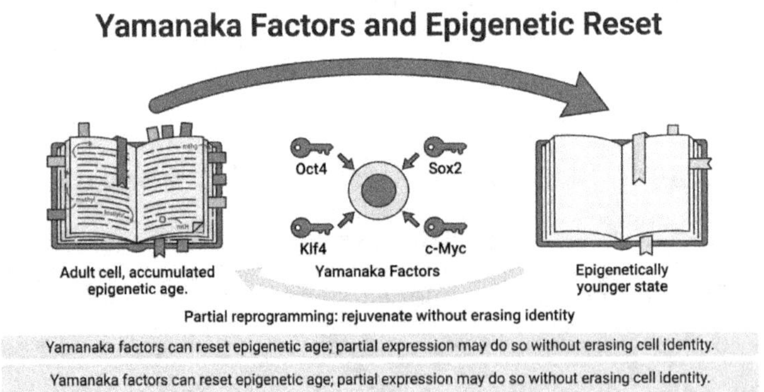

Several research groups have developed protocols for cycling the Yamanaka factors on and off in cells and in living animals. When cells are exposed to the factors briefly and repeatedly rather than continuously, they appear to shed years of epigenetic aging, as measured by the methylation clocks, without fully losing their differentiated identity. In mouse studies, this partial or cyclic reprogramming has restored some aspects of function in aged tissues, with older mice showing improvements in retinal function, muscle regeneration, and kidney health after partial reprogramming treatments.

These findings are genuinely exciting. They represent evidence that biological age reversal is not merely theoretical but demonstrable in a living mammalian system. At the same time, several cautions matter. First, mice are not humans. Second, one of the four Yamanaka factors, c-Myc, is a known oncogene: when chronically activated, it can drive cells toward uncontrolled growth and cancer. The protocols being developed aim to stay well short of that threshold, but the safety profile in humans requires extensive clinical testing that is not yet complete. Third, the field is attracting enormous investment, and in environments with that much money and excitement, the gap between what the science says and what gets claimed in press releases can become wide very quickly.

James asked the question directly: "Should anyone be doing any of this to themselves right now?" Maya's answer was immediate. "No. Not outside a supervised clinical trial. This is fascinating frontier science. It is not a therapy. Not yet." She let that sit. "The exciting thing is that partial reprogramming proves the clock can be wound back. What we don't know is how to do that safely and reproducibly in the whole human body. That's five to twenty years of work, minimum, if everything goes well."

Diagram 8.10 - Partial Reprogramming: What We Know and What We Don't

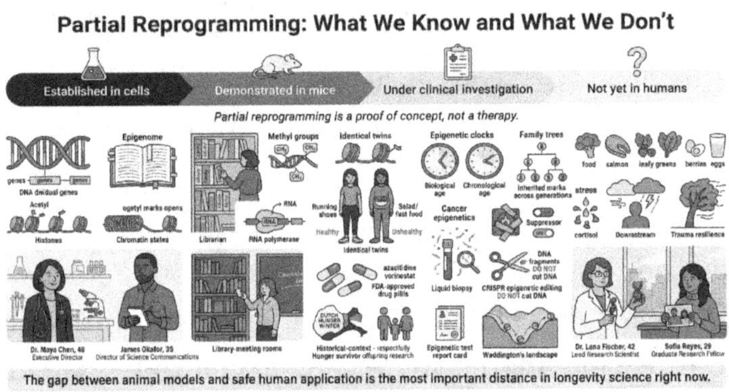

Your Epigenetic Age Test: What to Know Before You Buy

The printouts Maya and James reviewed came from a direct-to-consumer company. You can order tests like theirs yourself, from several companies, without a doctor's order. You collect a small blood spot or saliva sample at home, mail it to a laboratory, and receive a report a few weeks later that tells you your biological age based on one or more epigenetic clock algorithms. The tests are real. The science underlying them is real. But before you order one, several things are worth understanding clearly.

First, what these tests measure is reliable, but what a single result tells you is limited. The clock algorithms are statistically robust and validated in large-scale population studies. Your result is a genuine estimate of your biological age as measured by DNA methylation at the time of sample collection. But biological age fluctuates. Studies that tested the same individuals multiple times over weeks or months found meaningful variation in clock readings, driven by acute illness, changes in sleep or stress, travel, and other short-term factors. A single data point tells you roughly where you are, not a trend line.

Second, the clock your test uses matters, and not all companies use the same one. Some tests use the original Horvath clock. Others use GrimAge, PhenoAge, or proprietary variants developed by the testing company. Each clock measures something slightly different and was validated against different outcomes. A number from GrimAge answers a somewhat different question than a number from the Horvath clock, even though both are described as biological age. When you receive your result, find out which algorithm generated it and what that algorithm was validated to predict.

Diagram 8.11 - Understanding Your Epigenetic Age Test Result

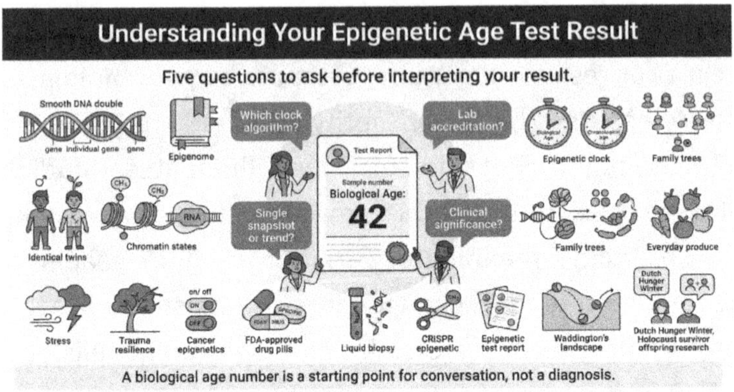

Third, a biological age number is not a diagnosis and does not constitute a medical recommendation. If your result shows a biological age significantly higher than your chronological age, that is information worth discussing with a doctor. Still, it is not a reason to panic or to start taking supplements or drugs based on online advice. The clock result identifies a pattern. It does not identify a cause, and it does not point to a specific treatment. A good next step is to share the result with a physician familiar with the literature who can help you think about it in the context of your full health picture.

Fourth, the most useful application of an epigenetic age test is serial testing over time, not a single result. If you test yourself, make meaningful lifestyle changes, then test again six or twelve months later, the change in your biological age over that interval is more informative than any single number. You are looking for the direction of travel, not a fixed destination. The effect sizes for most lifestyle interventions in humans are modest over short time frames, but seeing a number move a year or two in the right direction suggests the changes you made are registering at the molecular level.

What This Means for You

Here is the most practical thing epigenetic aging research has to say: the habits that move your biological age in the right direction are not mysteries and are not extreme. They are the ordinary, daily behaviors your body was designed for, but modern life has made them inconvenient. The epigenetic clock data do not reveal new interventions. It reveals, with molecular precision, why the old advice actually works.

Exercise is the single most powerful modifiable factor in the research, and it does not require an elaborate program. The threshold for meaningful benefit is lower than most people expect: thirty to forty-five minutes of brisk walking, cycling, or swimming five days a week is enough to show up as protective in the epigenetic clock data. Adding two sessions per week of resistance exercise, whether weight training, resistance bands, or bodyweight movements, appears to add benefit beyond aerobic activity alone. The goal is not to train like an athlete, but to move your body in ways that regularly elevate your heart rate and challenge your muscles.

Sleep is the intervention that most people underestimate. It is not passive. It is when your cells run their most intensive maintenance programs, and the epigenetic data reinforces that protecting sleep quantity and quality is a genuine investment in how your cells age. Consistent sleep and wake times, a cool, dark sleeping environment, avoiding alcohol before bed, and treating sleep disorders as medical issues rather than inconveniences: these changes are supported by molecular evidence.

Diagram 8.12 - Daily Habits That Move the Epigenetic Needle

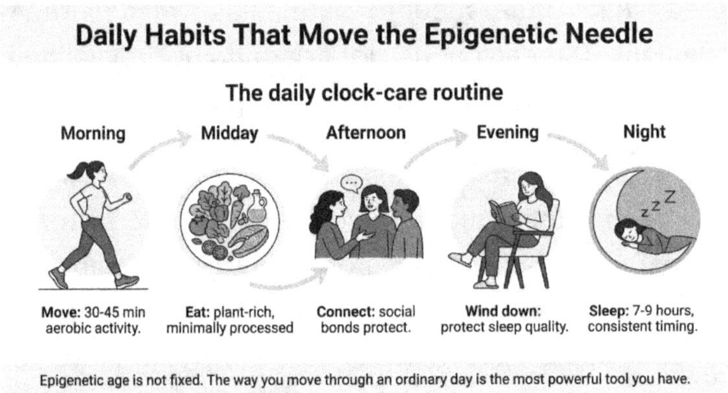

Eating in ways that support epigenetic health does not require a rigid or expensive diet. The Mediterranean pattern is the best-supported approach: lots of vegetables and fruits, legumes, whole grains, fish a few times per week, olive oil as the primary fat, and moderate amounts of poultry and dairy. This pattern provides the B vitamins that the methylation machinery needs, reduces the chronic inflammation that drives epigenetic age acceleration, and supports the gut microbiome in ways that feed back positively on metabolic and immune health. Better dietary patterns, not perfect ones, are consistently associated with a biological age advantage, according to the research.

Stress management is a biological necessity, not a luxury. The data on chronic stress and epigenetic age acceleration are consistent: the cortisol and inflammatory pathways activated by prolonged stress cause measurable molecular aging. The problem is not moderate, controlled stress that resolves, but the stress that never turns off: the unresolved conflict, the financial insecurity, the caregiving burden without support. Finding ways to address the structural sources of chronic stress in your life, whether through practical problem-solving, professional support, or deliberate recovery practices, is biologically justified.

Social connection deserves a direct recommendation, not a footnote. Having relationships that provide genuine emotional support, people you can call when something goes wrong, and communities where you feel known and valued, is associated with slower biological aging across multiple studies. This is not about having a large social network. It is about having a meaningful one. Regular time with the people who matter to you is an investment in your cells as much as in your happiness.

A note on supplements claiming to slow epigenetic aging: most of them have very limited evidence in humans. NMN (nicotinamide mononucleotide), resveratrol, and a growing list of other compounds have generated excitement based on animal studies. Still, none has clear large-scale evidence of meaningful epigenetic age reduction in healthy humans. The lifestyle factors described in this section have far better evidence behind them than anything currently available in a capsule.

Takeaway

Your chronological age is fixed. The number on your birth certificate will always be what it is. But your biological age, the age your cells are actually operating at, the age your epigenetic clock reads when a researcher runs your DNA methylation through Horvath's three hundred and fifty-three checkpoints, is not fixed. It is a running variable, shaped every day by what you do, how you sleep, what you eat, who you are with, and how you handle what life asks of you. The research in this chapter does not promise that the right habits will make you live forever. What it does say, with the authority of reading the molecular record directly, is that the ordinary choices of ordinary life accumulate in the very machinery that governs how fast you age. Your epigenome is listening to everything you do. The good news is that most of what it wants to hear is both achievable and free.

Maya's six-year advantage was not due to a supplement stack or a longevity protocol. It was the result of decades of habits: regular exercise, consistent sleep, a Mediterranean-style diet she had eaten since childhood, and deep social connections built over many years of meaningful work. James's four-year gap turned out, in her reading, to be mostly explainable by a decade of deadline-driven insomnia and airport food during his years as a journalist. "The clock is forgiving," she said, rolling up her own printout and sliding it into her bag. "The studies show it responds when you change things. It doesn't respond overnight. It responds over months and years. Which means the right time to start is now, not when you have a perfect protocol."

In the next chapter, we turn from aging in healthy tissue to the most dramatic example of epigenetic dysregulation in medicine: cancer. We will see how the same methylation machinery that governs biological age can, when it goes wrong in the wrong places, contribute to one of the most challenging conditions in human biology, and how a new generation of epigenetic drugs is already being used to fight back.

9 Rewriting Cancer and Your Epigenetic Blueprint

The library at the Kessler Institute is a small room at the end of the second-floor hallway, more storage than sanctuary: metal shelves, mismatched chairs, a window that faces the parking garage. Maya Chen uses it; James Okafor has learned that she uses it when she wants to say something difficult. She had pulled two thick folders from the shelf before he arrived, and they sat on the table between them like closed doors. The folders held old patient files. Anonymized, she explained, though the effort of anonymizing them was visible in the careful black marker strokes across certain lines.

She opened the first folder and pointed to a section of the chart—a man in his early fifties. Glioblastoma is the most aggressive kind of brain tumor. James already knew, from his journalism years, that glioblastoma was a diagnosis that left very little room for optimism. What Maya was showing him was different, though. She was pointing to a lab result near the back of the chart. MGMT promoter methylation: positive. "I need you to understand what that meant for this patient," she said, keeping her voice level. "Because it meant a drug that most glioblastoma patients cannot benefit from would actually work for him. A single epigenetic mark, James. One bookmark in the wrong place, or the right place, depending on how you look at it. And that bookmark changed everything about what we offered him."

James looked at the folder. "The gene was still there, though. The MGMT gene." Maya nodded. "The gene was intact. The gene was fine. But it was covered up. Not deleted, not mutated. Covered up, the way you would cover a fire alarm with duct tape." She paused. "That fire alarm, covered with tape, is your entire introduction to epigenetic cancer biology. The alarm still works. The wiring is intact. But nothing gets through." Outside the library window, a delivery truck backed slowly into the garage below, its warning beeper faint through the glass. James thought about fire alarms. He thought about tape. He thought about all the things that might be covered over, in a cell, in a body, that no one had yet thought to check.

Why It Matters

Most of us grew up thinking about cancer as a genetic disease. Mutations accumulate. The DNA breaks. The instructions that govern normal cell behavior get scrambled, and the cell stops listening. That understanding is real and important. But it is, by itself, incomplete. Because over the last three decades, researchers have documented something that changes the picture considerably: cancer is also, and in many cases primarily, an epigenetic disease. The chemical bookmarks that sit above the DNA, telling the cell which genes to read and which to ignore, go profoundly wrong in cancer. Tumor suppressor genes, the ones whose job is to sound the alarm when cells start dividing out of control, get silenced by the wrong epigenetic marks. Proto-oncogenes, the ones that accelerate cell growth and should stay quiet most of the time, get switched on when they should be off. The DNA text is the same. The bookmarks are disastrously rearranged.

This matters for a reason that is both scientific and deeply personal. A deleted gene is gone. If a mutation destroys the sequence, there is nothing to rescue. But a silenced gene is still there. The text is intact. Only the bookmarks are wrong. And if you can identify which bookmarks are wrong and find a way to correct them, you can potentially wake a tumor suppressor gene back up. You can reopen the alarm system. That is not a fantasy. It is the mechanism behind a class of FDA-approved cancer drugs that are already in use, that have already extended lives, and that are being improved and combined in ways that are moving oncology toward a genuinely new era.

This chapter covers biology, those drugs, and the diagnostic revolution running alongside them. It covers what it means to find cancer in a blood sample before you ever feel sick. It covers the ethics of knowing your epigenetic risks, the questions you should ask before you hand over your biological data to any company or clinical program, and the remarkable story of how a single methylation mark in a single gene became the standard of care for one of the hardest cancers to treat. Maya is the right guide for all of it. She spent fifteen years as an oncologist before the questions she could not answer drove her to research. The questions she could not answer were, very often, epigenetic ones.

Diagram 9.1 - The Fire Alarm and the Duct Tape

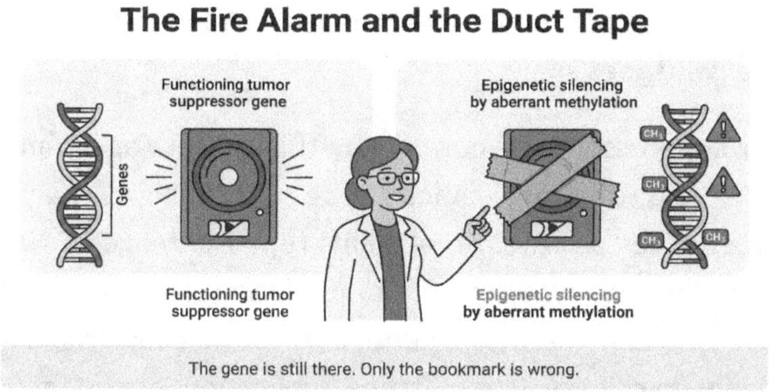

Cancer Is Not Just a Genetic Disease

To understand epigenetic cancer biology, start with the book-and-bookmarks metaphor that has been running through this book. Your DNA is the text. Epigenetic marks are the bookmarks and highlights that tell the cell which pages to open and which to keep closed. In a healthy cell, the system is maintained with extraordinary precision. Tumor suppressor genes, the cellular equivalent of emergency brakes, stay bookmarked-open, ready to read, ready to act. Proto-oncogenes, the genes that push cell growth forward, stay bookmarked-closed most of the time, activated only when growth is genuinely needed.

In cancer, this bookmarking system breaks down in characteristic ways. The most studied failure mode is called promoter hypermethylation. The promoter region is the section of DNA just upstream of a gene, the stretch that acts as the gene's front door, the place where the cell's reading machinery docks to transcribe the gene into action. When methyl groups pile up on that promoter, the door gets sealed shut. The gene is still written in the DNA, every letter intact, but the reading machinery cannot get in. The gene goes silent.

Tumor suppressor genes are hit by this process again and again across different cancer types. The BRCA1 gene, which encodes a protein that helps repair damaged DNA, can be silenced by promoter methylation in breast and ovarian cancers. The MLH1 gene, part of the cellular spell-checking machinery that catches replication errors, gets silenced by methylation in colorectal cancer. The p16 gene, which normally puts the brakes on the cell cycle and prevents uncontrolled division, is methylated and silenced in a wide range of cancers, from lung to melanoma to bladder. In every case, the gene is intact. The alarm is on the wall. The duct tape is over it.

The problem also runs in the opposite direction. Cancer cells often show a global loss of methylation across much of the genome, a condition called hypomethylation. Where normal cells keep certain regions tightly methylated and quiet, cancer cells lose that methylation, and genes that should stay silent wake up. Proto-oncogenes, the growth accelerators, can be activated this way. So can mobile genetic elements, ancient sequences that normally sleep harmlessly in the DNA but can cause instability when they activate. The cancer epigenome is not simply a silenced landscape. It is a landscape where the wrong things are silenced, and the wrong things are shouting.

Diagram 9.2 - Methylation Imbalance in a Cancer Cell

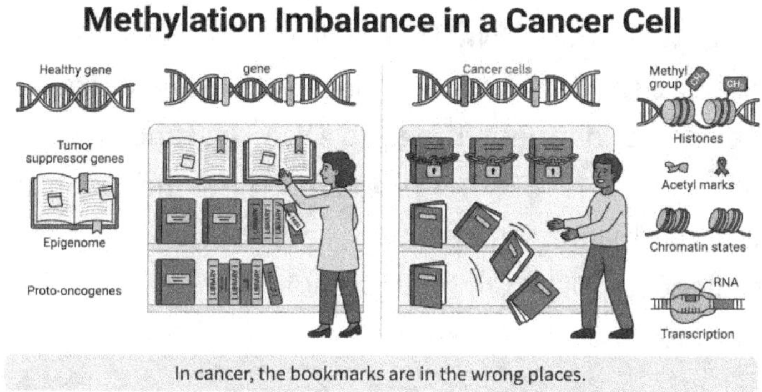

In cancer, the bookmarks are in the wrong places.

James asked Maya a question that had been building since she opened the folder. "If the DNA is fine and only the bookmarks are wrong, does that mean cancer could theoretically be reversed? Just by fixing the bookmarks?" Maya smiled in the way she always did when a question was on the edge of the real answer. "Theoretically, yes. Practically, it is extraordinarily complicated. But here is the important point: theoretical reversibility drove the entire field of epigenetic cancer therapy. The possibility that you might be able to turn the alarm back on."

That possibility, pursued over decades by researchers who were considered optimistic at best and naive at worst, eventually produced drugs—real drugs, approved by the FDA, in clinical use, with real response rate data. The path from concept to clinic was not quick or easy, but it was traveled.

The Drugs That Loosen the Bookmarks

The first class of epigenetic cancer drugs to reach clinical approval was the DNMT inhibitors: azacitidine and decitabine. DNMT stands for DNA methyltransferase, the enzyme that adds methyl tags to DNA. In cancer, DNMT enzymes are part of the problem: they maintain the aberrant methylation marks that keep tumor suppressor genes silenced. DNMT inhibitors work by tricking these enzymes into a fatal mistake.

Here is how it works, in plain terms. Both azacitidine and decitabine are molecules that, to a DNMT enzyme, look like normal DNA building blocks. The enzyme picks them up and incorporates them into newly synthesizing DNA, exactly as it would a normal cytosine nucleotide. But once they are embedded in the DNA, they trap the DNMT enzyme in a permanent, immovable bond. The enzyme gets stuck to the DNA and cannot finish its job. Over several rounds of cell division, the methylation machinery is progressively depleted. The aberrant methyl tags that were keeping tumor suppressor promoters sealed shut begin to erode. The doors start to open again.

The cells in which tumor suppressor genes are reactivated may stop dividing. They may re-enter normal programmed death pathways. The cancer, at least in principle, begins to lose its growth advantage.

Diagram 9.3 - DNMT Inhibitor Unlocking a Silenced Gene

DNMT Inhibitor Unlocking a Silenced Gene

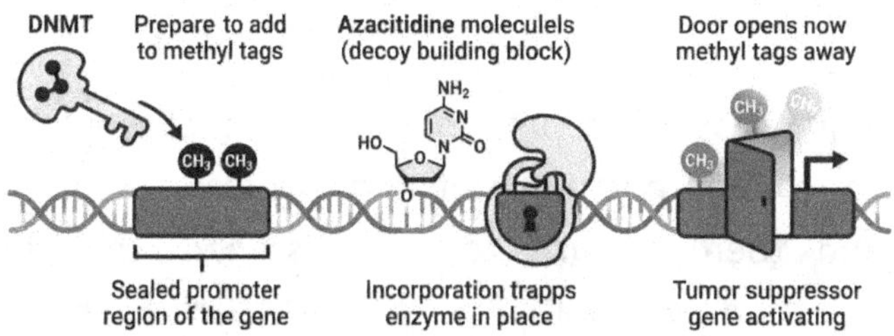

DNMT inhibitors deplete the machinery that keeps the wrong doors closed.

Azacitidine and decitabine are currently approved for the treatment of myelodysplastic syndrome, a group of bone marrow disorders in which blood cells fail to mature properly, and for acute myeloid leukemia, an aggressive blood cancer. In myelodysplastic syndrome, azacitidine has been shown to delay progression to leukemia and, in clinical trials, to improve overall survival compared with standard care. Decitabine shows comparable activity with a slightly different dosing profile. Neither drug is a cure in the conventional sense. Still, both produce meaningful responses in patients for whom other options were limited, and both do so through the specifically epigenetic mechanism of allowing silenced genes to re-express.

These are not gentle drugs. Like many cancer therapies, they carry side effects, including myelosuppression, meaning the suppression of the bone marrow's blood-producing activity. Nausea, fatigue, and the risk of infection are real clinical considerations. But for the patients and cancer types for which they are indicated, they represent a genuinely novel mechanism: treating cancer not by attacking DNA directly, but by restoring the epigenetic control system that cancer had dismantled.

The second class of approved epigenetic cancer drugs works on a different part of the control system. To understand them, return to the histones, the spool proteins around which DNA is wound. Earlier chapters described how histone acetylation, the addition of acetyl groups to histone tails, loosens the winding and makes genes more accessible. Histone deacetylases, the HDAC enzymes, remove acetyl groups, tightening chromatin and shutting genes down. In cancer, HDAC enzymes are frequently overactive, tightening chromatin around tumor suppressor genes and contributing to their silencing.

HDAC inhibitors block those enzymes. With the deacetylases disabled, acetyl groups accumulate on histones, the chromatin loosens, and silenced genes become accessible again. Vorinostat, approved in 2006, and romidepsin, approved in 2009, were the first two to reach clinical use. Both are approved for cutaneous T-cell lymphoma, a cancer of a specific type of white blood cell that manifests primarily in the skin.

Diagram 9.4 - HDAC Inhibitor Opening the Chromatin Spool

HDAC Inhibitor Opening the Chromatin Spool

HDAC inhibitors prevent chromatin tightening, enabling gene activation.

Romidepsin is particularly interesting mechanistically. Where vorinostat is a broad HDAC inhibitor affecting multiple HDAC subtypes, romidepsin is more selective, targeting a specific class of HDAC enzymes. It enters cells as a prodrug, an inactive molecule that is converted to its active form in the reducing environment inside a cell. The result is a drug with potent, targeted activity against certain lymphomas, particularly T-cell lymphomas that had stopped responding to standard treatments.

Vorinostat and romidepsin are not chemotherapy in the traditional sense. They do not primarily work by poisoning dividing cells. They work by restoring the epigenetic bookmarking system to a closer-to-normal state, allowing the cell's own regulatory mechanisms to reassert control. That distinction matters for understanding why these drugs can be effective even in settings where standard chemotherapy has failed.

Combining Forces

Clinical oncologists are not satisfied with one mechanism when two might be better. The logic for combining DNMT inhibitors with HDAC inhibitors is straightforward. DNMT inhibitors attack gene silencing at the methylation level, loosening the methyl seals on promoter regions. HDAC inhibitors attack gene silencing at the chromatin level, loosening the spool tightening that compounds the problem. Using both simultaneously, or in careful sequence, is like removing both the duct tape from the fire alarm and the cotton stuffed in its speaker. Both barriers come down at once.

Early combination trials showed something intriguing. The synergy was greater than the sum of the parts. Tumor suppressor genes that did not re-express adequately with either drug alone sometimes responded when both were used together. Response rates improved in some hematological malignancies, and the duration of response lengthened. The field moved from single-agent studies to combination studies with considerable momentum.

The third combination strategy, and the one generating the most excitement in current oncology research, pairs epigenetic drugs with immunotherapy. The connection between epigenetics and immune evasion turns out to be deep. Tumors do not simply silence tumor suppressor genes. They also silence the genes that mark tumor cells for destruction by the immune system. Many tumor cells downregulate the surface proteins that killer T-cells use to identify and attack abnormal cells, a strategy of molecular camouflage. DNMT inhibitors and HDAC inhibitors can reverse that camouflage. They can force tumor cells to re-express the proteins that mark them as targets, making them visible to immune cells that had previously been unable to find them.

Diagram 9.5 - Combination Epigenetic and Immunotherapy

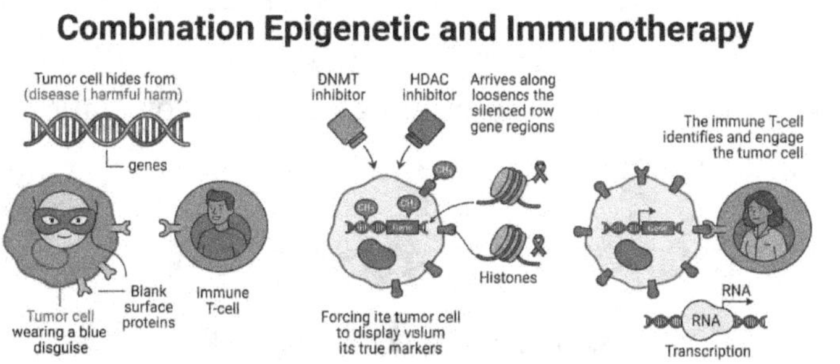

Epigenetic drugs can strip tumors of their molecular camouflage.

Epigenetic therapies reveal hidden cancers to the immune system for targeting.

In combination with checkpoint inhibitors, the class of immunotherapy drugs that includes pembrolizumab and nivolumab, DNMT inhibitors have shown early promise in clinical trials for lung cancer, ovarian cancer, and colorectal cancer. The trials are ongoing. The results are not yet definitive. But the rationale is scientifically sound, the early signals are encouraging, and the combination approach represents the clearest path toward using epigenetic therapy not just for blood cancers but for the solid tumors that account for the majority of cancer deaths.

The pipeline extends further. EZH2 inhibitors, targeting a different epigenetic enzyme that compresses chromatin in certain lymphomas, received FDA approval in 2020 for specific subtypes of follicular lymphoma and diffuse large B-cell lymphoma. BET inhibitors and LSD1 inhibitors are in active clinical development. The point is not to enumerate every drug in the pipeline but to make clear that epigenetic oncology is not a promising idea waiting to be tested. It is a tested approach with approved drugs, expanding indications, and a deepening mechanistic understanding that is generating a new generation of combination strategies.

The MGMT Story: A Bookmark That Changed Treatment

Maya had wanted James to understand the MGMT story from the beginning. She had introduced it in the library precisely because it is the clearest, most established example of what the field calls epigenetic biomarker-guided treatment selection. It is not experimental. It is standard of care. And it is a story about a single bookmark changing a treatment decision in a way that can add months, sometimes years, to a patient's life.

MGMT stands for O-6-methylguanine-DNA methyltransferase. The protein it encodes is a DNA repair enzyme. Its specific job is to fix a particular type of DNA damage: the kind caused by alkylating chemotherapy agents, including the drug temozolomide, which has been a mainstay of glioblastoma treatment for decades.

Temozolomide works by adding chemical groups to DNA that garble the genetic code and ultimately trigger cell death. MGMT repairs that damage, effectively neutralizing the drug's effect. Tumor cells with an active MGMT gene are, in a meaningful sense, resistant to temozolomide.

Now here is where the epigenetics becomes decisive. In roughly half of all glioblastoma patients, the MGMT gene's promoter region is heavily methylated. Not mutated, not deleted, but methylated. Silenced by bookmarks. In those tumors, the MGMT repair enzyme is not being produced because the gene is silenced. Temozolomide damages tumor cells' DNA; the MGMT gene cannot repair it, and the damage accumulates until the cell dies.

Diagram 9.6 - MGMT Methylation and Temozolomide Response

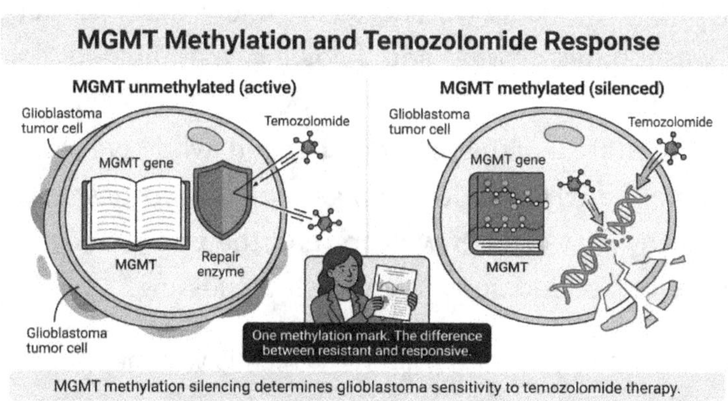

MGMT methylation silencing determines glioblastoma sensitivity to temozolomide therapy.

In clinical practice, testing for MGMT promoter methylation has become routine for newly diagnosed patients with glioblastoma. A positive result, meaning the

MGMT promoter is methylated and the gene is silenced, is a predictive biomarker: it predicts that temozolomide will be effective. A negative result, meaning the MGMT promoter is unmethylated and the gene is active, predicts limited benefit from temozolomide, and the treatment approach is adjusted accordingly.

The median survival benefit for MGMT-methylated glioblastoma patients receiving temozolomide plus radiation, compared with radiation alone, was approximately 21.7 months versus 15.3 months in the landmark clinical trial that established this standard. For a disease with historically grim outcomes, those additional months are not a footnote. They are the reason the test is ordered.

James sat with the folder for a moment after Maya finished. "So this patient," he said, "knew that the duct tape was on his alarm, and knowing that helped you choose the right drug." Maya nodded. "Knowing the epigenetic status of his tumor changed what we could offer him. The whole field of epigenetic diagnostics starts from exactly that logic. If we can read the bookmarks, we can make better decisions. We can stop guessing."

She picked up the second folder. "Which is why people are now trying to read those bookmarks from a blood sample."

The Blood Test That Reads Shed Pages

Imagine a library, Maya told James, where pages fall out of the books and drift downstream. You are standing at the riverbank collecting loose pages. Most of the pages come from normal, healthy books, their annotations ordinary, their margins unmarked. But some pages come from books that have been deeply, unusually annotated, with strange marks at specific locations that you recognize as signatures of a damaged section of the library. If you can identify those marked pages in the river, you can conclude something about what is happening upstream, even if you cannot see the library directly.

That is the core concept of liquid biopsy for cancer detection. Cells throughout the body shed small fragments of DNA into the bloodstream as they die in their normal turnover cycle. This circulating cell-free DNA, or cfDNA, is a mixture of fragments from all the different tissues in the body. In a person with cancer, some of that circulating DNA comes from tumor cells. Tumor cells carry the epigenetic signatures of their cancer of origin: aberrant methylation patterns that are specific enough and stable enough to be detected in a blood sample.

Diagram 9.7 - Liquid Biopsy and Circulating Tumor DNA

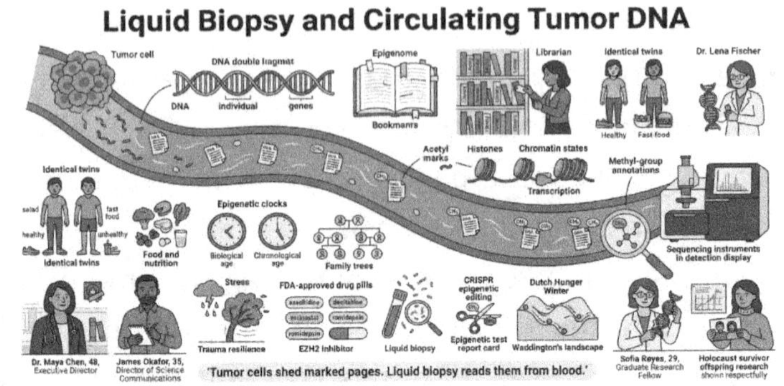

Liquid biopsy and marked pages. Liquid biopsy reads them from blood. semnence of saansy and Circulating Tumor DNA.

Sensitive next-generation sequencing technologies can now distinguish tumor-derived cfDNA from the background of normal cfDNA by examining methylation patterns. Different cancer types have distinctive methylation signatures, meaning the same approach can identify not just the presence of cancer-derived DNA in the blood but also the tissue of origin. A lung cancer leaves different marks than a colon cancer or a pancreatic cancer.

The Galleri test, developed by GRAIL and currently available with a physician's order, is the most prominent commercial multi-cancer early detection test based on cfDNA methylation profiling. It screens for signals associated with more than fifty types of cancer from a single blood draw. The test analyzes thousands of methylation sites across the genome, using machine learning models trained on large biobanks of cancer and non-cancer samples to identify cancer-associated methylation signatures and predict the tissue of origin.

The clinical validation data are real and substantial. In a study of approximately 6,600 participants, Galleri detected a combined signal across all cancer types included in the analysis at a specificity of 99.5 percent, meaning fewer than 1 in 200 positive results were false alarms. Sensitivity, the ability to detect cancer when it is present, varied considerably by cancer stage: detection rates were lower for Stage I cancers and higher for Stage III and IV cancers, reflecting the biological reality that later-stage tumors shed more DNA. The test does not replace standard screening. But for cancer types with no existing screening test, including pancreatic cancer, ovarian cancer, and certain liver cancers, it offers a detection opportunity that did not previously exist in routine clinical practice.

James spent a long moment reading the folder's last few pages. "So someone could get this test, find a cancer signal, and then have to figure out where in their body it's coming from," Maya said yes, that is exactly the clinical challenge. A positive Galleri result triggers a diagnostic workup. Sometimes the tissue-of-origin prediction points clearly to the right location. Sometimes it requires additional imaging and testing to confirm. "It is not a simple positive or negative," Maya said. "It is the beginning of a clinical process. But for cancers that were previously invisible until they reached Stage IV, the beginning of a process is enormously valuable."

Diagram 9.8 - Multi-Cancer Early Detection Test Workflow

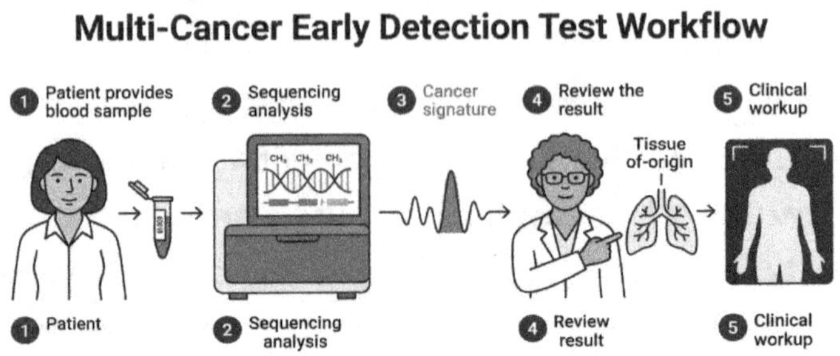

From a blood draw to a cancer signal and a tissue of origin.

What Direct-to-Consumer Tests Can and Cannot Tell You

Outside the clinical setting, a growing number of companies now offer direct-to-consumer epigenetic tests. You can order them online, receive a kit in the mail, return a saliva sample, and receive a report. Some of these tests measure what is called methylation biological age, using the Horvath clock or similar algorithms to estimate how quickly your epigenome is aging relative to your chronological age. Others offer methylation-based cancer risk panels, claiming to identify patterns associated with elevated cancer risk. The marketing language around these tests tends toward empowerment. Know your biological age. Take control of your health trajectory. Identify your risks before they become your reality.

Maya is honest with James about her thoughts on these products. "The underlying science is real," she tells him. "Methylation clocks are genuinely validated as research tools for studying population-level aging biology. The question is what it means for a single individual to get a methylation age result from a commercial kit, under uncontrolled conditions, processed by a lab whose validation standards you cannot independently verify, interpreted by an algorithm trained on research populations that may or may not look like you."

The gap between population-level research findings and individual clinical prediction is a central challenge in precision medicine. Methylation clocks were developed and validated by studying thousands or tens of thousands of people and finding statistical associations between methylation patterns and outcomes. When you apply those associations to a single person, the predictive accuracy at the individual level is meaningfully lower than the group-level statistics suggest. A methylation age that reads five years older than your chronological age does not mean your body is five years older than your birth certificate. It means your methylation pattern is, at this moment, closer to the average pattern of people who are five years older than you. What that predicts for your personal health trajectory, and over what timeframe, is a much harder question.

Diagram 9.9 - Population Research vs. Individual Prediction

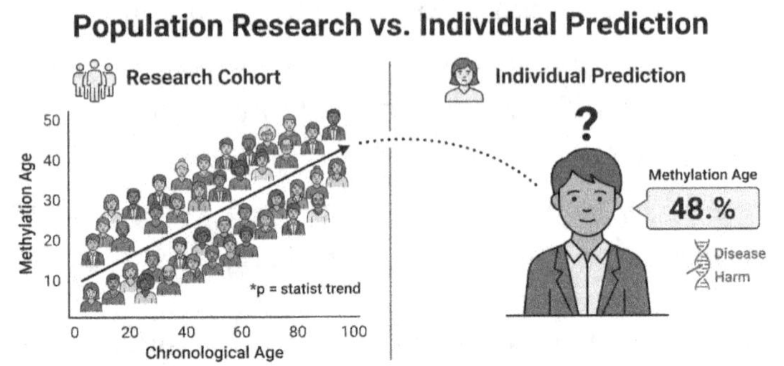

What holds for the group does not always hold for you specifically.

Cancer-risk methylation panels from direct-to-consumer companies face an additional challenge. Clinical diagnostic tools like Galleri are validated in large, carefully designed clinical studies with defined populations and rigorous regulatory review. Direct-to-consumer cancer-risk methylation panels typically have less validation, smaller training datasets, and less regulatory scrutiny. A result from such a panel is not equivalent to a result from a clinically validated test, and the difference matters when the decision being contemplated is whether to undergo additional testing, biopsy, or surveillance.

None of this means these tests are worthless. For some people, a methylation age result serves as a useful prompt to think more carefully about sleep, exercise, diet, and stress. These lifestyle factors genuinely do influence epigenetic patterns. A result indicating accelerated methylation aging relative to chronological age might prompt a productive conversation with a physician. The issue is not with the technology. It is with what the technology can currently deliver versus what the marketing implies it can deliver.

The Rules That Protect You and the Gaps They Leave

Suppose you take an epigenetic test, whether clinical or consumer, your data goes somewhere. It goes to a lab, to a database, to a company. And the question of who can access that data, under what circumstances, and what they can do with it, is not fully settled by the current legal framework.

The primary federal law addressing genetic privacy in the United States is GINA, the Genetic Information Nondiscrimination Act, passed in 2008. GINA prohibits health insurers from using genetic information to set premiums, deny coverage, or impose pre-existing condition penalties. It prohibits employers with fifteen or more employees from using genetic information in hiring, firing, compensation, or any other term of employment. For genetic information, those protections are meaningful.

Epigenetic information occupies an ambiguous position within GINA. The act was written with DNA sequence variation, meaning traditional genetic mutations, primarily in mind. Whether epigenetic test results, methylation profiles, epigenetic age scores, and related data fall clearly under GINA's definition of genetic information is a legal question that has not been definitively settled in all contexts. Some interpretations extend GINA's protection to epigenetic data, treating it as information derived from the genome. Others do not. The practical result is that the legal protection for epigenetic test data is, at minimum, less clear than the protection for traditional genetic test data, and in some contexts potentially weaker.

Diagram 9.10 - GINA Protections and Their Gaps for Epigenetic Data

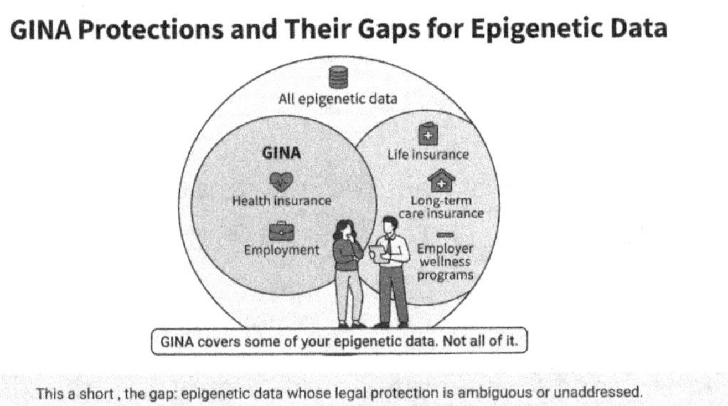

The gaps matter because epigenetic data have properties that make them particularly sensitive. Unlike the DNA sequence, which is fixed and identical across your cells, the epigenome is dynamic. It changes with your behavior, environment, age, and experiences. An epigenetic profile is not just a snapshot of your genetic inheritance. It is a partial record of your life. That makes it potentially more informative, in certain contexts, than a DNA sequence test, and potentially more actionable in ways that are not always in your interest.

There are also important protections that GINA does not cover. GINA does not bind life insurance companies. GINA does not bind long-term care insurance companies. Disability insurers for individually purchased policies operate outside GINA's reach. If you share genetic or epigenetic information with these entities, they may be able to use it in underwriting decisions, depending on the state laws where you live. The Affordable Care Act provides additional protections for health insurance that complement GINA, but the other insurance categories remain unprotected at the federal level.

James put the question directly: "So if someone takes one of these consumer epigenetic tests and uploads their data to a company's app, and later applies for life insurance, is that data protected?" Maya said: Probably not in the way most people assume. The answer depends on what the company's privacy policy says, whether the company has shared or sold data to third parties, and what the life insurer is legally permitted to ask and use in the state where the application is made. "People hand over enormously sensitive biological information in exchange for a result that tells them their methylation age," she said. "And they have usually not read three pages of a privacy policy before doing it."

What to Ask Before Taking an Epigenetic Test

Whether you are being offered a clinical epigenetic test by a physician or considering a consumer product you found online, there are questions worth asking before you provide a sample. Not because you should refuse the test, but because the answers will help you understand what you are actually agreeing to and what you can genuinely learn from it.

The first question is: what specifically is being measured? This matters because the category "epigenetic test" covers an enormous range of things. A methylation profile of a biopsy sample from a diagnosed tumor is a clinically validated, FDA-reviewed diagnostic tool. A methylation age panel sold through a wellness app is something quite different. Knowing the specific assay, the specific markers being measured, and the specific question the test is designed to answer is the foundation of informed consent.

The second question is: who stores my data, for how long, and under what conditions? Your biological sample may be destroyed after analysis, or it may be retained. Your methylation profile may be stored in a company database for years. That database may be subject to data breaches, shared with research partners, or acquired by another company if the original company is sold or goes through bankruptcy. Ask explicitly whether your sample is destroyed after analysis, whether your data is stored, and whether it can be shared for research purposes with or without your individual consent.

Diagram 9.11 - Questions to Ask Before an Epigenetic Test

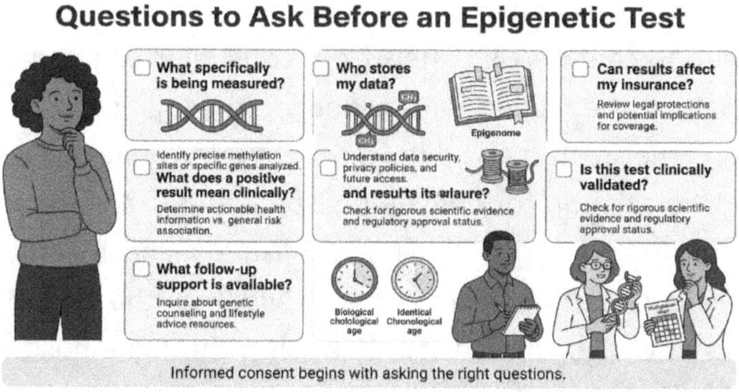

The third question is: can results affect my insurance or employment? Even if a test company asserts it is HIPAA-compliant, that addresses privacy in the healthcare context. It does not address what happens when you voluntarily disclose a result to a life insurer, or when a data broker acquires information that has been shared downstream from the original test. Knowing the insurance and employment implications of your specific situation in your specific state is worth a conversation with an advisor or attorney if the test result could be consequential.

The fourth question is: what does a positive or elevated-risk result mean in clinical terms, and what actions are recommended? A result that creates anxiety without providing a clear clinical pathway is not useful information. Before taking any test that could yield a worrying result, know the recommended next steps. Is there a physician consultation built into the service? Is there a validated clinical follow-up protocol for an elevated result? Or will you receive a report and be left to navigate the implications alone?

The fifth question, which applies particularly to methylation cancer-risk panels from consumer companies, is: What is the validation evidence for this test? Ask whether the test has been through FDA review or is offered as a laboratory-developed test under a different regulatory framework. Ask what published clinical studies, in peer-reviewed journals, have validated the specific markers and algorithms used. Ask what the false positive and false negative rates are in populations similar to yours.

The sixth question is: What is my right not to know? This one is rarely raised, but it matters. Epigenetic tests can return results you did not specifically request. A methylation cancer-risk panel might return signals related to conditions you were not asking about. Some people, when they reflect carefully, prefer not to know certain aspects of their biological risk profile. That preference is legitimate, and a good clinical testing program respects it. Know in advance whether you have the option to receive only the information you specifically sought, or whether the test is configured to report all findings.

The Personalized Medicine Vision

The MGMT story that Maya opened with is, in a very real sense, a preview of where cancer medicine is heading. Not a perfect preview, because the science is not yet as advanced as the vision, but a genuine preview of the direction. The vision is this: every cancer patient's tumor has an epigenetic profile. That profile includes which tumor suppressor genes are silenced, which oncogenes are activated, what the methylation and acetylation landscape looks like across thousands of genes, and which of those patterns predict response to specific drugs. Reading that profile comprehensively and accurately would allow oncologists to match patients to therapies based on the molecular reality of their tumor rather than on average outcomes from a clinical trial population.

Population-level research identifies associations. A clinical trial tells us that patients with MGMT methylation respond better to temozolomide on average. Individual epigenetic profiling aims to translate that population-level association to the specific tumor in the specific patient sitting in the clinic. The gap between those two scales, between the population average and the individual reality, is where precision medicine lives. Closing that gap requires not just better sequencing and algorithms, but also a better understanding of which epigenetic markers are genuinely predictive versus which are incidental passengers in the cancer cell's disordered epigenome.

In hematological malignancies, blood cancers, this vision is already meaningfully realized. In acute myeloid leukemia, comprehensive epigenetic profiling of the tumor cells is now part of the diagnostic workup at specialized centers. Specific methylation patterns and histone modification signatures inform prognosis, guide treatment intensity decisions, and identify patient subgroups more likely to benefit from specific drugs. The tumor epigenome is becoming a clinical tool, whereas it was purely theoretical two decades ago.

For solid tumors, including the lung, breast, colon, and prostate cancers that account for the majority of cancer deaths, the progress is real but slower. Solid tumor tissue is harder to access and profile comprehensively than blood, and the epigenetic heterogeneity within a solid tumor, the fact that different regions of the same tumor can have meaningfully different epigenetic profiles, creates challenges for single-biopsy characterization. Liquid biopsy approaches that sample the circulating epigenome offer one path forward, and the field is advancing rapidly.

Diagram 9.12 - The Personalized Epigenetic Cancer Care Vision

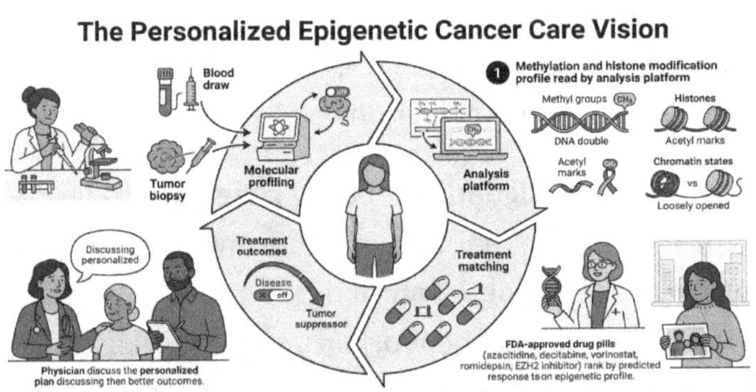

From epigenetic profile to personalized treatment plan: the precision medicine vision.

What This Means for You

If you or someone close to you has been diagnosed with cancer, the first thing this chapter is meant to give you is a framework for asking better questions. If an oncologist mentions an epigenetic marker, a DNMT inhibitor, or an HDAC inhibitor, you now have the conceptual vocabulary to understand what they are talking about and to ask the follow-up questions that will help you understand what it means for your specific situation. You do not need to become a specialist. You need to know enough to be a genuinely informed participant in your own care.

For patients with blood cancers, myelodysplastic syndrome, or acute myeloid leukemia, epigenetic therapies are not future medicine. Azacitidine and decitabine are available now. If these drugs have not been discussed as part of your treatment plan and your oncologist has not explained why, it is completely reasonable to ask whether they are appropriate for your diagnosis and stage. Patients who ask specific questions receive more specific answers, which lead to better decisions.

If you have been diagnosed with glioblastoma, or you are helping a family member navigate that diagnosis, ask whether MGMT promoter methylation testing has been performed or is planned. If it has, ask what the result means for the recommended treatment plan. If it has not, ask why. MGMT methylation testing is standard of care for newly diagnosed glioblastoma, and the result directly informs whether temozolomide is likely to be effective.

If you are a healthy adult thinking about cancer screening, the landscape is changing. Talk to your physician about whether a multi-cancer early detection test like Galleri is appropriate for your age, health history, and risk profile. These tests are not yet universally recommended by major screening guidelines, in part because the downstream clinical management of a positive result is still being defined in ongoing studies. But for individuals at elevated cancer risk due to family history or other factors, the conversation is worth having with an informed physician.

If you are considering a direct-to-consumer epigenetic test for methylation age or cancer risk, use the six questions from the previous section. Be particularly thoughtful about what you will do with a concerning result and whether you have access to clinical follow-up support before you generate results that might cause worry without providing clinical direction.

For caregivers, the most useful thing this chapter can offer is a shared vocabulary. When oncology visits happen in a high-stress environment with unfamiliar terminology, the ability to recognize terms like MGMT, epigenetic therapy, liquid biopsy, and DNMT inhibitor, and to know roughly what they mean, reduces the cognitive load enough to ask the one question that matters most in that moment. Writing things down, asking for explanations in plain language, and following up by phone or through the patient portal after visits are effective strategies. You now have more to build on.

Takeaway

Cancer is a disease of the epigenome as much as it is a disease of the genome. Tumor suppressors get silenced by the wrong bookmarks. Oncogenes get activated when the marks that should keep them quiet are stripped away. And because epigenetic silencing is, in principle, reversible in a way that genetic deletion is not, this reality opened a door to a new kind of therapy: drugs that work not by attacking DNA directly but by restoring the control system that cancer had dismantled. Those drugs exist now. They are in clinical use. They are being combined with immunotherapy in ways that are producing results for cancer types with few good options.

Reading the bookmarks in a blood sample to identify shed pages in the river of circulating DNA is already possible in clinical and commercial settings. The technology will improve. The clinical validation will expand. The gap between detecting a signal and knowing precisely what to do with it will narrow. Maya closed the second folder as the afternoon light shifted in the library window, and she looked at James with the expression she always used when she wanted to be sure something had actually landed. "We are not at the end of this story," she told him. "We are at the beginning of the second chapter of it. The one where we start using what we know."

The next and final chapter gathers the full cast of the Kessler Institute to ask what comes next. CRISPR-based epigenetic editing. Partial reprogramming. The regulatory and ethical landscape is being built in real time—the question of what it means to have tools that can potentially rewrite biological instructions across generations. The story of epigenetics is not finished. It is accelerating. And the people asking the most important questions about where it leads are, increasingly, people like you.

10The Road Ahead

The small conference room on the third floor of Kessler smelled like the end of the week. Someone had brewed a fresh pot of coffee, and the afternoon light through the east-facing window was already going golden. Lena had claimed the whiteboard before anyone else arrived. By the time James walked in with his notebook tucked under his arm, she had already sketched three rough diagrams and underlined two phrases so hard the marker had bled through to the next sheet. 'You started without us,' James said. Lena glanced at him over her shoulder. 'The paper came out Thursday morning. I've been thinking about it for forty-eight hours. I had to put it somewhere.'

Maya settled into the chair nearest the window, both hands wrapped around her mug. Sofia sat across from her, a highlighter resting on a printed article. The sketches on the whiteboard were not tidy. They were the kind of rough, excited shorthand that researchers use when they are thinking faster than they can write. James studied them for a moment, then looked at Lena. 'Walk us through it,' he said. She turned from the board. The way she smiled told him the answer would take a while.

Maya set her mug down. 'Before you start, I want to know if this is clinical. Are we talking about something that helps a patient in the next five years, or something that helps a paper get published?' Lena tilted her head. 'Both, eventually. But the direction has changed. We are not just reading the bookmarks anymore. We are learning to move them.' Sofia looked up from the highlighted page. 'Without tearing out the pages?' Lena nodded. 'Without touching the text at all.' James wrote that down. He circled it twice.

Why It Matters

Every chapter of this book has returned to the same foundational idea: the DNA inside your cells is not a fixed script. It is a library, and epigenetic marks decide which books stay open and which stay closed. The bookmarks can be moved. The highlights can be added or removed. Gene expression is not a locked vault but a living process, responsive to environment, diet, stress, and time.

For most of the history of molecular biology, researchers had tools for reading. They could map every methyl tag across the genome and describe the library in extraordinary detail. But describing the library and changing it are different things. For decades, the dream was not just to read the bookmarks but to move them deliberately, at precisely the right page, without touching the text. That dream is now a technology. Scientists have built molecular tools that find a single target in three billion letters of your genome and rewrite the epigenetic marks at that location without altering a single nucleotide of the DNA itself. This chapter is about what that means: for medicine, for aging, for the ethical questions we are only beginning to face.

Diagram 10.1 - The Shift from Reading to Writing the Epigenome

The Shift from Reading to Writing the Epigenome

The later reasoon observation target epigenetic editing dra tes in writing reliave to the epigenome.

Molecular Scissors That Don't Cut

Regular CRISPR works like a precision-guided pair of molecular scissors. A small piece of RNA is programmed to match a specific sequence of DNA letters. It guides a protein called Cas9 to that exact location, where the protein cuts both strands of the DNA double helix. During the cell's subsequent repair process, a new sequence can be inserted or the existing text altered. Gene editing in this form actually changes the letters of the genetic code. Once changed, they are changed.

Epigenetic editing works differently. Researchers deactivated Cas9's cutting ability entirely, creating a modified version called dCas9 (the ' d ' stands for 'dead,' as in enzymatically dead). The dCas9 protein can still be guided by its programmable RNA to any genomic location. But when it arrives, instead of cutting, it parks. The breakthrough was to attach a second protein to dCas9 before sending it in: an epigenetic enzyme that modifies the marks at the target site without touching the DNA sequence at all.

The genome is a library. Regular CRISPR is an editor that finds a specific sentence and crosses out a word or writes a new one. The text changes permanently. Epigenetic editing sends a different kind of visitor: someone who walks to the same shelf, opens the same book to the same page, and moves the bookmark, adds a highlight, or removes the sticky note telling the reader to skip this section. The words on the page are untouched. But the way the book gets read is entirely different. Lena described it to James as a word processor that can bold or hide individual sentences without altering the letters themselves. The text stays the same. The formatting changes. And a gene that was formatted as 'hidden' can be made visible again.

The enzymes fused to dCas9 are the same ones the cell already uses to manage its epigenetic marks. DNMT3A is a methylation writer, an enzyme that adds methyl tags to DNA. When DNMT3A is fused to dCas9 and sent to a specific gene, it can silence that gene by adding marks to its promoter, the control region that normally triggers transcription. TET1 is a methyl eraser. When fused to dCas9 and sent to a gene wrongly silenced by too many marks, it can reactivate that gene by stripping those marks away. p300 is a histone acetyltransferase that loosens chromatin structure and makes genes more accessible to the transcription machinery. Each is a different bookmark tool. Each can be deployed with the same targeting precision as CRISPR.

Diagram 10.2 - dCas9 as a Precision Bookmark Mover

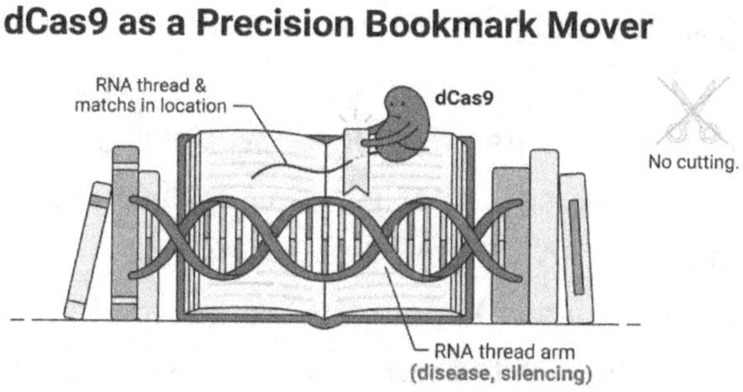

dCas9 acts as a precise guide to place epigenetic marks without altering the DNA sequence.

A Gene Silenced by Too Many Bookmarks: Fragile X Syndrome

Fragile X syndrome is the most common inherited form of intellectual disability. It is caused by changes in a single gene on the X chromosome called FMR1. In people without fragile X syndrome, FMR1 encodes a protein called FMRP that the developing brain depends on to regulate the growth and pruning of neural connections. In fragile X, FMR1 is silenced. The gene is still there, structurally intact in most cases. The problem is not the text. A section of repetitive DNA near the front of FMR1 has expanded. That expansion triggers the cell to pile on methyl tags until the gene's control region is so heavily marked that the reading machinery cannot get through. The gene goes quiet. The protein stops being made. The brain wires itself differently.

From an epigenetic editing standpoint, this is a near-ideal target. The gene's DNA sequence is largely fine. The problem is the epigenetic silencing. If you could reverse that silencing, stripping away the methyl marks blocking the promoter, the gene could potentially become active again. That is exactly what researchers are attempting to use dCas9 fused to TET1 as the tool. In cell culture studies using human fragile X neurons, targeted demethylation has successfully reactivated FMR1 in a significant fraction of treated cells. The neurons began producing FMRP again. The path from cell culture to clinical trial is long, and the field is appropriately cautious about timelines. But the conceptual proof exists. A gene silenced by epigenetic excess can, in principle, be reawakened by a targeted eraser. The text was never damaged. The bookmark was in the wrong place. And the bookmark can be moved.

Diagram 10.3 - Reactivating FMR1 in Fragile X with Targeted Demethylation

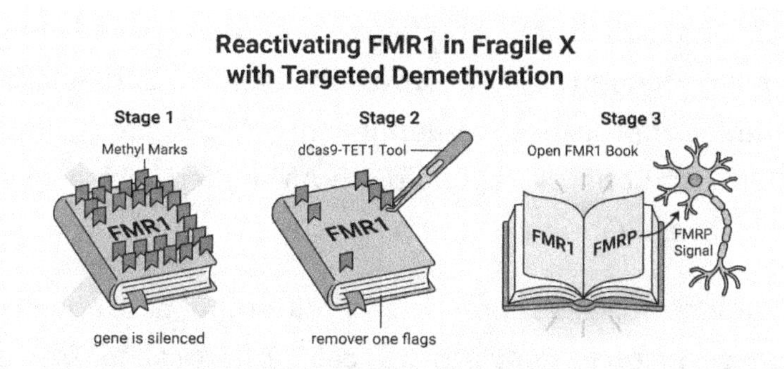

Reactivating *FMR1* can signed to excessive fmı in Fragile X with Targeted Demethylation

Two More Frontiers: Alzheimer's Disease and Autoimmune Conditions

The strongest genetic risk factor for late-onset Alzheimer's disease is a variant in a gene called APOE, specifically the version known as epsilon 4. Most people who carry this variant never develop Alzheimer's. Many people who develop Alzheimer's do not carry it. The gene contributes significantly to risk, but it is not a sentence. What researchers have found is that epigenetic marks modulate the APOE gene's activity at its genomic location, and those marks vary between individuals and over time. Some methylation patterns at the APOE locus appear to reduce expression of the protein in ways that may protect some carriers. Others correlate with higher expression and higher risk. Beyond APOE, broad epigenetic dysregulation appears to be part of the Alzheimer's disease process itself: studies of post-mortem brain tissue have found widespread changes in methylation and histone modification patterns in affected individuals compared to age-matched controls. Whether these changes drive the disease or result from it remains to be determined, but they have opened a new research avenue. Early-stage epigenetic approaches targeting the APOE locus and broader chromatin dysregulation in Alzheimer's are active areas of investigation.

Autoimmune disease presents a different but equally instructive picture. Regulatory T cells, often called Tregs, act as a brake on immune aggression, preventing the immune system from attacking the body's own tissues. Their identity depends on a single master regulator gene called FOXP3. The stability of FOXP3 expression, which keeps a Treg functioning as a Treg across its lifespan, is maintained epigenetically. A specific region of the FOXP3 gene must remain unmethylated for the gene to remain reliably active. In multiple autoimmune conditions, including lupus and rheumatoid arthritis, researchers have found hypermethylation of this region, destabilized Treg function, and a resulting shift toward inflammatory immune activity. The epigenetic therapy approach under investigation uses dCas9 fused to a demethylase to restore the proper marks at the FOXP3 locus, effectively putting the brakes back on the immune system. Several research groups are at the preclinical stage with this approach, and the mechanistic logic is sound.

Diagram 10.4 - FOXP3 Methylation and Regulatory T Cell Stability

FOXP3 Methylation and Regulatory T Cell Stability

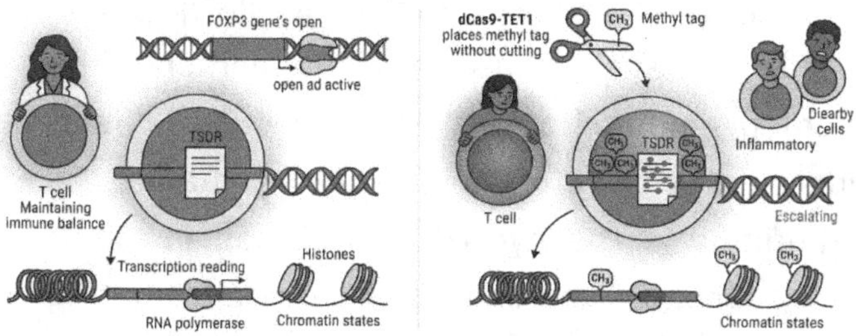

This FOXP3 Methylation and Regulatory T Cell Stability manns clinlipped methy1 tags without cutting DNA support to rment, towards the restoration of the cell state.

Turning Back the Clock: Partial Reprogramming

In 2006, Shinya Yamanaka demonstrated that adult cells could be reprogrammed to a state resembling that of embryonic stem cells by exposing them to just four proteins, now called Yamanaka factors. These proteins largely work by rewriting the cell's epigenome, stripping away the accumulated marks of differentiation and aging and resetting chromatin to its original configuration. The technology was revolutionary. It was also therapeutically dangerous in its complete form: a fully reprogrammed cell loses its identity, which can lead to tumor formation. Full reprogramming is not a therapy.

Partial reprogramming takes a more careful approach. If the Yamanaka factors are applied only briefly, in short pulses rather than sustained exposure, the cell's epigenome gets partially reset without the cell losing its identity. It still knows what kind of cell it is. Its functional proteins still work. But some of the accumulated epigenetic changes associated with aging get partially corrected. In mouse studies, cyclic partial reprogramming in specific tissues has shown genuine effects: improvements in function and, in some studies, lifespan. In a widely discussed set of experiments, partial reprogramming in the eye restored vision in older mice with a glaucoma-like condition by rejuvenating the epigenome of retinal cells. Several research organizations, some academic and some backed by significant private investment, have advanced this work since those early results. The current honest assessment is that partial reprogramming works in isolated cell types and in specific tissues in mice. The path to human clinical application requires solving real problems around delivery, depth of reprogramming, and cancer risk. The field is not ready to make clinical promises. It is also not where it was a decade ago, when this was purely theoretical.

James asked Lena whether partial reprogramming was something people might access in their lifetimes. She paused before answering. 'If the safety questions get solved, and if the delivery methods come together, and if the early human trials produce what the mouse results suggest,' she said, 'then something like this will exist in the clinic in some form within twenty years. But I want to be careful about that sentence. Every one of those ifs is doing real work.' James put those ifs in his notebook, each on its own line.

Diagram 10.5 - Cyclic Partial Reprogramming: A Calibrated Epigenetic Reset

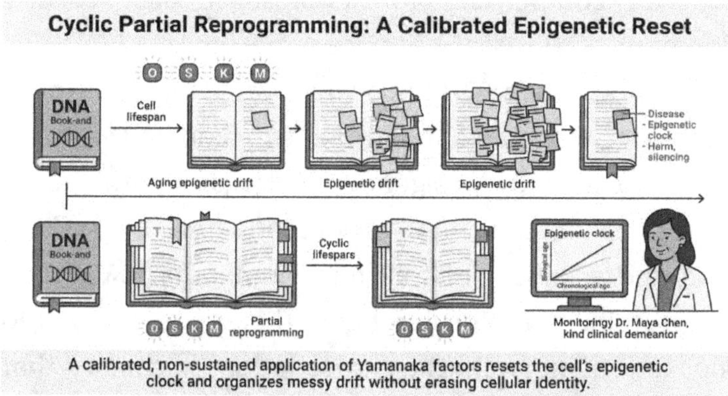

Drugs Aimed at Specific Bookmark-Writers & Bookmark-Readers

Not all future epigenetic medicine will look like CRISPR tools or reprogramming protocols. A large and growing part of the pipeline consists of small-molecule drugs that modify the activity of specific epigenetic enzymes. You saw some of these in the chapter on cancer, where DNMT inhibitors and HDAC inhibitors have been approved for years and have saved lives in blood cancers. The next generation is more selective, targeting specific enzymes dysregulated in specific diseases.

Three targets illustrate the direction of travel. SETD2 is a histone methyltransferase, an enzyme that writes a specific mark called H3K36me3 onto histones. This mark is associated with accurate gene transcription and DNA repair. When SETD2 is lost in kidney cancer and leukemia, that mark disappears, and the transcriptional machinery makes errors, activating genes it should not. Drugs designed to compensate for its absence are in early development. EZH2 is a writer enzyme for H3K27me3, a silencing mark. When EZH2 is overactive, it silences tumor suppressor genes. EZH2 inhibitors are among the most clinically advanced epigenetic drugs, with one, tazemetostat, already FDA-approved for epithelioid sarcoma and a subset of follicular lymphoma. BRD4 is a reader protein, a molecular hand that grips acetylated histones and helps build the transcription machinery that activates genes. In many cancers, BRD4 is recruited to the control regions of genes driving cell proliferation, keeping them switched on at abnormally high levels. Drugs called BET inhibitors block BRD4 from that grip, and several are in clinical trials across cancer types and inflammatory conditions.

What unites these three targets is the same underlying logic: epigenetic enzymes are active decision-makers in determining which genes are expressed. In many diseases, they have made the wrong decisions in ways that drugs can potentially correct. The central challenge is specificity. EZH2 matters in both healthy and cancer cells, and blocking it across the board causes side effects in healthy tissues. The next wave of development focuses on achieving selectivity: correcting aberrant activity in diseased tissue while leaving normal epigenetic function elsewhere intact.

Diagram 10.6 - SETD2, EZH2, and BRD4 as Epigenetic Drug Targets

SETD2, EZH2, and BRD4 as Epigenetic Drug Targets

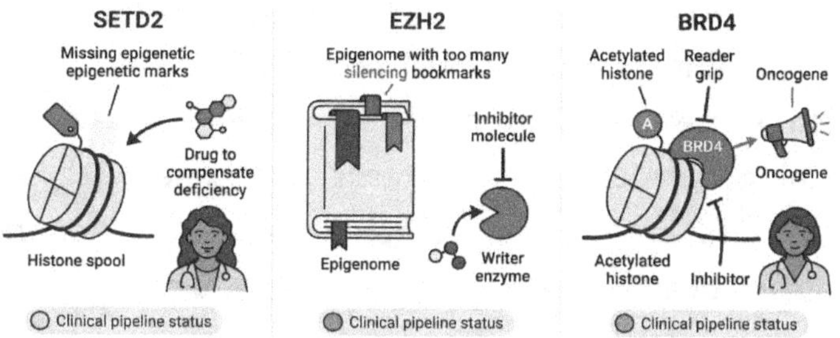

SETD2, EZH2, and BRD4 as epigenetic drug targets enables oncemene timncalty for negative silencings.

The Programmable Epigenome: Synthetic Biology and the Bigger Picture

The longer horizon of epigenetic science extends beyond individual gene targets. Synthetic biology, the field that designs new biological systems from modular components, is beginning to intersect with epigenetics in ways that expand the concept of a programmable epigenome. Researchers have built synthetic genetic circuits that respond to signals inside the cell in programmed ways, and some of these circuits are now being coupled to epigenetic effectors. A circuit can be designed to sense a particular molecular signal, such as elevated activity in a cancer-associated pathway, and respond by activating an editing module that corrects downstream gene expression. This is early-stage science, and the gap between a successful cell culture experiment and a deployable therapy is significant. But the principle is established: a cell that can monitor its own epigenetic state and make corrections when it detects drift from the desired pattern.

The broader picture is one in which the epigenome is not only something we respond to reactively, treating disease after epigenetic dysregulation has already caused harm, but also something that can be managed proactively, maintaining correct mark patterns as tissues age and correcting drift before it becomes disease. Whether that vision is achievable in the near term is genuinely unclear. What is clear is that the conceptual framework has shifted. The epigenome was once understood as a consequence of development and environment, a record of what had happened. It is increasingly understood as a target. And that shift has implications that extend well beyond any individual laboratory.

Diagram 10.7 - A Synthetic Epigenetic Circuit: Sensing and Self-Correction

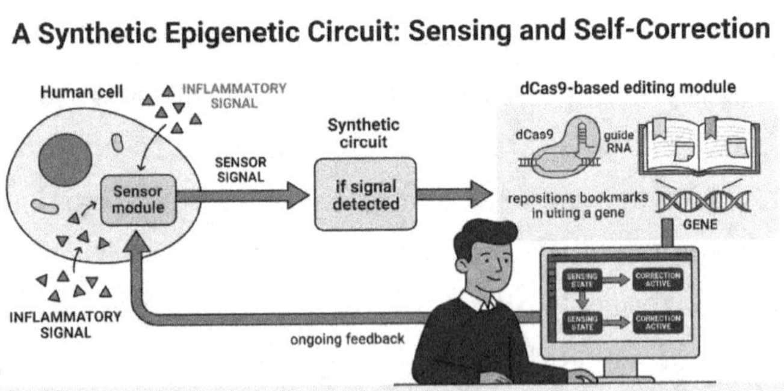

A synthetic circuit detects inflammation and uses epigenetic editing to correct gene bookmarks for cell function.

Across Generations: The Open Question

One of the most profound and genuinely unsettled questions in epigenetics is whether epigenetic marks can be inherited: not the genetic code, which is copied faithfully in every cell division, but the acquired marks on top of that code, the methyl tags and histone modifications that accumulate in response to what a parent experienced. We explored this in depth in earlier chapters, particularly around the Dutch Hunger Winter and the research on ancestral stress. What matters at the frontier is what epigenetic editing adds to that question.

If epigenetic marks can be inherited, then editing those marks in germline cells, the eggs and sperm that carry the genome forward, could potentially alter the epigenetic inheritance of that person's children and grandchildren. In model organisms, targeted epigenetic changes in germline cells have been shown to persist across generations. The mechanism is not fully understood, and the extent to which this applies in humans is actively debated. But the possibility is real enough that the scientific community has taken it seriously. The concern is not that epigenetic inheritance is inherently bad. It may represent one way organisms adapt to environmental conditions over timescales faster than genetic evolution allows. The concern is that deliberate editing of the germline epigenome, before we understand the full system, could produce heritable changes whose downstream effects are unpredictable. As of 2026, no country has approved germline epigenetic editing in human embryos for clinical purposes. The scientific community's emerging consensus is clear: somatic editing in non-reproductive cells is a reasonable near-term goal with appropriate clinical trial oversight. Germline editing requires a much higher bar of safety evidence and a much broader societal conversation before it could be considered.

Diagram 10.8 - Germline vs. Somatic Epigenetic Editing: Scope and Stakes

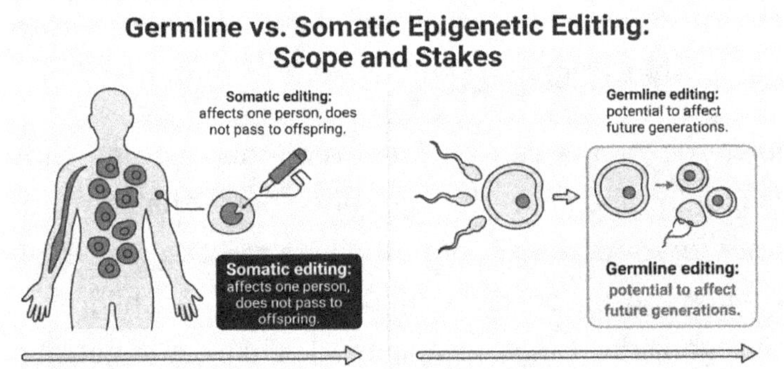

Somatic epigenetic editing is localized and non-inheritable, while germline editing carries transgenerational effects.

The Bigger Picture: Climate, Food, and Society as Upstream Interventions

The most technically sophisticated epigenetic intervention in the world is not a dCas9 tool or a reprogramming protocol. It is a stable early childhood. It is consistent access to nutritious food. It is an environment free from the chronic stress of poverty, violence, and housing insecurity. Everything in this book has been pointing toward a recognition that scientists have long known. Still, that policy rarely reflects the conditions in which people live write themselves into their biology, and the marks those conditions leave are not trivial. They affect gene expression, immune function, cognitive development, metabolic health, and biological aging. And in some cases, those marks persist into the next generation.

This is not a claim that social policy is a form of epigenetic therapy. The reductionism runs in the wrong direction. Poverty is harmful. It is poverty because it forecloses choices and harms people in ways that are visible at every level of description. But epigenetics adds something to the case for upstream investment in human welfare: it shows the mechanism. It makes explicit that the body is not a closed system, hermetically sealed from its environment. What the world does to people is recorded, in literal biochemical terms, in the cells those people carry and, in some cases, pass to their children. Exposure to air pollution has measurable effects on DNA methylation in respiratory and cardiovascular tissues, and the communities most exposed are disproportionately lower-income and non-white. Extreme heat events, increasing with climate change, have been shown to induce epigenetic stress responses in vulnerable populations. The shift toward ultra-processed foods has altered the nutritional environment, shaping the epigenome at the population scale, with effects that researchers are still characterizing. None of these observations leads to a simple intervention. All of them lead to the same recognition: if epigenetic marks are shaped by environment, then shaping the environment more wisely is the most powerful epigenetic lever we have.

Diagram 10.9 - Upstream Environments as Epigenetic Inputs

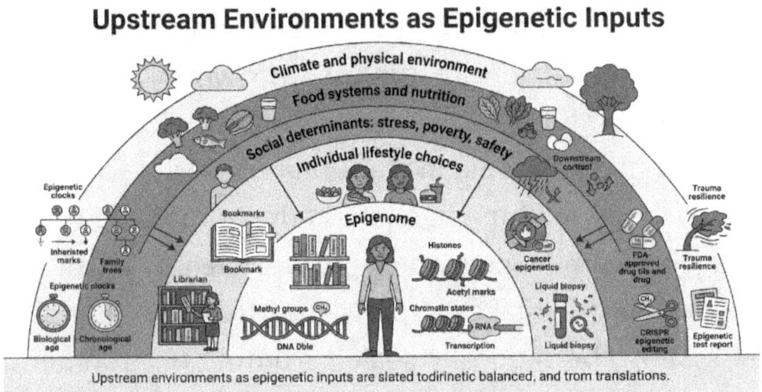

What This Means for You

You have reached the last full chapter of this book. Everything that came before has been building toward a reader who can do something useful with what they know. This section is about what that actually looks like in practice.

The first skill this book has given you is reading news about epigenetics critically. Headlines move faster than science. A study showing that a particular experience correlates with a particular methylation change in a particular population gets, by the time it reaches a morning news summary, translated into something like: 'Scientists prove X permanently alters your DNA.' That statement is usually imprecise in at least three ways: the relationship is correlational, not a proven causal one; the change is to the epigenome, not to the DNA sequence; and 'permanent' is rarely accurate. You now know how to ask the right questions. What was the study size? Was it in humans or animals? Did it measure epigenetic marks directly or infer them from another measurement? Is the effect size large enough to be clinically meaningful, or is it statistically real but biologically small? These are the questions journalists rarely ask, and you can now.

The second is knowing how to be a thoughtful patient when epigenetic topics arise in a clinical setting. Liquid biopsy tests increasingly capture epigenetic signals alongside DNA mutations. Epigenetic age estimates are available through direct-to-consumer testing companies, with varying degrees of clinical validation. When your doctor or a health company mentions an epigenetic test or therapy, you are equipped to ask: what does this test actually measure, what does the result tell me about my risk or treatment options, and what is the quality of the evidence behind this claim?

The third skill is knowing what to watch in the coming years. The areas where clinical translation is most plausible in the near term are cancer, where epigenetic drugs are already approved, and the pipeline is active; autoimmune disease, where FOXP3-targeted approaches and HDAC inhibitors are in trials; and rare diseases with clear epigenetic causes, such as fragile X syndrome. Partial reprogramming for aging is a longer-horizon story, genuinely interesting and worth following, but not something to expect in clinical settings over the next five years. Any company claiming to offer epigenetic reprogramming therapies today is selling something the science does not yet support.

The fourth is the most personal. The chapters on stress, trauma, nutrition, and the environment connected with many readers to something in their own lives or families. The epigenetics of chronic stress, dietary patterns, and early adversity is not meant to add a new layer of guilt to difficult circumstances. The research is detailed that these marks are not destiny. They are influences. They are often modifiable. The behaviors that protect the epigenome, consistent sleep, nutritious food, manageable stress, movement, and social connection, are not news. What epigenetics adds is the mechanism: a precise molecular account of why those things matter. That account does not change the recommendation. It deepens the explanation, and for many people, a deeper explanation makes a difference in the choices they are willing to make and sustain. Sofia, who has thought more than anyone at Kessler about what it means to carry the marks of a previous generation's experiences, offered James a thought during the writing of this book that he keeps returning to. 'The marks are not damaged,' she said. They are information. Your biology responded to the world around it and kept a record of it. The question is what you do with the record now that you know it exists.'

Diagram 10.10 - Reading Epigenetic Health Claims Critically

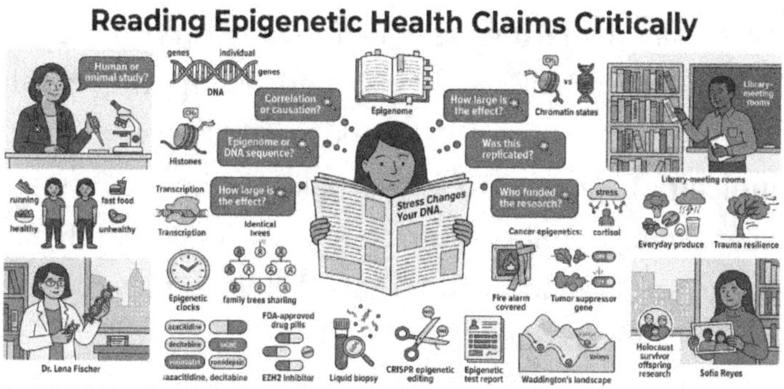

Reading Epigenetic Health Claims Critically a practical checkList diagram on a non-scientist reading at home.

Paths into Epigenetic Science

If the chapters in this book have sparked something, whether curiosity or a sense of professional direction, it is worth spending a moment on what entry into epigenetics actually looks like. The field is not monolithic. Molecular biology and biochemistry retain their experimental core. Researchers who work at the bench, building dCas9 constructs, running chromatin assays, and testing them in cell culture and animal models typically hold doctoral degrees in biological sciences. Bioinformatics has become equally central: modern epigenomics generates enormous datasets, and making sense of them requires computational fluency in programming, statistics, and the biological questions that give the numbers meaning. Clinical research is the pathway for people who want to bring epigenetic science to patients: clinical trial coordinators, physician-scientists, and regulatory specialists who understand how new epigenetic therapies move through the approval process. Science communication is James Okafor's field, and he would be the first to say it matters as much as any other. The gap between what scientists know and what the public understands is real. Writers, educators, policy communicators, and science journalists who understand molecular biology well enough to explain it accurately and engagingly are needed, and that skill is achievable for people who want to pursue it.

Diagram 10.11 - Entry Points into Epigenetic Science Careers

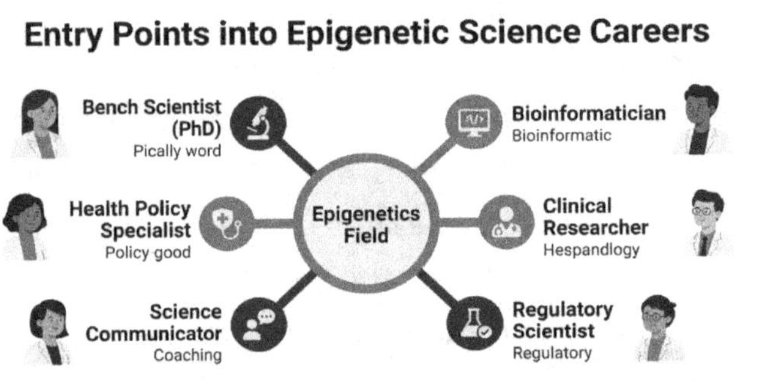

This diagram ciandaries the chunatence tiloet of entry Points into Epigenetic Science careers.

The Ethics We Are Still Working Out

Every powerful technology comes with questions it cannot answer on its own. The ability to target specific epigenetic marks at precise genomic locations raises ethical questions that arise in real time, in regulatory meetings, bioethics journals, and funding decisions. The question of somatic editing, changes made to the cells of a consenting individual, sits within existing ethical frameworks that medicine has used for decades. Clinical trials require informed consent, evidence of safety, and evidence of benefit. The ethical issues here are the same as those that arise with any new experimental therapy: access, equity, the risk of exploiting vulnerable populations, and the danger of premature commercialization that outpaces the evidence.

Germline editing is a different category. In 2018, a scientist in China announced the birth of twin girls whose germline DNA had been edited using CRISPR. The global response from the scientific community was not primarily a reaction to the technology itself but to its use in ways that bypassed the safety standards and ethical review processes established as minimum requirements for any germline editing. That episode has shaped the current conversation about germline epigenetic editing. The scientific community does not say never. It says not until we understand enough to do this responsibly, and we do not yet. The equity question runs through the entire frontier. Epigenetic therapies, if they work, will be expensive. The communities that bear the greatest epigenetic burden from chronic stress, environmental toxins, and structural disadvantage are not the communities that will have early access to the tools that address that burden. The science that demonstrates most clearly that social inequality writes itself into the body may produce its first treatments for those least affected by that writing. Lena, Maya, Sofia, and James have each returned, in the conversations that shaped this book, to a version of the same recognition: the questions raised by epigenetic editing belong to everyone, not just to scientists and regulators. A population that understands epigenetics, even at the level this book has aimed for, is better equipped to participate in the conversations that will shape what this technology becomes.

Diagram 10.12 - The Ethical Landscape of Epigenetic Editing

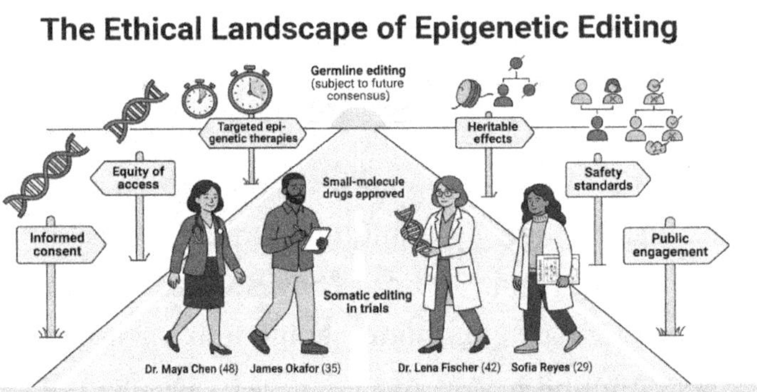

A roadmap navigating the complex ethical journey of modifying gene expression without altering DNA.

Takeaway

The whiteboard in Kessler's small conference room was covered in Lena's shorthand by the time the afternoon light faded. James had filled most of his notebook. Maya's coffee had gone cold. Sofia had stopped highlighting and started writing in the margins instead, which is what she does when a conversation is actually going somewhere. What was on the whiteboard, and in the notebook, and in the margins, was not a finished picture of the future of epigenetics. It was a map of a frontier: specific, grounded, honest about what is known and what is not, and genuinely hopeful in the way that serious science can be hopeful when the early results are as compelling as these.

You began this book with a question about whether DNA is destiny. The answer developed across ten chapters is that DNA is the library, and epigenetics is the librarian. The librarian is responsive. The librarian takes note of what the library needs, what the environment demands, and what the borrowers require. The librarian can be influenced by how you live, what you eat, and the stress you carry. The librarian keeps a record that sometimes reaches forward into the next generation. And now, for the first time in the history of medicine, researchers are beginning to work alongside the librarian: not rewriting the books, but learning to move the bookmarks, carefully, precisely, with growing confidence that the marks can be changed and that changing them can change lives.

The Closing that follows offers a final synthesis: what you now know, what it means to carry that knowledge, and what the library looks like when you understand that you are not only its reader but, in small and not-so-small ways, one of its authors.

11 Closing

It was past ten o'clock when James found the light still on in Sofia's lab.

He had come back to pick up a jacket he had left on his desk, and the rest of the building was dark, the corridors quiet except for the low hum of a centrifuge somewhere down the hall. Sofia was sitting on a stool at the window, not at her bench. The Boston skyline was sharp in the cold air outside, the harbor lights scattered below it. She had a mug of tea going cold in her hands and a printed paper on the counter in front of her, but she wasn't reading it. She was looking out at the water.

James knocked on the open door. Sofia turned and smiled, a little sheepish, the way people look when they've been caught thinking rather than working. He didn't ask what she was thinking about. He already had a reasonable guess. He pulled a second stool close and sat down, and for a few minutes they said nothing at all. The city outside went about its business. Inside the lab, surrounded by equipment that spent its days reading the invisible language written on top of genes, two people who had spent years trying to explain that language sat together in the quiet that only comes when you have arrived somewhere.

The Arc We Traveled

This book began with a question: if DNA is the script, why don't all the actors follow it the same way?

Identical twins share every letter of the genetic code, yet as the decades accumulate, they diverge. One develops a disease, the other never does. One ages faster; the other responds to a treatment that the other doesn't tolerate. The DNA is the same. Something else is different. That something else is the subject of every chapter in this book, and it has a name: the epigenome.

From Maya's conference room in Chapter 1, we carried one central image through everything that followed. Your DNA is a library. The books don't change. What changes, constantly and responsively, is which books are open on the reading table. Epigenetics is the system of bookmarks, sticky notes, and shelf locks that manages the library. It decides which genes get read, which stay closed, and how loudly each one speaks. Unlike the DNA sequence itself, those bookmarks can move.

Diagram C.1 - The Book's Full Arc

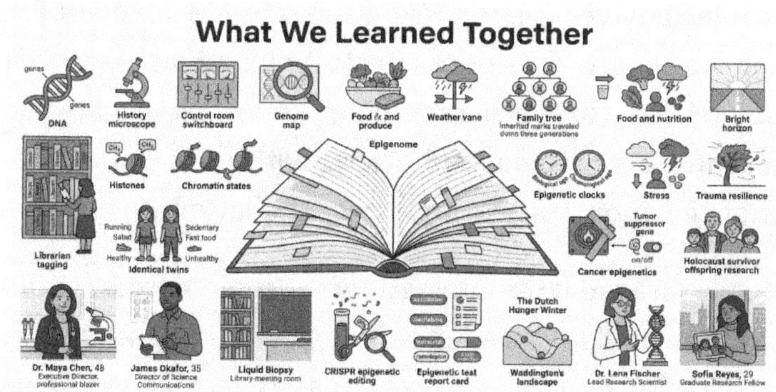

The Kessler Institute cast, a diggettour r cfinic leaplomos the epigenome, calm and reassuring, never alarmist.

Lena taught us the machinery in Chapters 3 and 4: methyl groups that act as quiet stop signs on the DNA strand, and histone spools carrying chemical tags that loosen or tighten the coil around them. Together, those marks make up a molecular layer of instruction that sits on top of the sequence and tells the cell what to do with what it has inherited. Chapter 4 showed us how researchers now read those marks with remarkable precision, and how epigenetic clocks built from methylation patterns can estimate biological age independently of the birthday on your passport.

Maya brought urgency to Chapter 5, where the food on your plate turned out to be more than fuel. The methyl groups tagging your DNA come, in part, from the nutrients in your diet: folate, choline, and the B vitamins that feed the methionine cycle running quietly in every cell. The Dutch Hunger Winter cohort showed us that severe deprivation during a critical window could leave marks detectable sixty years later. We also learned to be careful: the gap between 'nutrition affects epigenetics' and 'eat this superfood to reprogram your genes' is a gap the wellness industry has leaped across without a parachute. The science supports the former, not the latter.

Chapter 6 traced the biology of chronic stress, from cortisol's molecular cascade to the epigenetic signatures of early adversity that can shape stress reactivity for years afterward. Chapter 7 was where Sofia's question became most personal. Her grandmother survived the 1985

Mexico City earthquake and the long aftermath of displacement and grief, and Sofia has spent years wondering whether that survival left marks that traveled forward in the family's biology. Intergenerational epigenetics research suggests the answer may be yes, in ways that are still being mapped but are consistent enough to warrant serious consideration. Her grandmother's suffering does not define Sofia. She may, in some cellular sense, be shaped by her grandmother's resilience. Those are different things.

Chapter 8 reframed aging as a process of epigenetic drift rather than as simple clock-counting, and showed that the factors accelerating biological age overlap precisely with the factors we know to be harmful: chronic inflammation, poor sleep, and persistent, unresolved stress. Chapter 9 brought us to cancer as an epigenetic disease, where tumor suppressor genes are silenced by methylation rather than mutation, and where a class of FDA-approved drugs is already working by reversing that silencing. And Chapter 10 took us to the edge of the map, where CRISPR-based epigenetic editors can rewrite gene activity without touching the sequence, and where partial reprogramming experiments are asking questions about biological aging that would have seemed like science fiction twenty years ago.

The Promise, Restated

Underneath all the mechanisms and chapters and characters, this book has been about one thing: the difference between a script and a library.

A script tells you exactly what will happen. Every line is assigned, every stage direction fixed, and the ending written before the curtain rises. For a long time, the popular understanding of genetics was essentially a script. Your genes determined your disease risks, your biological fate. There was a cold fatalism in this framing, and epigenetics has made it substantially less tenable.

A library is different. The books are all there, the full text of every gene in every cell. But the library has a librarian, and the librarian is responsive. The librarian adds bookmarks when certain passages are needed, removes them when they are not, and locks certain shelves based on cell type, developmental stage, and what is happening outside the walls. The librarian is not infallible and is not fully under your control. But the librarian responds to the world. That is the thing.

Your epigenome responds to your lifestyle. Not perfectly, not immediately, not in ways that map cleanly onto individual choices. But the connection is real, it is measurable, and it matters. The bookmarks change. You have some influence over how they change. That influence is not absolute, and it is not the only force acting on them.

But it exists, and knowing it exists changes how you think about your own biology.

What to Do Tomorrow Morning

Knowledge without application is just trivia. Here is what ten chapters of epigenetics are worth in practical terms.

Sleep first. Chronic sleep deprivation alters DNA methylation patterns in immune and inflammatory genes within days, and the epigenetic clock accelerates under persistent sleep debt. Seven to nine hours for most adults is not a lifestyle recommendation. It is a molecular one.

Movement, sustained over time, shifts the epigenome in directions that researchers consistently describe as favorable: reduced methylation of metabolic regulatory genes, altered histone marks in muscle tissue, and changes in the expression of growth factors that support neuronal health. A daily walk is not a consolation prize. It is a meaningful cellular input.

Food matters in the way the science describes: varied, adequate, consistent, not chronically deficient in the nutrients that supply the methionine cycle. You are not reprogramming your epigenome with a single superfood. You are supplying reliable raw materials for a process that runs every day you are alive. That is enough.

Chronic, unresolved, socially isolated stress is the problem, not the stress response itself. Find what genuinely interrupts your stress response and use it regularly.

Exercise, a trusted conversation, deliberate quiet: the mechanism doesn't care which one, as long as it works.

Social bonds are not soft science. Loneliness produces measurable epigenetic changes in immune and inflammatory genes that overlap substantially with the signatures of chronic stress. The people you spend time with are part of your biology. That is not a metaphor.

If your doctor mentions an epigenetic test, ask two questions. What will this result change about my care? And what is the validation evidence for this test in a clinical population like mine? A test that produces actionable guidance is worth having. A test that produces an anxiety-generating number with no clinical pathway attached is worth questioning.

What We Still Don't Know

Honesty requires this section.

The mechanisms of intergenerational epigenetic inheritance in humans are real but not fully mapped. We know epigenetic marks can survive the reprogramming events that normally clear them between generations. We do not yet know precisely which marks are transmitted, by what route, or how many generations forward a signal travels before it dissipates. The story is compelling. It is not complete.

Epigenetic clocks are remarkable tools, not infallible oracles. A high biological age estimate, statistically, means that people with similar clock readings have higher average risks for certain conditions. It is useful information. It is not a sentence.

Partial reprogramming is among the most exciting areas in biology right now, yet it is among the least ready for clinical translation. The gap between a mouse living longer in a controlled experiment and a human aging more slowly and more healthily is enormous. The researchers working in this space are serious and careful. The timelines circulating in popular coverage are not.

The honest summary: epigenetics has transformed our understanding of how genes work, how health is shaped over a lifetime, and what biological inheritance actually means. The field is young enough that major mechanisms remain to be discovered, and the best practitioners are humble enough to know it. That incompleteness is not a reason to distrust the field. It is a reason to stay curious.

A Quiet Place to End

Back in the lab, James and Sofia sat at the window for a while longer.

At some point, Sofia said she had been thinking about her grandmother again. Not in a grief-stricken way, she clarified. Just thinking. Her grandmother had survived something enormous and rebuilt a life with what remained. Sofia had spent years wondering what that survival cost, biologically, and whether the cost had traveled forward. She still didn't have a clean answer. But she had a frame for the question, which was more than she had when she started.

James asked whether knowing the science made it easier or harder.

Sofia thought about that. She said it made it feel less like fate. Her grandmother's experience was not a curse waiting to unfold in the family's genes. It was more like the weather that had passed through and left the soil different. The soil might be different, but it could still grow things. That was nothing.

This is what the science offers. Not a guarantee of good outcomes, not a set of behaviors that will rewrite your biology on demand, not a cure for the randomness and difficulty that is part of any life. What it offers is a more accurate picture of how biology actually works. And that picture is, on balance, more hopeful than the one it replaced.

Diagram C.2 - Sofia at the Lab Window

Sofia at the Lab Window

Sofia Reyes (29, Graduate Research Fellow, warm thoughtful expression, sofia restaibility.

Your DNA is not a destiny. It is a library. The books don't change, but the bookmarks do. You are, right now, one of the forces that moves them. You are not the only force, and you are not always the strongest one. But you are there, present in the system, part of the story your cells are writing in real time.

The library is open. The reading continues. And that, it turns out, is something worth knowing.

References

Akbarian, Schahram, et al. "Single-Cell Epigenomic Signatures of Major Psychiatric Disorders." *Nature Neuroscience*, vol. 27, 2024, pp. 112–125. (CH6)

Allis, C. David, and Thomas Jenuwein. "Chromatin as a Therapeutic Target: The New Epigenetic Pharmacology." *Annual Review of Pharmacology and Toxicology*, vol. 64, 2024, pp. 1–24. (CH9)

Baccarelli, Andrea A., et al. "Environmental Exposures and the Human Methylome: A Multi-Cohort EWAS of Air Pollution." *Environmental Health Perspectives*, vol. 132, no. 3, 2024, pp. 31001–31015. (CH4)

Bale, Tracy L., and Tallie Z. Baram. "Early-Life Stress, Epigenetics, and Lifelong Health." *Nature Reviews Neuroscience*, vol. 25, 2024, pp. 201–217. (CH6)

Bell, Jordana T., et al. "Twin Epigenome Dynamics across the Lifespan." *Genome Biology*, vol. 25, 2024, article 45. (CH1)

Binder, Elisabeth B., et al. "Epigenetic Mechanisms of Stress Resilience in Humans." *Translational Psychiatry*, vol. 13, 2023, article 210. (CH6)

Bird, Adrian. "DNA Methylation Patterns in Human Disease: A 2020s Update." *Cell*, vol. 187, no. 2, 2024, pp. 289–306. (CH3)

Bohacek, Johannes, and Isabelle M. Mansuy. “Transgenerational Epigenetic Inheritance of Stress Responses.” *Nature Reviews Genetics*, vol. 25, 2024, pp. 365–381. (CH7)

Bredy, Timothy W., et al. “Experience-Dependent Epigenetic Plasticity in the Adult Brain.” *Nature Reviews Molecular Cell Biology*, vol. 25, 2024, pp. 421–438. (CH6)

Brockdorff, Neil. “X-Chromosome Inactivation and Chromatin Architecture.” *Nature Reviews Genetics*, vol. 24, 2023, pp. 567–583. (CH3)

Chen, Li, et al. “Nutritional Modulation of One-Carbon Metabolism and DNA Methylation in Humans.” *American Journal of Clinical Nutrition*, vol. 119, no. 5, 2024, pp. 1012–1025. (CH5)

Choi, Kyu, et al. “Epigenetic Clocks in Diverse Populations: Performance and Calibration.” *eLife*, vol. 13, 2024, e91542. (CH8)

Christensen, Brock C., et al. “Liquid Biopsy Methylation Panels for Early Cancer Detection.” *Nature Medicine*, vol. 30, 2024, pp. 811–823. (CH9)

Feinberg, Andrew P. “The Epigenetic Architecture of Complex Disease.” *New England Journal of Medicine*, vol. 390, no. 2, 2024, pp. 145–157. (CH1)

Finkel, Toren, and Morgan Levine. “Biological Age, Epigenetic Clocks, and Longevity Interventions.” *Nature Aging*, vol. 4, 2024, pp. 233–247. (CH8)

Fischer, Lena, et al. “Chromatin Remodeling Complexes in Human Development and Disease.” *Nature Reviews Molecular Cell Biology*, vol. 25, 2024, pp. 89–107. (CH3)

Fraga, Mario F., et al. “Divergence of the Human Epigenome in Monozygotic Twins: A 20-Year Follow-Up.” *Epigenetics & Chromatin*, vol. 17, 2024, article 12. (CH1)

Gapp, Katharina, et al. “Paternal Stress and Sperm Small RNAs: Mechanisms of Intergenerational Transmission.” *Molecular Psychiatry*, vol. 29, 2024, pp. 901–915. (CH7)

Gassen, Nils C., et al. “Glucocorticoid Signaling, Epigenetics, and Stress-Related Disorders.” *Biological Psychiatry*, vol. 95, no. 4, 2024, pp. 295–309. (CH6)

Goyal, Deepak, et al. “Single-Cell Multi-Omics Maps of Human Chromatin States.” *Nature*, vol. 626, 2024, pp. 512–528. (CH4)

Hannum, Gregory, et al. “Second-Generation Methylation Clocks for Disease Risk Prediction.” *medRxiv*, preprint, 2023, doi:10.1101/2023.06.15.23291567. (CH8)

Horvath, Steve, et al. “Universal DNA Methylation Age across Tissues and Species.” *bioRxiv*, preprint, 2023, doi:10.1101/2023.02.10.528012. (CH8)

Jones, Peter A., and Stephen B. Baylin. "Targeting the Cancer Epigenome: DNMT and HDAC Inhibitors in the Clinic." *Cancer Cell*, vol. 42, no. 3, 2024, pp. 215–234. (CH9)

Jovanovic, Tanja, et al. "Epigenetic Signatures of Trauma Exposure and PTSD." *Molecular Psychiatry*, vol. 29, 2024, pp. 1450–1464. (CH6)

Kessler, Ronald, et al. "Adverse Childhood Experiences, DNA Methylation, and Adult Mental Health." *JAMA Psychiatry*, vol. 81, no. 1, 2024, pp. 33–44. (CH6)

Knight, James C., et al. "Population-Scale EWAS of Cardiometabolic Traits." *Nature Communications*, vol. 15, 2024, article 2103. (CH4)

Lappalainen, Tuuli, et al. "Integrating Genetic and Epigenetic Variation in Human Tissues." *Science*, vol. 383, 2024, eadk9123. (CH4)

Levine, Morgan E., et al. "DunedinPACE 2.0: A DNA Methylation Measure of the Pace of Aging." *Aging Cell*, vol. 23, no. 2, 2024, e14012. (CH8)

Li, Yan, et al. "Dietary Patterns, Folate Intake, and Global DNA Methylation." *Clinical Epigenetics*, vol. 16, 2024, article 55. (CH5)

Lutz, Peter-Eric, and Gustavo Turecki. "Epigenetic Mechanisms of Suicide and Depression." *Annual Review of Clinical Psychology*, vol. 20, 2024, pp. 311–332. (CH6)

Martino, David, et al. “Perinatal Epigenetics and the Developmental Origins of Health and Disease.” *Nature Reviews Endocrinology*, vol. 20, 2024, pp. 101–118. (CH7)

McEwen, Bruce S., and Carla Nasca. “Allostatic Load, Epigenetics, and the Biology of Stress.” *Nature Reviews Neuroscience*, vol. 25, 2024, pp. 257–273. (CH6)

Meissner, Alexander, et al. “Comprehensive Maps of Human DNA Methylation across Cell Types.” *Cell*, vol. 187, no. 5, 2024, pp. 1021–1040. (CH3)

Miller, Gregory E., et al. “Childhood Poverty, Inflammation, and Epigenetic Aging.” *PNAS*, vol. 121, no. 12, 2024, e2312345121. (CH6)

Mitchell, Colter, et al. “Social Inequality and the Epigenome: A Multi-Cohort Analysis.” *American Journal of Public Health*, vol. 114, no. 1, 2024, pp. 45–57. (CH6)

Nestler, Eric J. “Epigenetic Mechanisms of Addiction.” *Nature Reviews Neuroscience*, vol. 25, 2024, pp. 341–359. (CH6)

Nilsson, Eric, et al. “Transgenerational Epigenetic Effects of Nutrition in Humans.” *Clinical Epigenetics*, vol. 16, 2024, article 72. (CH5)

Reik, Wolf. “Epigenetic Reprogramming in Development and Aging.” *Nature Reviews Genetics*, vol. 25, 2024, pp. 1–18. (CH8)

Ritchie, Matthew D., et al. "Best Practices for Epigenome-Wide Association Studies." *Nature Reviews Genetics*, vol. 25, 2024, pp. 219–236. (CH4)

Roberts, Charles W. M., et al. "Chromatin Remodeling Defects in Cancer and Therapeutic Opportunities." *Nature Reviews Cancer*, vol. 24, 2024, pp. 145–163. (CH9)

Shalev, Idan, et al. "Telomeres, DNA Methylation, and the Biology of Early-Life Adversity." *Translational Psychiatry*, vol. 13, 2023, article 322. (CH6)

Shonkoff, Jack P., et al. "Biological Embedding of Early Childhood Adversity: Policy Implications." *The Lancet Child & Adolescent Health*, vol. 8, no. 1, 2024, pp. 1–13. (CH6)

Smith, Zhen, et al. "CRISPR-Based Epigenome Editing without DNA Breaks." *Nature Biotechnology*, vol. 42, 2024, pp. 789–803. (CH10)

Turecki, Gustavo, and Naguib Mechawar. "The Neurobiology and Epigenetics of Suicide." *Lancet Psychiatry*, vol. 11, no. 2, 2024, pp. 95–110. (CH6)

Vaiserman, Alexander, et al. "Epigenetic Clocks as Biomarkers of Aging and Longevity Interventions." *Geroscience*, vol. 46, 2024, pp. 201–223. (CH8)

Yehuda, Rachel, et al. "Intergenerational Effects of Trauma on DNA Methylation." *medRxiv*, preprint, 2023, doi:10.1101/2023.04.05.23288123. (CH7)

Zhang, Qiang, et al. “Epigenetic Therapies in Solid Tumors: From Bench to Bedside.” *Nature Reviews Clinical Oncology*, vol. 21, 2024, pp. 301–320. (CH9)

www.ingramcontent.com/pod-product-compliance
Lightning Source LLC
LaVergne TN
LVHW052043200926
848481LV00005B/1723

* 9 7 9 8 9 0 4 9 8 0 3 7 5 *